NATIVE AMERICAN PROPHECIES

BY
SCOTT PETERSON

PARAGON HOUSE
370 Lexington Avenue, New York, N.Y. 10017

First edition, 1990

Published in the United States by

Paragon House
370 Lexington Avenue
New York, N.Y. 10017

Manufactured in the United States of America
Cover design and illustration © Peter Thorpe 1991

Library of Congress Cataloging-in-Publishing data

Peterson, Scott, 1955–
    Native American prophesies / by Scott Peterson. — 1st ed.
       p.   cm.
    ISBN 1–55778–205–9 (HC) : $22.95. — ISBN 1–5578–417–5
(PBK) : $12.95
    1. Indians of North America—Religion and mythology. 2. Indi-
ans of Mexico—Religion and mythology. 3. Human ecology—
Religious aspects. 4. Prophesies. I. Title.
E98.R3P36   1990
299′.75—dc20   90–7793
                                                         CIP

Excerpt on p. 77 from APOLOGIES TO THE IROQUOIS by
Edmund Wilson. Copyright © 1959, 1960 by Edmund Wilson.
Reprinted by permission of Farrar, Straus and Giroux, Inc.
10 9 8 7 6 5 4 3

NATIVE AMERICAN
PROPHECIES

For
NATASHA

CONTENTS

•

•

PREFACE

The two years it took to research and write this book were the culmination of a spiritual and intellectual quest that began during my boyhood in Arizona. In one of my earliest memories I accompanied my father, a true lover of nature, to the top of a rugged mesa where we discovered in the ruins of an Indian village a *mano* and *metate.* These ancient stone appliances, used to grind corn, fired my curiosity about the Native people that still inhabit the land we call America. Over the years, I absorbed everything I could about them. Then, while in high school, a friend of the family went to live among the Navajos and became a member of the Native American Church. Now a professor at Arizona State University, Kathleen Ferraro's stories and insights were grist for my mill and fueled my sense of wonder.

The Indians I met and the material I read about them told me that they were far different from the stereotypical images of Hollywood. Some, though certainly not all, passed along bits of wisdom that were like adobe bricks used in the building of my own mental house. As a second-generation American, baptized Russian Orthodox as Maxim Gregori Persianoff, confirmed as a Lutheran, and for a period of years agnostic, I have long been preoccupied with the questions so many others have pondered throughout time. Why are we on earth? What is our relationship to the Creator and the cosmos?

As a baby boomer, I have also been keenly aware that many

important trends that have been building for generations appear to be coming to a head during my lifetime. None of these are more critical to our future than what we human beings are doing to the earth.

The collection of Native American prophecies and histories contained between the covers of this book is but a brief introduction to a rich and varied body of wisdom. My hope is that by the time you have read through these pages, you will be as affected by them as I have been in writing them. Due to practical considerations, I was unable to write about three additional Native North American prophets, Chief Seattle of the Suquamish Nation; Tenskawtawa, the Shawnee Prophet; and Tecumseh, his wise older brother. I aspire to giving these great leaders their due in the future.

Many people deserve thanks for helping to make this work a reality. I am most grateful to Helene Chirinian, Q. Pierce, Raney Draper, and Jack Artenstein who got the ball rolling; Jerry Bathke who provided me with some key introductions; and Myrna Plost and Robert Fiveson for their support. My appreciation also goes out to the UN's Environmental Programme in Geneva and Richard Hansen of Project RAINPEG for their invaluable assistance. Thanks, too, to John Blizek, who listened to me ruminate for hours on end and provided me with invaluable feedback; Rosa Morales for her translations; my father and mother, Gregg and Anita Peterson, who were unflagging in their encouragement; and my wife, Natasha, without whom this book would never have been written.

The primary library resources consulted during the course of my research were UCLA's University Research Library, the Southwest Museum's Braun Research Library, and the Los Angeles Central Library.

Finally, I want to thank my editor at Paragon House, Andy DeSalvo, who had the courage to believe. And most of all, I want to acknowledge Annie Kahn, Hunbatz Men, Sun Bear, and my Hopi friends Eugene Sekaquaptewa of Hotevila, and Thomas and Clifford Balenquah of Bacobi, who shared with me the wisdom of their peoples and their reverence for the earth.

Scott Peterson

INTRODUCTION

An old prophecy, attributed to the Hopi Indians of northern Arizona, declares that Native American medicine, or spirituality, would fall into disrepute, and that for over a hundred years most Indians themselves would not believe in it. Then, one day, the great grandsons and great granddaughters of the white oppressors would seek out the few remaining medicine men and women left, and they would say, "Teach us, because we have almost destroyed the Earth."

This book was written as a contribution toward the fulfillment of that prophecy. For there is much that we as a civilization can learn from Native American reverence for the earth. Ever since French philosopher René Descartes proclaimed nearly four hundred years ago that men are the masters and possessors of nature, Western civilization has operated with little respect for our planet. Our luxurious cradle has provided us with incalculable bounty and taken all of the punishment we have meted out. The land was so rich, the water so abundant, the air so pure, that it was only quite recently that we began to question whether or not it would last.

Many Native Americans have tried, and are trying, to warn us that we must get back in sync with the planet from which we all spring. For generations, no one listened. Then sometime in the 1980s, influenced by growing scientific evidence, the five hottest days of average global temperature ever recorded, and an unending series of ecological megadisasters, it became apparent to even the ultra apathetic that we have reached an environmental turning point.

George Bush, in the heat of his presidential campaign, declared 1988 to be "the year the earth spoke back!" Yet despite that stirring sound bite, he has yet to face up to the startling dimensions of our problem. For it is not just air and water pollution that we now face, but a staggering, interlocked crisis of a global nature. The holes torn in our planet's stratospheric ozone layer by our use of chlorofluorocarbons (CFCs) and the frightening pace of deforestation caused by greed contribute to global warming. Together, they are presenting us with a challenge the magnitude of which humankind has never known.

The United Nations, in a report issued in July 1990, urged Bush to act. Based on sober scientific evidence, the United Nations Environmental Programme concluded that the rate of global warming of the environment was twice as bad as had been previously estimated. Heated by accumulated greenhouse gases like carbon dioxide from cars, factories, and the burning of tropical forests, the earth's atmosphere is predicted to grow hotter in the next fifty years than it has in the last one hundred thousand. This will mean that the oceans will expand in size flooding coastal areas around the globe. Hurricanes will grow in intensity; prime crop lands will migrate toward the poles. Already, the U.S. Department of Agriculture is conducting studies on what strains of crops will best be able to endure the new conditions.

The noble struggles of the developed nations to clean up the environment since the early 1970s have had some beneficial effect. But rising levels of global economic prosperity and the pollution that have accompanied it has made our overall problem worse. Never before have we mixed such huge amounts of toxic chemicals into our atmosphere. Like a chef concocting a soup without a recipe, what the final result will be is still not known. But all indications are that the taste is likely to kill us.

A chilling example of our gargantuan gamble is taking place in southern California. The air quality of the South Coast Air Basin, comprised of four counties including Los Angeles, is without a doubt the worst in the nation. Ozone and carbon monoxide pollution frequently reach maximum levels nearly three times the national standard set to protect public health. Fine particulate matter

(PM_{10}) reaches levels of nearly twice the national standards. The Los Angeles basin is also the only area in the nation still exceeding the nitrogen dioxide health standards.

To bring the region's air quality down to maximum federal and state standards, the South Coast Air Quality Management District (AQMD) and the Southern California Association of Governments adopted a policy on March 17, 1989, calling for their attainment no later than December 31, 2007. The plan calls for the world's most stringent controls on emissions from motor vehicles, industry, and consumer products. Critics have claimed that the measures are so severe that oil refineries will have to move out of the basin and furniture manufacturers will be forced to shut down because of the restrictions on the use of paints and solvents. That American institution, the backyard barbecue, is even threatened due to plans to ban the sale of lighter fluid.

Yet, in testimony before the Senate Energy and Natural Resources Committee, meeting in special session in Santa Monica on May 20, 1989, AQMD executive officer James M. Lents testified that according to a previously secret computer modeling study, even with the planned 80 percent emission reduction, ozone levels by 2007 could still be double the federal standard due to the effect of global warming. In essence, all of the hard-fought gains would be wiped out.

Of course, the conclusions of computer models are open to debate. Lents's testimony, however, is cited here not as an ironclad prediction of the future, but rather as an example of how we are sailing in uncharted seas. In September 1988, British prime minister Margaret Thatcher addressed an audience of scientists, doctors, diplomats, and government officials about this dilemma. A former research chemist, Thatcher warned that we may have "unwittingly begun a massive experiment with the system of the planet itself."

Perhaps most fearsome is the fact that in order to curb the catastrophic environmental changes that we are already encountering, we must develop a whole new way of living, one that is driven by ways of creating wealth that do not depend on ravaging our now fragile planet. That path of sustainable development is our only hope. Yet it is far different from the path pursued since the dawn of the Industrial Revolution some 150 years ago.

The American public seems aware of the problem. A poll conducted by Media General–Associated Press and released in June 1990, indicated that four out of five Americans say "pollution threatens the quality of their lives." We have been at it for the last twenty years, though during the Reagan administration, halfheartedly at best; in Eastern Europe, the Soviet Union, and Latin America the campaign to Save the Earth has hardly begun.

Now, before it is too late, it is time to redouble our efforts at reducing pollution and look in new directions, at ideas previously rejected, to see if there is some way to find a means out of the mess we have gotten ourselves into. One of those ways is by taking Native American reverence for the earth to heart.

The Native Americans who speak through this book are of one mind when it comes to what is missing from the current environmental movement. That missing link is a unified approach, an attitude toward the earth. In the pages that follow, this is expressed most succinctly by Sun Bear. "I believe that environmental issues have to become a spiritual thing," he says. "People have to think of the earth in a spiritual way. Taking responsibility for the earth must be ingrained from the time they're still children."

Looking out at the beautiful Lukachukai mountains from her hogan's eastern door, Navajo medicine woman Annie Kahn puts it another way: "Earth Mother, Father Sky, and the Dawn is Grandfather. I am a member of this family. I care for this whole family. Once I have said, 'the earth is my mother,' I am earth's child. I take responsibility for all people. When my parents died, I didn't feel alone because I still had Mother Earth and Father Sky. People in the cities especially haven't recognized water, the earth, the mountains as part of our lives. But they are."

The Hopi traditional village leaders are even more direct: "We have accepted the responsibility designated by our prophecy to tell you that almost all life will stop unless men come to know that every one must live in Peace and in Harmony with Nature. Only those people who know the secrets of Nature, the Mother of us all, can overcome the possible destruction of all land and life."

To put things into perspective, this book begins with a historical examination of a few of this continent's greatest Native American prophets and prophecies. Each of the stories work as independent units. First are the Maya, whose influence upon Native American thought cannot be overstated. Today, some four million Mayan-speaking people live in an area stretching from Mexico's Yucatan Peninsula south through El Salvador, though the culture that remains is but a shadow of their once magnificent civilization. By the time the first Europeans set foot on this continent, more than six hundred years had passed since the mysterious demise of the Classic Maya. Although they revived somewhat under the Toltecs in the five hundred years preceding the Spanish Conquest, they never again regained their cultural supremacy.

What has come down to us are mere fragments of their once prodigious body of prophecies as well as tantalizing glimpses of how they conceived of and honored their God Behind the Gods, Hunab Ku. These bits and pieces are provided as a jumping off point for the further examination of other Native American prophecies and earth wisdom. As will become apparent, each of the cultures profiled owe their own debts to the Maya. In some cases, this may be for no other reason than their shared emphasis of what Swedish expert Ake Hultkrantz has termed the "direct experience of spiritual power through dreams and visions. . . . Probably no other cultures have given visions such importance in daily religious life as those of native North America."

Despite the fact that Hunab Ku has never been identified as purely male or female, "he" is often used when referring to this deity in order to avoid needless complication. The Mayan understanding of God changed in some significant ways under the bloodthirsty Aztecs, though their obsession with prophecy was equally intense. Aztec emperor Moctezuma Xocoyotzin's belief that Hernando Cortez's arrival was the fulfillment of the prophecy of Topiltzin-Quetzalcoatl's return is one of the great stories of history and is told here from a new perspective.

The chapter on Deganawidah, on the other hand, takes a slightly different slant. In these pages, the vision is of a new way of living. Deganawidah is a prophet who, through the power of his ideas, changed the lives of other people from his own time to our own. Creator of the federal system of government and a union called the League of Five Nations, which was one of the most democratically advanced societies the world has ever seen, Deganawidah's ideas were borrowed by Benjamin Franklin and woven into the fabric of the United States. He is the great, unsung first philosopher of America. And it is deplorable that today his name is completely unknown.

Native Americans, like other human beings, have a dark side. An example of this is related in the story of Wovoka. Starting out with the finest of motivations and concern for his downtrodden brethren, this great Indian prophet experienced a powerful vision in which he claimed to have gone to heaven and spoken with God. The prophecy that he enunciated afterward told of the coming regeneration of the worn-out earth, the return of the buffalo, and the end of the white race. Yet to sustain the adulation that soon swelled around him, he committed ever greater lies, ultimately succumbing to the corruption of celebrity, and sparked the Last Indian War.

It is true that Native Americans were not perfect stewards of their environment. The horse, for example, native to the Americas, had been killed off by them and was completely unknown when reintroduced by the Spanish in the early 1500s. Yet, in general, they have paid more respect to nature than any other culture. Said in a variety of ways, their message is a simple one: The earth is our Mother. We must take care of her.

Whether or not that message will be heeded remains uncertain. The way that Indians have been shunted aside and ignored, that Deganawidah has gone uncredited, that the Supreme Court in 1990 took away the ancient right of Native Americans to use peyote in religious ceremonies, bodes ill for any expectation that society will embrace their finest ideas. Yet there are glimmers of hope.

We are living through one of the most important turning points in history, the end of one epoch and the beginning of another. Some of the prophecies in this book may directly affect your life and the lives of your loved ones. Others had impact only in their own time and place. Either way, they form a collection of powerful warnings. Believe them if you will. Ignore them at your peril.

CHAPTER ONE

THE MAYAN ROOTS
OF PROPHECY

Over a hundred Mayan men and women walked slowly out of the isolated mountain village of San Francisco el Alta in central Guatemala. Their sandals made impressions in the dust as they stepped quietly along a worn dirt path, through tall grasses and a forest of pine trees, until they arrived at a huge stone blackened by countless applications of smoke from an incense known as copal.

The women, dressed in colorfully embroidered huipile blouses; and the men, wearing drab, store-bought ladino trousers and shirts, waited reverently as the presiding *kukulcán,* or head priest, moved to the front of the assembly. They had journeyed from throughout Mesoamerica to be present for the ceremony about to begin, marking the end of a Mayan calendrical cycle. The seriousness of their meeting was reflected on their bronze faces. A cool breeze began to blow as a few musicians played a plaintive song on vertical flutes and shell horns. The Maya sang along with the ancient words they knew by heart. Then the priest lit the pungent copal and initiated an age-old ritual to honor the god of creation, Hunab Ku.

Most people think that the Maya are long gone, a historical curiosity that died out with the Spanish Conquest. But that is not the case. Today, over four million people stretching from Mexico's Yucatán Peninsula and the states of Chiapas and Tabasco, through Belize, Guatemala, Honduras, and El Salvador speak twenty-eight Mayan dialects. Although Mayan civilization—the superpower of its time—did indeed perish, and many of the ancient religious rituals have been forgotten, the essence of Mayan culture lives on, as evidenced by the gathering described above that took place early in March 1990.

Recognized even less, however, is how Mayan ideas influenced the Native peoples of North America. For as we shall see through the course of this book, the Mayan tradition of prophecy and conception of the cyclical nature of time is reflected in the beliefs of many, if not all, of the Indian nations. And the Mayan understanding of the place of humankind in the cosmic scheme of things and the sacredness of all creation is nothing less than the foundation upon which Native American thought is built.

•

Archeologists have uncovered evidence of human occupation in the Mayan lowland areas of coastal Belize as early as 9000 B.C. By 2500 B.C., permanent agricultural settlements had sprung up in these same areas, and by 1000 B.C. the inhabitants had penetrated the jungle lowlands of what is known today as Guatemala's Department of the Peten—the heart of the Mayan Golden Triangle.

It is impossible to say just when these early people gelled into what can be called the Maya, since with almost every major new archeological field study, the date of their genesis is pushed back in time. Until recently, it was believed that the greatest achievements of Mayan civilization—feats such as hieroglyphic writing, zero-based mathematics, the most advanced astronomy in ancient America, sophisticated art and architecture, and an elaborate system of roads and trade—were developed toward the end of what scholars had termed the Late Formative period, or around 200 A.D. But recent finds made by the Regional Archeological Investigation of the North Peten of Guatemala (RAINPEG) have caused that date to be dramatically revised.

Deep in a rain forest 350 miles north of Guatemala City and three days by foot from the nearest road, a team of investigators have been sweeping away the dust of time at the ancient city of Nakbe and finding amazing things. "We now have evidence of complex architecture being constructed sometime between 600 and 400 B.C.," explains Richard Hansen, a research associate with the University of California at Los Angeles's Institute of Archeology and project director of RAINPEG.

Previously, it had been believed that society during that early era was one of simple villages. Yet Nakbe has shown the age of Mayan civilization had been seriously underestimated.

"We've found occupation and settlement from 1000 to 600 B.C.," said Hansen, in a telephone interview from Guatemala City. "Then there's a tremendous jump in sophistication. The buildings at Nakbe that we've discovered—from 600 to 400 B.C.—have a minimal amount of sculpture but range up to twenty meters in height. We're trying to determine exactly what the factors were that allowed that jump from a small village level society to a massive, full-blown city with major pyramids."

Over the years, there has been a lot of uninformed speculation that some outside force swept into the area and raised the Natives to a higher level of cultural sophistication. Extraterrestrial intervention has been suggested. So have other cultures, including Egyptian, Chinese, Pacific Islander, even the lost tribes of Israel. But there has never been one shred of evidence to back up any of these claims. Not a single object manufactured outside of the Americas has ever been unearthed at a Mayan site. And it is racist to believe that the Natives were *incapable* of such advances.

Hansen instead cites three factors that are believed to have provided an impetus to Mayan development. One of them is trade. "Nakbe is located at the most distant point from rivers or coastal shorelines of any city yet found," he states. "Because of the isolation and the difficulty of getting things into the area, an organization was required. Once that was formed, it gave them a jump on the guys that had everything easily available to them."

Another factor is the location itself. Because there are no rivers and the environment is so difficult, it created a need for an administration. "In the dry season," Hansen continues, "they don't have enough water. In the rainy season, they have too much water and the swamps are inundated. So that required the formation of a government to build the causeways to go across the swamps," he says. On six major pyramids, water collection aqueducts that run off the architecture have also been uncovered. The large-scale water collection system is considered to be additional evidence that a government planned and constructed the city.

Around 300 B.C., there was a quantum leap in the size of the structures and their decoration. "Fabulous masks and panels are found on buildings from this period," states Hansen. "The reason for the jump in cultural achievements appears to be that once they had an elite established, they developed a religious ideology. Of course, there's evidence of ritual long before that. But we've not seen the massive investment in architectural labor until around 300 B.C. That's when we see a tremendous effort, involving millions of cubic yards of construction material, taking place."

Exactly how great an effort is best understood by comparing Tikal, once considered the largest Mayan city, to Nakbe. Also located in the Guatemalan lowlands, Tikal was excavated and restored by the University of Pennsylvania from 1956 to 1969. Primarily constructed late in the Classic Period (A.D. 300 to 900), the center of the city contains five major temple-pyramids. Yet, according to Hansen, "you can fit all of the pyramids of Tikal inside one of the pyramids at Nakbe. And we're one thousand years earlier. So it's clear that in many cases the Early Maya eclipsed the Classic Maya in, for example, the size and sophistication of their architecture."

MAYAN RELIGION

Who was the divinity that the Maya moved so much earth to honor? If one judges by the total number of gods, the conclusion might be that Mayan religion is complex beyond comprehension. Major deities, to mention just a few, include Chac, the rain god; Itzamna, credited with the invention of books and writing; Yum Kaax, the god of agriculture; and patrons of the numbers, days, months, and twenty-year periods known as *katuns.*

One god, however, exists above all the others in the Mayan pantheon and has unfortunately been overlooked or misunderstood by most Western-educated scholars. The name of this supreme God Behind the Gods, say the Maya, is Hunab Ku. Focusing on this ultimate deity, the cloak of mystery falls away from Mayan religion, and its fundamental influence on Native American spirituality is there for all to see.

No representation of the Great Hand has ever been identified in any of the four surviving Mayan codices, the carvings that decorate their stone cities, or the polychrome pottery for which they are famous. In fact, few Maya have ever spoken about the subject.

Hunbatz Men, a traditional Mayan "daykeeper" in his forties, born in the Mexican Yucatán village of Espita, explained his people's silence in a series of interviews with the author. "We don't mention the name of God because, for the Maya, God is invisible. Don't mention the name. Keep him in your memory. You see, this is high respect for the creator. Only in the most sacred centers did the high priests speak about Hunab Ku."

Despite this similarity to the Judeo-Christian commandment of not taking the name of the Lord in vain, there is very little else in common between the two religious traditions.

"In the European cultures, if you want to do something or need something or if something bad happens in your life, you petition God through prayer," states Hunbatz. "If something good happens, people say, 'Thank you God.' But the Maya don't say that because, for us, God only gives you your body and your spirit. He is impersonal. That is why we say he is only the giver of movement and measure. Movement is your spirit. And your body is your measure."

When traditional Maya participate in a ceremony, they honor Hunab Ku and, by doing so, remind themselves about their relationship to him. In this chapter's opening paragraphs, it was related how Mayan pilgrims from throughout Mesoamerica gathered to perform their ritual in front of a huge stone. "That stone represents the beginning," Hunbatz explains. "We have been doing that same ritual for thousands of years before the Spanish came to this continent. Part of it is to make a confession for the community in front of the stone. Very old, traditional Maya believe in the elements. Those elements are made from the cosmic dust that was created by Hunab Ku in the beginning. Everything is made from that dust and he is represented by that stone. That's why we say the sun is my father. The earth is my mother. This belief is held in tiny villages throughout this continent. It's nothing new.

"The straight connection that we make with the earth is our spirit. Because the symbol of our spirit is the circle. And the symbol of the earth is the same. Everything has a spirit. My spirit is the reflection of the earth. I am in you and you are in me. We are all the same. It's in the stars, too. If I look at a tree, in my memory it's possible to say that's a manifestation of Hunab Ku," Hunbatz adds. "Because in the Maya culture, everything is sacred."

In A.D. 1525, the Spanish conquered the Quiche Maya in what is now Guatemala. The Yucatán fell in 1541 and the Maya abandoned their cities of stone, to retreat into the forests and hills. A Catholic priest by the name of Diego de Landa pursued them and used torture and execution in his attempt to stamp out what he saw as their pagan beliefs.

"De Landa tried to find Hunab Ku to destroy him," states the daykeeper. "But he couldn't find him because he is in every place. To destroy Hunab Ku, you need to destroy the Milky Way."

•

Traditionally, one member of a Mayan family is chosen while still a child to receive the wisdom of their ancestors and keep it secret. Hunbatz was chosen by his uncle—the holder of that knowledge in his generation—from among five brothers and two sisters. It was from this uncle, Teo Beto, who never left the tiny village of Espita for any length of time during his entire life, that the boy was given his Mayan name. Hunbatz means "teach" and "understand," while Men is the name of a Mayan day—the one on which he was born.

"When I was seven, my uncle began to take me to different sacred centers in that area," says Hunbatz. "Near Espita, maybe ten kilometers away, you have one big center named Xuenkal. In that center, some Indians continue to conduct rituals. They have never stopped. I first went there walking with my uncle, because there are no roads, and began my education.

"Over time came problems," he continues. "Most of my family believes in the Christian religion and not all of them keep the traditions of the Maya. When my mother and father tried to baptize me, my uncle said, 'No. We're not going to do that.'"

When Hunbatz was nine years old, he began to learn Spanish. Then, at the age of sixteen, he moved to Mexico City. Having a natural talent for drawing, he soon got work as a designer. "If sometimes I work doing that, it's only because I need money to live," he adds.

Soon, however, he began to feel conflicted. "My Spanish is more like the Indian Spanish," he says. "A lot of people made fun of that. Along with my name. And I had problems inside. The information my uncle gave me did not fit with the information of the new civilization. I began to make a lot of money and use it in a bad way. I was caught in the confrontation between two cultures. One day I said, 'I need to go back to my uncle.' So, when I was twenty-one, I went back to Espita. Because his initial teachings were very strong, I went back."

Accompanying the Maya's respectful reluctance to voice the name of the creator of the universe is a more sinister aspect. "In the United States, it's possible at any time to speak about all of this," Hunbatz states. "But in some places, it's not good. A lot of people in Mexico are killed only because they speak about this kind of knowledge.

"One of the ways people are attacked for spreading this kind of knowledge is by calling them *brujo* [which means devil]. There are a lot of small villages in Mexico where the priests will say, 'That guy who lives in that house is a *brujo*. He has a connection with Satan. So people would not like him and the problems begin. Some of the stupidest guys go to Catholic church. Then they drink some beer or alcohol and want to teach the *brujo* a lesson. Who are the intellectuals who make trouble for the Maya? The Church."

By and large, the governments of Mexico, Guatemala, Honduras, and El Salvador ignore Mayan worshippers. "If you have a big stone and a half a million people do their rituals there, the government isn't going to say anything," he states. "Because to try to get them out of there is going to cause problems. For them, this stone is not important because the cost would be too high to try and stop the rituals in front of it.

"We only have problems when we try to go to one of the archeological sites, because tourists go there and pay money and the government takes that. So, the official systems believe those places belong to them. But, in fact, it belongs to the people. In most of those countries, they say the Mayas may have made these sites but they don't exist any more. They're gone. But in Guatemala, 80 percent of the people are Indians and belong to the same families as the ancient Maya. Something is obviously wrong," he adds. "But that wrong was initiated by the colonialization."

SACRED GEOMETRY

During the long heyday of their civilization, the Maya did not limit their honoring of the God Behind the Gods solely to rituals. In city after city, they went so far as to construct ceremonial centers and pyramids to reflect the heavens that were created by him. At Uaxactun, for example, located in Guatemala's Peten, a pyramid was constructed on the west side of what is known by scholars as the Group E courtyard, facing due east. Three smaller temples were erected on a platform directly opposite. When viewed from the top of the pyramid, the sun rises rises directly over the middle temple on March 21, the vernal equinox; from behind the left-hand temple on June 21, the summer solstice; over the middle temple again on September 23, the autumn equinox; and from behind the right-hand temple on December 21, the winter solstice.

Similar alignments have been deciphered at nearly a dozen ancient centers within one hundred miles of Uaxactun, including Nakum, Uxul, Rio Bec, and Dzibilchaltun.

Uxmal, a large and important Classic era center in the northern Yucatán, also has documented astronomical placement of buildings, though in its case, they relate to Venus. From the main doorway of the beautiful Palace of the Governor, which is decorated with more than 350 Venus symbols, the perpendicular line of sight runs directly to a large pyramid several kilometers distant called Nohpat. Archeoastronomer Anthony Aveni has calculated that Venus would have risen directly over Nohpat "at the time of its maximum southerly eight-year excursion about A.D. 800 when the Palace of the Governor was erected." From another building known as the House of the Magician, a sight line passes directly over the center of two other buildings and the ceremonial ballcourt to align with a point on the horizon where Venus sets at its most southerly position.

"The temples and pyramids are like a big book," says Hunbatz Men. "Uxmal was a special place for women. Kabah is a special place for men to make rituals. That is the reason you see at a center different architecture. Each architecture is for specific work. But all the pyramids incorporated sacred geometry."

CULTURAL DIFFUSION

Starting before and running through the first millennium of the Christian era, while Europe was in feudal darkness, the civilization of the Maya was the dominant cultural force of the Americas. By way of its traders and travelers, Mayan ideas spread northward across the roiling waters of the Gulf of Mexico, up along the mighty Mississippi, and into the verdant, green heartland of the North American continent.

Artifacts found during the excavation of the Adena Estate near Chillicothe, Ohio, to cite just one example, are graphic testimony to the sway they held over other Native Americans. One of the most famous items discovered is the Waverly Tablet, carbon dated to A.D. 100. Carved out of stone, it is remarkably similar in style to Mayan designs of the same period. The Adena, Hopewell, and Mississippian cultures that populated the valleys of the Mississippi River and its tributaries for fifteen hundred years were also prodigious pyramidal mound builders.

Poverty Point, an ancient city discovered in 1953 in northeastern Louisiana, also dates from this era. Situated not far from the banks of Bayou Macon near the Mississippi River, the complex contains six mounds constructed in concentric half-octagons. Measuring three-quarters of a mile in diameter, they allow for accurate prediction of the spring and fall equinoxes.

The most compelling evidence of Mayan influence, however, is the shared belief among all Native Americans of the sacredness of creation itself. No other culture that ever existed on earth has surpassed the Native American reverence for nature. The honor bestowed upon Mother Earth is a shining thread that weaves together the many-colored fabrics of the peoples examined in this book. And underlying that respect is the God Behind the Gods, known by a variety of names, but always unseen and all-powerful. This Great Spirit created all things and is reflected in all things. That is why a tree is as worthy of honor as a human being, an animal, or the stars.

THE CALENDARS

One of the most basic factors underlying Mayan development was the shift from hunting and gathering of wild game, fish, and foods to highly organized corn agriculture. This was accomplished by the slash and burn, or milpa, process in which the forest was cleared with a stone ax, left to dry, burned, then planted. The surpluses that were produced enabled segments of the population to turn their attention to matters other than the procuring of food. Key to this success was the creation of a calendar that allowed for the precise timing of planting and harvesting.

The calendars were derived from careful observation of the heavens by generations of astronomer-priests. Though the original calendar must have been quite simple, and may have been created by others, it was refined by the Maya into a sophisticated series of interlocking time-keeping devices that were the most advanced in ancient America. It is one of their greatest intellectual achievements. To thoroughly examine them would take up this entire volume and thus is best left to others. Yet to achieve a basic understanding of the importance of prophecy to the Maya and how it was derived, we must first understand how they perceived time.

The Western conception of time is like a line stretching out into infinity. Every event along that line is something new. For the Maya, however, time is like a circle. The past will repeat itself in the future. Everything that happens at this point in time occurred at the same point in the last cycle, and will repeat itself endlessly at the same point in the cycles to come. Small cycles, furthermore, are components of even larger ones.

The two most basic calendars are the Haab, meaning solar or "vague" year of 360 days, which is broken down into eighteen months of 20 days apiece; and the Tzolkin, or sacred almanac of 260 days, comprised of thirteen months of 20 days apiece. Every fifty-two years, the same day comes up simultaneously on each calendar. This cycle, equaling seventy-three Tzolkin and fifty-two Haab years, is known as the Calendar Round.

The Haab and Tzolkin are still used by the Maya in remote areas of the Yucatán, Guatemala, and other regions of Central America. According to Hunbatz Men, they are synchronized in one of two ways. One is by adding 21 days every fourth year (5 days for each year, plus 1 more for leap year). The other is to add 273 days every fifty-two years (5 days for each year, plus 13 more for the leap years.)

Why fifty-two years? Because every fifty-two years, the Pleiades star group, known to the Maya as Tzek'eb ("rattlesnake's rattle") reappears at exactly the same spot on the horizon. This conspicuous cluster of stars is among the brightest in the night sky and has been used for eons by developing civilizations throughout the world to time agricultural operations. Like the solar and sacred calendars, the fifty-two year "century" was subsequently adopted by cultures throughout Mesoamerica. As we shall see, the Aztecs' New Fire ceremony was constructed around the reappearance of this star group.

The Tzolkin (meaning "pieces of the sun") calendar intermeshes the numbers one through thirteen with twenty named days, moving forward like two interlocked gears. Each of its 260 days has its own prophecy. "The priests of the Mayas used the Tzolkin for the divination of truth," says Hunbatz. "To know the destiny of the people. For prophecy. Because through this calendar it is possible to know the future and the past, too."

Though most of the Mayan books that contained these prognostications were destroyed by the Spanish, those that survived were copied by hand in Latin script. Known as the *Books of Chilam Balam,* with a supplemental name of the Yucatán village to which they belonged, eighteen or more are thought to have existed at one time. Several, though, have been lost. Still others have never been revealed to the Western world. Hunbatz, for example, speaks of *The Book of Chilam Balam of Espita,* which is unknown to scholars.

The following excerpt from a Tzolkin almanac is taken from the *Book of Chilam Balam of Tizimin* and is provided to give the reader a taste of their flavor. Like most of the Chilam Balam books, this one is laden with Christian references and these have been omitted here. Furthermore, only those dates with additional characteristics besides "lucky" and "unlucky" are reproduced. Obviously, the month being labeled as "May" highlights the fact that what has been passed down to us is only a fragment of the original hieroglyphic manuscript.

May

13 Oc	lucky	A day of rain	
2 Eb	unlucky	A handful of food	
3 Ben	unlucky	Searching through the forest	
		Recalling the sins of our fathers	
4 Cib	unlucky	Perchance going into the forest	
		[for food]	
7 Caban	unlucky	Luring the deer with good things	
		[into traps]	
8 Eznab	unlucky	When men sing	
9 Cauac	lucky	For the lords of the land	
11 Imix	unlucky	For the caciquedom	
12 Ik	unlucky	A spirit in the hearts of men	
1 Kan	unlucky	A calm upon the spirits	
		The moon is completed	
2 Eznab	lucky	The count of strong suns	
6 Muluc	lucky	For people to visit on this day	

For centuries, the Tzolkin almanacs controlled the actions of everyone. Merchants and war parties, for example, would delay journeys until an auspicious date. The Tzolkin was also consulted when a child was born. If a male child was born on the days Kan or Chuen, he would become a craftsman. Those born on Hix and Cib would be warriors. Doctors were born on Edznab. Other days would predestine a life as a murderer, thief, and so forth. Such forecasts could be mitigated, however, by offerings to various deities.

Just why the Tzolkin was created remains an enigma lost in time. It is remarkably close in duration, though, to the average length of a woman's pregnancy, as well as the interval of appearance by Venus as the morning and evening star.

According to Hunbatz Men, there were once seventeen calendars—the penultimate one having a duration of twenty-six thousand years. Though a complete explanation is exceedingly complex, suffice it to say that because the earth wobbles like a top, its plane of rotation moves relative to its plane of revolution about the sun. This movement causes the equinox points to shift over time through the constellations that stretch in a band around the earth's plane of revolution. One entire circuit takes twenty-six thousand years to complete.

Hunbatz Men, however, ties this interval to the Pleiades. "The calendar of twenty-six thousand years is the calendar of the Pleiades," he quietly maintains. "For the Mayas know we belong to these stars. We are here in our solar system. The center of the Pleiades is there. Every twenty-six thousand years, we complete one cycle around the Pleiades.

"Some cycles we can witness during our lives," he continues. "It's possible to see the cycle of the woman. The cycle of the moon. The twenty-eight-year cycle of the sunspots. Every year, we see the changes on the earth. In our lives, it's possible to see the Pleiades in the same place two times at most. But others we are not going to see. The big one, for example, of 260 years. Larger still are the cycles of 1,040 and 5,200 years. All of them and more are within the calendar of 26,000 years."

Long and Short Counts

The Maya employed two additional, time-keeping methods not used by any other Mesoamerican people. Known as the Long Count and Short Count, they serve to underline what has been called the Maya's "obsession with time." The periods involved are

Tun	18 months or 360 days or 1 year
Katun	7,200 days or 20 years
Baktun	144,000 days or 400 years
Pictun	2,880,000 days or 8,000 years
Calabtun	57,600,000 days or 160,000 years
Kincultun	1,520,000,000 days or 3 million years
Alautun	23,040,000,000 days or 60 million years

As the names of these time periods are formed from the root word "tun," which means "stone," it is obvious that what has been referred to as the Mayan "worship of time" is in actuality yet another way of honoring Hunab Ku.

Long Count dates were written vertically through combinations of just three symbols: a dot equivalent to one, a horizontal bar equal to five, and a zero represented by a shell and several other emblems. Sometimes the dots and bars were stylized. Occasionally, drawings of the grotesque heads of gods were substituted.

The Long Count begins on the date 4 Ahau 8 Cumku, or as expressed in Arabic numerals, 0.0.0.0.0. After one day had elapsed, the Long Count advanced like an automobile's odometer to 0.0.0.0.1., and so on. Using what is known as the Thompson correlation, we can translate 4 Ahau 8 Cumku as being August 9, 3114 B.C. As the calendars of other cultures began, at least in theory, with a certain major event such as the birth of Christ, or when Allah directed Mohammed to flee from Mecca, one would think the same occurred to initiate the Mayan calendar. But what that was is a total mystery. "That's something that's extremely puzzling to us," says Richard Hansen.

Thirteen baktuns of 400 years—or 5,200 years—make up a Mayan Great Cycle. Thus, knowing the starting date, we are able to deduce that the current cycle will end on December 21, 2012. One of the prophecies that has survived concerns the end of this Great Cycle. It has been translated by Makemson from *The Book of Chilam Balam of Tizimin.*

Prophecy of the End of the Great Cycle

> When the original thirteen baktuns were created, a war was waged which caused the country to cease to exist. Little by little, however, our enemies came to hear the prophecies of Ahau; but finally even the hope of hearing Ahau is brought to an end, because of the words of opposition. When the need arises for the high authority at the head of the mat to safeguard our children, then we will feel deeply the tragedy of being captives in war; also when we are ordered to obey. . . . And when over the dark sea I shall be lifted up in a chalice of fire, to that generation there will come the day of withered fruit. . . . The face of the sun will be extinguished because of the great tempest. Then finally ornaments shall descend in heaps. There will be good gifts for one and all, as well as land, from the Great Spirit wherever they shall settle down. Presently Baktun thirteen shall come sailing, figuratively speaking, bringing the ornaments of which I have spoken, from your ancestors. Then the god will come to visit his little cones. Perhaps "After Death" will be the subject of his discourse.

Like many Native American prophecies, and all of the Mayan prophecies that remain, the meaning of this one is obscure and open to interpretation. Is the reference to the "day of withered fruit" a warning about the death of the earth? What are the "ornaments that shall descend in heaps?" Surely missiles and bombs, an obvious choice, cannot bring "good gifts for one and all." Yet the final line seems to be a warning of death and destruction.

Using the Long Count, the Maya recorded dates of historical events in books, on buildings, and on upright stone slabs known as stelae in the ceremonial courtyards. This "stelae cult," as it has sometimes been called, involved the erection of a carved, stone monument at the end of each katun, or twenty-year period, and sometimes even at ten-year intervals. Until recently, the earliest one found had been at Chiapa de Corzo, dated 36 B.C., though RAINPEG is deciphering one from Nakbe that is much older.

Some stelae refer to dates of astonishing antiquity. Stelae D at the ancient city of Quirigua bears the date 7 Ahau 3 Pop, which preceded the erection of the monument by some four hundred million years. Another at Coba, in the Yucatán, refers to an event that occurred forty-two nonillion years before—that is 42 followed by thirty-two zeros.

The number of Mayan centers setting up stelae inscribed with Long Count dates reached a peak in A.D. 790, a date considered to be the pinnacle of Classic Maya civilization. After that, there was a precipitous decline. At Copan, southernmost of the great Classic cities located in what is now Honduras, the last dated monument was erected in A.D. 800. Quirigua, its rival, planted its last stelae in A.D. 810. Uaxactun lasted until A.D. 849, and Seibal to 889. The last stelae found is from Tonina and is inscribed with the Mayan date for A.D. 909.

Shortly after these dates, the magnificent lowland centers were largely abandoned. Precisely why is still a matter of debate, though one prominent theory holds that the priestly elite, mesmerized by their intellectual pursuits, became so detached from the common people and their concerns that a revolution that destroyed society ensued. Another theory blames barbarian hordes from the north of the Valley of Mexico. Whatever the cause, Mayan civilization in the central area fell back to the level of the village. In the Yucatán and

Guatemalan highlands, it revived to some extent under the influence of the Toltecs in the Postclassic Era (A.D. 925 to 1540), yet never again achieved the sophistication in engineering, design, and mathematics of the Classic Period.

The Short Count operated simultaneously with the Long Count and became the primary method of timekeeping during the Postclassic Era. Not anchored to any specific date in time, it cycles over and over like the minute hand of a clock. The Short Count is made up of thirteen katuns, or 260 Mayan years. Because of the mathematical relationship between the 7,200 days of the katun and the 260 days of the Tzolkin, a katun always ends on the day Ahau. At each repetition, however, the attached number decreases by two. Each katun was named for the Ahau day on which it ended and was thought to be ruled over by a favorable, unfavorable, or indifferent deity.

For nearly two millennia, at the end of each katun a city's calendar priest would record the significant happenings in a book made out of the inner bark of a ficus tree then lacquered with a preservative like jesso. These events would include everything from major storms and natural calamities to the actions of rulers, wars, and insurrections to list just a few. Then the priest would fold up the paper lengthwise like a fan, tie it up with two cords, then shelve it in an archive. The record of the katun might not be looked at again until the same point in time during the next 260 year cycle, or a multiple of that cycle, when it might be consulted for advice on how to deal with a similar natural or man-made situation. Although details would vary, it was believed that the broad outline was relevant.

Regularly, people would gather to listen to the priests read aloud from these books and other sacred texts. The contents of some were chanted to the accompaniment of a drum. Others were sung, and still more were acted out dramatically. Unfortunately, none of the chronicles survived the Spanish Conquest. But upon these histories were based the katun prophecies, a few of which have been preserved in the Chilam Balam books.

An example is the general prophecy for Katun 13 Ahau, a date that turns up once every 260 Mayan years, and will next occur on May 30, 2052. It is reproduced here in part from *The Book of Chilam Balam of Tizimin,* this time translated by Brinton.

Prophecy of Katun 13 Ahau

> Eat, eat, thou hast bread;
> Drink, drink, thou hast water;
> On that day, dust possesses the earth,
> On that day, a blight is on the face of the earth,
> On that day, a cloud rises,
> On that day, a mountain rises,
> On that day, a strong man seizes the land,
> On that day, things fall to ruin,
> On that day, the tender leaf is destroyed,
> On that day, the dying eyes are closed,
> On that day, three signs are on the tree,
> On that day, three generations hang there,
> On that day, the battle flag is raised,
> And they are scattered afar in the forests.

Priests and Prophets

Armed with the Tzolkin almanacs, the katun prophecies, and other sacred books, the regular priests, known as *Ah Kin,* ("he of the sun,") would make divinations and sacrifices to various deities. For centuries, these sacrifices were usually turtles, fish, iguanas, turkeys, jaguars, and the like. On special occasions, dogs and human beings were offered. It was not until the Postclassic Era, however, when the Maya came under the influence of bloodthirsty Toltecs, that the famous sacrifices at the Cenote of Chichén Itzá and the ripping out of human hearts became commonplace.

"At Nakbe, we have found evidence of autosacrifice," says RAINPEG project director Richard Hansen. Penis perforation is one example. This ritual involved making a hole in the foreskin of the penis with a lance, then painting the image of a deity with one's blood. Ear, lip, and tongue autosacrifice is also depicted in artwork from other Mayan cities. "But I think that human sacrifice is a fairly late innovation."

Hansen continues, "Prior to the Toltecs, we have excellent information of sacrifice being carried out by the King of Quirigua, who captured and sacrificed the King of Copan. But I think that this was really more of an execution, just ritualized. When you say sacrifice, you're assuming all this gory pageantry. And it may have been that way. But by the same token, the guys that were sacrificed may have been deemed worthy of an execution and they just ritualized it."

Priests who specialized in prophecy were known as the *chilam* ("mouthpiece" or "interpreter of the gods") and their proclamations were widely quoted in politics. Bishop Diego de Landa, in his *Account of the Affairs of Yucatán* written in 1566, relates that the prophets "were so highly esteemed by the people that they carried them about on their shoulders." Besides consulting his books, a *chilam* would arrive at his prognosis through visions that could only be received on specific days. Often, it appears, these would be aided by such drugs as tobacco mixed with lime, peyote, or hallucinogenic mushrooms.

When he was about to receive a vision, a *chilam* would retire to a room in his house and lie down on his back. Falling into a trance, he would then receive divine inspiration from a god or spirit who was thought to have descended to the roof of his house. Afterward, other priests would assemble and listen to the oracle with heads bowed. The *chilams* would frequently refer to historical events. They were stirring enough about the future to capture the imagination yet vague enough to allow for wiggle room.

Chilam Balam, for whom the famous books are named, lived in the village of Mani during the end of the fifteenth and beginning of the sixteenth centuries. Balam, in Yucatec Mayan, means "jaguar." Chilam translates as "prophet." So, Chilam Balam means Jaguar Prophet. However, since Balam is also a common family name in the region, the manuscripts could also be interpreted as being titled, *The Book of the Prophet Jaguar.*

Originally, Chilam Balam's book was written in Maya hieroglyphic writing. But in 1562, Diego de Landa burned some twenty-seven of these books in the village of Mani. "We found a great number of books in these letters of theirs," he later wrote in his *Account,* "and because they contained nothing but superstition and the devil's falsehoods, we burned the lot, which upset them most grievously and caused them great pain."

Other Catholic priests did the same. Afterward, naturally, the books that escaped the fire were carefully concealed. When they wore out from constant use, transcriptions were made by Mayan scribes educated by the Spanish. By that time, few people could read the hieroglyphic writing any longer, so they were written in Latin script. Then, they were then passed down through the generations from hand to hand.

Chilam Balam's final and most famous prophecy concerns the Itzas, believed by the great Mayanist J. Eric Thompson to be a branch of the seafaring Chontal Maya who invaded and occupied the abandoned Classic Mayan city now known as Chichén Itzá around A.D. 918. Some sixty years later, a second invasion force of Toltecs arrived at Chichén Itzá from the Valley of Mexico and took power. The Toltecs were extremely militaristic, fond of human sacrifice, and brought with them the worship of the Feathered Serpent god, Quetzalcoatl—known to the Maya as Kukulcán. This god will be examined in detail in the next chapter. But for now, it is important to understand that the Feathered Serpent worshiped at Chichén Itzá was a corruption of what had originally been an enlightened being.

In time, the Itzas threw off their veneer of foreign influence and restored much of their Mayanism. But the arrival of the Spanish signaled the beginning of the civilization's end.

For centuries, Chilam Balam's final prophecy has been interpreted by Eurocentric thinkers as foretelling the coming of the Europeans with a new religion. But many Maya today view it far differently. The following rendition is taken from *The Book of Chilam Balam of Chumayel.*

Prophecy of Chilam Balam

On the day 13 Ahau the katun will end in the time of the Itza, in the time of Tancah [Mayapan], lord. There is the sign of Hunab-ku on high. The raised wooden standard shall come. It shall be displayed to the world, that the world may be enlightened, lord. There has been a beginning of strife, there has been a beginning of rivalry, when the priestly man shall come to bring the sign [of God] in time to come, lord. . . . A new day shall dawn in the north, in the west. Itzamna Kauil shall rise. Our lord comes, Itza. Our elder brother comes, [oh] men of Tantun. Receive your guests, the bearded men, the men of the east, the bearers of the sign of God, lord. Good indeed is the word of God that comes to us. The day of our regeneration comes. You do not fear the world, Lord, you are the only God who created us. It is sufficient, then, that the *word* of God is good, lord. [He is] the guardian of our souls. He who receives him, who has truly believed, he will go to heaven with him. Nevertheless [at] the beginning were the two-day men.

Let us exalt his sign on high, let us exalt it [that we may gaze upon it today] with the raised standard. Great is the discord that arises today. The First Tree of the World is restored; it is displayed to the world. This is the sign of Hunab-ku on high. Worship it, Itza. You shall worship today his sign on high. You shall worship it further-more with true good will, and you shall worship the true God today, lord. You shall be converted to the word of Hunab-ku, lord; it came from heaven. Oh it is he who speaks to you! Be admonished indeed, Itza. They will correct their ways who receive him in their hearts in another katun, lord.

Believe in my word itself, I am Chilam Balam, and I have inter-preted the entire message of the true God [of] the world; it is heard in every part of the world, lord, the word of God, the Lord of heaven and earth. Very good indeed is his word in heaven, lord.

He is ruler over us; he is the true God over our souls. But those whom [the word] is brought, lord: thrice weighed down is their strength, the younger brothers' native to the land. Their hearts are submerged [in sin]. They are frequent backsliders, the principal ones who spread [sin], Nacxit Xuchit in the carnal sin of his compan-ions, the two-day rulers. [They sit] crookedly on their thrones; crookedly in carnal sin. Two-day men they call them. For two days [endure] their seats, their cups, their hats. They are the unrestrained lewd ones of the day, the unrestrained lewd ones of the night, the rogues of the world. They twist their necks, they wink their eyes, they slaver at the mouth, at the rulers of the land, lord. Behold, when they come, there is no truth in the words of the foreigners to the land. They tell very solemn and mysterious things, the sons of the men of Seven-deserted buildings, the offspring of the women of Seven-deserted buildings, lord.

Who will be the prophet, who will be the priest who shall inter-pret truly the word of the book?*

According to many Maya, the prevailing interpretation of the Jaguar Prophet's declaration has been entirely wrong. "The proph-

*From *The Book of Chilam Balam of Chumayel,* by Ralph L. Roys, With an Introduction by J. Eric S. Thompson. New edition copyright © 1967 by the University of Oklahoma Press.

ecy means that in the new time, the Itzas—meaning the Mayas—and their knowledge are going to come back," declares Hunbatz Men. "The first tree of the world is the holy Ceiba tree of the Maya. Hunab Ku will be recognized as creator."

When Hunbatz attended the convocation of Mayan elders early in March 1990, in the village of San Francisco el Alta, they conferred about the prophecies.

"The conclusion was that at this time, we need to do more rituals," he states. "More rituals everywhere. We're going to go again to the very old, sacred places and make rituals there. The pyramids belong more to the Indians than to some official system like the government. So we're going to go to more of those places, to reopen our sacred centers again for people to try to understand the knowledge that is there. We need to take in the knowledge of the Sun. To understand what we have in our memory. With that energy, we are going to wake up those centers, activate them, and wake up society."

CHAPTER TWO

THE AZTECS: CULT OF THE FIFTH SUN

I am like the quetzal bird, I am created in the house of the
 one only God; I sing sweet songs among the flowers; I
 chant songs and rejoice in my heart.

The fuming dew-drops from the flowers in the field
 intoxicate my soul.
I grieve to myself that ever this dwelling on earth should
 end.
I foresaw, being a Mexican, that our rule began to be
 destroyed, I went forth weeping . . . .
Let me not be angry that the grandeur of Mexico is to be
 destroyed.
The smoking stars gather together against it; the one who
 cares for flowers is about to be destroyed.
He who cared for books wept, he wept for the beginning
 of the destruction.

—"A Song of Lamentation," No. 25,
from *Ancient Nahuatl Poetry*

Before the arrival of the Spanish in central Mexico, ominous
signs appeared that many Native Americans interpreted as the
foretelling of impending doom. The first of these was a comet, or
"smoking star," that Aztec emperor Moctezuma Xocoyotzin (Moctezuma II) observed from the roof of his royal palace in Tenochtit-

lán. It appeared in the east at midnight, as bright as the dawn, then stretched across to the very center of the heavens.

Such "tongues of flames" were always considered evil omens by the Aztecs, or Mexicas as they called themselves. But this one was particularly frightening to Moctezuma in light of the startling warning by Nezahaulpilli, the wise astronomer-king of the allied city-state of Texcoco, that a sign would soon appear in the heavens signaling the beginning of the end.

According to a prophecy that had been in widespread circulation for centuries throughout the Valley of Mexico, a part-man, part-god named Ce Acatl Topiltzin, or Quetzalcoatl, would one day return to reclaim his kingdom which had been "guarded" by the Aztecs since his departure from the abandoned Toltec capital of Tollán. (In the language of Nahuatl, used throughout the central highlands, *Ce Acatl* means "One Reed," the date of Topiltzin's birth.) For political reasons, Moctezuma, who was himself regarded as a god upon whom men could not gaze, claimed that he was only keeping the empire for Topiltzin-Quetzalcoatl until his return.

A great teacher and innovator, the Toltec ruler-god Topiltzin-Quetzalcoatl had stood in opposition to the militarists of Tollán, believing that flowers, butterflies, and snails might be sacrificed to God, but never human beings. As we shall demonstrate, it was because of this uncompromising stand that he was forced to flee Tollán.

Quetzalcoatl was one of many connections to the classic artistic and intellectual heritage of the Toltecs that gave the insecure Aztec ruling class the legitimacy they felt was needed by a great power. After all, only two hundred years before they had been nomadic barbarians—a fact about which they were only too aware. Yet their regard for the great civilizer was insincere. For while the Feathered Serpent's temples had been allowed to deteriorate, the sacrifice of humans to Huitzilopochtli, Aztec God of the Sun, proceeded at a ferocious pace and the skulls piled up.

About thirty years old, tall and slender, with a rather long face, Moctezuma sported a sparse, black beard and wore his dark hair over his ears. As he contemplated the smoking star, he pulled on his beard nervously. Throughout his brief reign as Cemanahuac Tlatoani, or "Ruler of the World," he had been on guard for signs of Quetzalcoatl's return. Tradition held that he had been making arrows while away. And if he returned in the year One Reed, still ten years in the future, he would strike down kings. Could it be, wondered the Great Lord as he observed the comet, that he was about to live through what had been foretold?

Moctezuma observed the comet for most of the night. Then, the next morning, he visited the King of Texcoco, Nezahaulpilli, at his sumptuous palace and asked for the learned man's help in understanding the meaning of the awesome celestial event. As related to chronicler Fray Diego Duran shortly after the Spanish Conquest, he was told

Nezahaulpilli's Prediction

> Oh lord, your vassals, the astrologers, soothsayers and diviners have been careless! That sign in the heavens has been there for some time and yet you describe it to me now as if it were a new thing. . . . That brilliant star . . . is an ill omen for our kingdoms; terrible, frightful things will come upon them. In all our lands and provinces there will be great calamities and misfortunes, not a thing will be left standing. Death will dominate the land! All our dominions will be lost and all of this will be done with the permission of the Lord of the Heights, of the Day and the Night and of the Wind. You will be witness to these things since it will all happen in your time.

Moctezuma repaired sullenly to the altar atop the magnificent Great Temple in the center of the sacred precinct of Tenochtitlán where, as head priest of Huitzilopochti, he offered the hearts and blood of countless human beings to the Sun. Despite his determined efforts to forestall the end of the age, other fateful signs appeared over the next ten years: The Temple of Huitzilopochtli spontaneously burst into flames that no amount of water could extinguish. Then a second smoking star, so bright it was visible in the western sky during the day, split into three parts, provoking such great paranoia amongst the populous that they talked of nothing else night and day.

Another time, Duran tells us, some hunters brought Moctezuma a strange bird they had snared on Lake Texcoco. The bird was ashen in color, and shaped similarly to a brown crane. Imbedded in its head, however, was a round, obsidian mirror. When the anxiety-ridden sovereign peered into the mirror, he glimpsed the stars and heavens, then a massive army riding upon the backs of deer. Shaken, Moctezuma consulted his astrologers and wise men. But when he looked into the mirror a third time, the bodeful images disappeared.

Inauspicious events accumulated. And the great Moctezuma, ruler of thirty-eight provinces and an estimated fifteen million souls, wept.

So it was he was not surprised that in the year Ce Acatl, known to us as A.D. 1519, it was reported that strange and powerful beings had arrived upon the eastern shore. Burdened by the prophecies, the apprehensive ruler secretly dispatched emissaries bearing gifts. In doing so, he initiated a fateful chain of events that would result in the fulfillment of the auguries of doom, the destruction of his empire, and the proclamation of a final Aztec prophecy that reverberates in Mexico today. For the visitors turned out to be led not by the enlightened Quetzalcoatl returning to reign over his domain on the year of his birth, but rather a cunning Spanish rebel with dreams of fame and fortune by the name of Hernando Cortez.

•

To fully understand Moctezuma Xocoyotzin's fearful obsession with the future, we must first travel back approximately five hundred years further in time, to what Western civilization considers to be the close of the first millennium. There, at the dawn of Aztec history, we are told that the tribe occupied seven caves, sometimes referred to as "barrios," in a land known as Aztlan. At that time, Aztlan was most probably a distant province of the then powerful and influential Toltec Empire.

Whether driven out by drought, disgust for the Toltec yoke, or the desire to achieve their *anecuyotl,* or destiny, as conquerors of the world, the Aztecs headed south. Priests carried their religious relics in four sacred bundles. During this period of migration, the Aztecs, like the Hopis far to the north, settled in various locations, sometimes for years at a time. One of these places was Coatepec, not far from the Toltec capital of Tollán, which itself was located just to the north of the Valley of Mexico.

After the Aztecs had been at Coatepec for some time, differences surfaced as to whether or not the tribe should move on. One faction, the "Four Hundred Southerners" (four hundred meaning, in Nahuatl, "infinite"), who were followers of Coyolxauhqui, the goddess of the moon, felt that the tribe should remain at Coatepec permanently under the tutelage of the Toltecs. Another powerful faction believed that only by leaving could they fulfill their destiny. The disagreement bubbled and brewed, then turned into a civil war that led to a climactic battle on Coatepec Hill.

BIRTH OF HUITZILOPOCHTLI

Although there are several versions of this pivotal event in Aztec history, one mythic rendition, passed down by pioneer ethnohistorian Fray Bernardino de Sahagun, claims the conflict started with a woman named Coatlicue. More than just a woman, Coatlicue was, in fact, goddess of the earth, and mother of the gods. While sweeping a temple one day, a ball of sacred feathers floated by which Coatlicue grabbed and secreted next to her breasts. In this way, it is said she became pregnant. As Coatlicue was already mother of the Four Hundred Southerners, who represented all the stars in the sky; and Coyolxauhqui, who was the moon; she was berated by her angry offspring for bringing great dishonor upon the family by her pregnancy. So, Coyolxauhqui urged her brothers to kill their mother as well as the illegitimate unborn child.

According to the myth, a sister of one of the Four Hundred informed the fetus of their siblings' plans. So, to save his mother's life, Huitzilopochtli sprang from his mother's womb, born for war.

> [He] attacked Coyolxauhqui,
> He cut off her head,
> which was left abandoned
> on the slopes of Coatepetl.
> The body of Coyolxauhqui
> went rolling down
> as it fell, dismembered,
> in different places fell her hands,
> her legs, her body.
> Then Huitzilopochtli rose up,

he pursued the Four Hundred Southerners,
he harassed them, he put them to
flight.

The struggle for dominance that occurred between two very real early Aztec factions had been elevated to a mythic battle between gods. As Huitzilopochtli represents the sun at noon, the myth resonated with and was validated by observation of the natural world. When it rises, the sun can be thought of as slaying the moon and chasing away the stars with its radiance. Yet more importantly, each time the story was told that Huitzilopochtli emerged from the womb, slew his sister, then cut off her head and rolled it down the hill, the violent pattern of Aztec culture was reinforced. As we shall see, this act of "divine retribution" was only one of a number of ways that the Mexica attempted to provide a religious justification for their astonishingly violent acts.

AZTEC MOTHER EARTH

Huitzilopochtli's mother, Coatlicue, was memorialized by the Aztecs in a colossal, eight-foot stone sculpture that is one of the most alarming statues ever created. Rather than being an accurate representation of a human being, the effigy instead is a collection of horrific ritual symbols. The figure has, first of all, been decapitated and out of its stump of a neck rise two contentious serpents. A necklace of human hearts and hands hang around her neck and mid-back, a skull with apron. Claws extend from her hands and feet, and around her waist is fastened a skirt of writhing snakes.

Buried after the conquest, the sculpture was rediscovered in 1790 under the Zocalo, or central square, in Mexico City—a space that also served as the central square during the time of the Aztecs. The representation of Coatlicue so frightened the Dominican professors that came into possession of it—they feared it would incite the Natives into a pagan frenzy—that they had it reburied on the grounds of the University of Mexico. It has since been exhumed and is on display at the National Museum of Anthropology.

This, then, was the Aztec's version of Mother Earth. She was thought to have created all life and received the dead back into her body. Far from being the nurturing, benevolent diety honored in other Native American cultures, however, Coatlicue was an intimidating power that reflected most of all the Mexica's bloodthirsty culture.

•

Huitzilopochtli's followers soon departed from Coatepec and headed south. Around A.D. 1165, they arrived in Tollán, capital of the Toltec Empire, where, according to Mexican scholar Eduardo Matos Moctezuma, "it is likely that they played a part in its collapse." Eventually, the Aztec wanderers settled in the Province of Colhuacan where they became vessels of a great lord named Achitometl. Colhuacan was a bastion of Toltec culture. In exchange for use of the land and his protection, Achitometl demanded that the Aztecs fight as his mercenaries in war and pay him tribute in the form of canoes and labor.

The Mexicas first established their reputation for outrageous religious and political behavior during this period. Once, after a battle in the service of Achitometl, the ruler asked for proof of the Aztec's claims of victory. The indignant warriors responded by delivering a bag of ears.

Later, with thoughts of elevating the lowly barbarian's stature, Achitometl offered one of his daughters in marriage to one of their leaders. The Aztecs thanked him graciously, and invited him to a festival of Huitzilopochtli. Imagine the reaction of the proud father, expecting to see his daughter as a bride, and instead, in the middle of the festivities, seeing a priest dance in front of his table wearing his daughter's flayed skin! This ghastly practice of skinning and wearing the victims of sacrifice for up to twenty days—thought to symbolize a corn in its husk and regeneration—came to be so popular that an entire month was dedicated to it. The principle ceremony was known as the Feast of Xipe Totec.

FOUNDING OF TENOCHTITLÁN

Fleeing the horrified and vengeful Colhuacans, the Aztecs were forced to seek refuge far to the south upon a tiny, unoccupied island in the marshlands in the middle of Lake Texcoco. There, in A.D. 1325, they founded their capital of Tenochtitlán. The marshy island belonged to the Azcapotzalcos, who demanded, in the time honored manner of Mesoamerican societies, tribute and mercenary labor in exchange for the right to stay. The Aztecs complied for they had finally found their home.

Solace was found in the wondrous physical setting of their new capital. Two snowcapped volcanoes, skirted with lush, green forests, loomed over the landscape. The shimmering sapphire lake teemed with fish, frogs, and birds. It has been said that location is everything and the Aztecs certainly had that. So they started a market and invited the peoples living around Lake Texcoco and the four connecting lakes to trade.

The ancestors of many of these people had once been under the dominion of the Toltecs and were still influenced by their advanced ways. In the years to come, they would have much to teach the barbarians from Aztlan about the classic heritage of that lost civilization. Considering the Toltec's achievements in art and architecture, in astronomy and the sciences, in agriculture, in the organization of their entire society, and the fact that—unlike after the fall of Rome—the Toltec language, religion, and tradition of polygamy had been kept alive after the fall of Tollán, the Mexica were keenly aware that they had a lot to live up to if they were ever to achieve greatness.

Fifty years would pass before they were organized enough to select their first sovereign, or *tlatoani* (Nahuatl for "speaker"). For another fifty years beyond that, the Aztecs lived as dependents of the Azcapotzalcos, forced to fight or donate labor on call, and deliver onerous loads of lake products, junipers, willows, and floating gardens of maize, chile, beans, and squash in tribute.

Time not spent in such servitude was used to construct Tenochtitlán. Swampland adjacent to the island was laboriously filled in, expanding the acreage. The city-to-be was divided into quadrants bisected by four roads. These roads were aligned, in the Mayan manner, to major celestial events and met at the Great Temple.

Though the city was built on top of a lake, it was not long before the supply of drinking water was insufficient to support the growing population. To address the problem, engineers proposed that a stone aqueduct be constructed to bring water across the lake from Chapultepec. The Azcapotzalcos, however, refused to grant permission for the project and in a fatal mistake, assassinated the Aztec's young *tlatoani,* Chimalpopoca.

In response, the Aztecs launched their war of independence. A hardened veteran of mercenary service named Itzcoatl was selected as the new *tlatoani* in 1427. Less than a year later, after a bloody struggle, the Azcapotzalcos were overthrown and the direction of the flow of tribute was reversed. With the momentum of victory behind him, Itzcoatl launched a campaign of military expansion in league with the great city-state of Texcoco and the lesser one of Tlacopan. The "Triple Alliance" went on to conquer the regions surrounding Lake Texcoco, then moved on to more distant provinces in order to fulfill their self-proclaimed destiny of "conquerors of the world."

They called their realm Anahuac. One of Moctezuma Xocoyotzin's titles was Cemanahuac Tlatoani, or Ruler of the World. The word Cemanahuac is a compound construction. "Cem" means union or conjunction, and "anahuac" translates as encircled by water, or within water. Thus, Cemanahuac means "the great earth encircled and surrounded by water." Or possibly "union with the land (Tenochtitlán) surrounded by water (Lake Texcoco)."

"More than fifty-two groups of Indians made up the Confederation of Anahuac," states Hunbatz Men. "At one time it included the Toltecs, all the Indians from the north, the Otomis, the Anasazi. It was the biggest confederation that ever existed in North America and included part of Central America and a lot of other places."

Anahuac, though, at the time of the Aztecs was not the democratically advanced, egalitarian state the Iroquois Confederacy was operating during roughly the same period far to the north. Although it is true that each conquered province was permitted to keep its own internal government, and ceded foreign affairs to the national level, they were also forced to erect a temple for Huitzilopochtli on an equal footing with the supreme, local god. On a federal level, the *tlatoani* was originally elected. But by the time the Spanish arrived, the Aztec Empire actually functioned like an absolute monarchy, with power passing from one member of the ruling family to the next, and all power in the hands of the Cemanahuac Tlatoani, the Ruler of the World.

The Aztecs: Cult of the Fifth Sun · 3 1

CULT OF THE FIFTH SUN

It was during the thirteen-year reign of Itzcoatl that the task of reinventing the Aztecs was undertaken. If their past as nomadic fighters was nothing to brag about, went the reasoning, then why not simply rewrite it? The society that these fierce warriors had forged needed sanction by the gods. In order to achieve it, the ancient codices containing historical accounts were ordered burned and a thorough reexamination of myths and legends was begun.

Spearheading the reform effort was a key councilor named Tlacaelel. Under his leadership, the royal households were refurbished and the military was restructured. The judiciary was reorganized with nonnoble judges to mete out equal justice under the exceedingly harsh laws. Drunkeness and adultery, for example, were punishable by death. Rigorous sumptuary laws were also promulgated. Only nobles were permitted to drink cocoa, and wear cotton clothes and elaborate jewelry. Merchants were allowed to indulge in such privileges only on their annual holiday. Any other time, they, like the commoners, could be executed on the spot.

Individual initiative, however, continued to play an important role in rejuvenating society. If you were a man, you could work your way up into the military aristocracy through courageous acts such as capturing prisoners for sacrifice. The successful merchant class also offered opportunities for advancement, and support for corporations involved in long-distance trade was strengthened.

Itzcoatl then sanctioned a new history of the people that was considered to be more accurately reflective of the supreme role that they had carved out for themselves. The philosophers and wise men who stitched together the new worldview allowed most of the old beliefs to survive. But important new ones had to be tailored from whole cloth.

One example concerns the Aztec's arrival upon the island and the founding of their capital. The reality of the tale was simply too undignified, Tlacaelel argued. So, after the theoreticians did their creative work and their ideas were duly deliberated upon, it was announced and maintained from that day forth that before the Aztecs had come to Tenochtitlán, Huitzilopochtli had appeared to a priest in a dream. Duran takes up the tale:

Prophecy of the Founding of Tenochtitlán

You will remember [said Huitzilopochtli] how I commanded you to slay my nephew, Copil, ordering you to remove his heart and toss it among the reeds and rushes. This you have done. Know now that his heart fell on a stone and from this sprang a prickly pear cactus. This cactus is so wondrously tall that it bears the nest of an eagle. Each day the eagle in his nest eats the finest and most beautiful birds of the land. In his lair on the cactus he stretches out his large and handsome wings to receive the heat of the sun and the freshness of the morning. You will always find the eagle on this tree that sprouted from the heart of my nephew Copil, and all around it you will see innumerable green, blue, red, yellow, and white plumes from the splendid birds on which the eagle feeds. The place of the cactus and the eagle I now name Tenochtitlán. Place near the Hard Prickly Pear Cactus.

Another example of Tlacaelel's reconceptualization concerned the ritual sacrifice of human beings. The offering of humans to the gods had long been practiced throughout Mesoamerica. But in no other society, with the exception, perhaps, of the Toltecs, did the ceremonial spilling of human blood play as central a role as among the Aztecs. Aside from the mystical idea of feeding the gods with that which is most precious, immolation had a very real political purpose. And that was the intimidation of current and potential subjects. Anger the Mexicas, refuse to pledge obeisance, fail to maintain tribute, and thousands of your finest young men could end up on the sacrificial stone. So, to sanctify what many saw as an abhorrent, barbaric practice, Tlacaelel and his wise men decided to rewrite the story of the creation of the present age.

Accepted as a given was the old belief that before this world there were four previous ages, or Suns. Four-Ocelotl ended when giants that inhabited the earth were killed off by ocelots or jaguars. Four-Ehecatl, the second Sun, was blown away by a hurricane. The third, 4-Quauhuitl, was destroyed by a fiery rain. And the fourth Sun, 4-Atl, ended in a flood. The fifth Sun is the Sun of Movement, 4-Ollin, and it was considered to be the Age of Earthquakes. Accordingly, the story went out that at the end of the previous age, the gods had gathered amidst the ancient pyramids of the sun and moon at Teotihuacán to consider how to restart the universe.

The gods knew that in order to ignite the Fifth Age one of them would have sacrifice himself in the enormous fire that was burning nearby. Naturally not wanting to die, the gods procrastinated. Finally, an ugly little deity named Nanahuatzin, "The Pimply One," threw himself into the flames and the sound of his roasting body filled the air. Challenged by his bravery, a second god followed the lead of the first. According to Sahagun, the gods then honored Nanahuatzin as he rose into the sky, "faltering from side to side," as the sun.

The Fifth Age had thus been energized by the blood of the gods and the universe was reborn, though it was a wobbly creation. Most important, however, was how this new view of creation related to those of flesh and blood who inhabited the earth. How could anyone object to human sacrifice, it was argued, since the gods had made the supreme sacrifice themselves. Tlacaelel insisted that it was inevitable that one day the age would end in an apocalypse. But it was possible to delay that fateful day by maintaining the life of the sun by providing it with that most precious of liquids, human blood. If such a practice were to cease, this insane logic reasoned, then the sun would fall from the heavens and the age would come to and end. According to a 1558 version of the Leyenda de los Soles:

Prophecy of the End of the Fifth Age

> The Fifth Sun, its sign 4-Movement, is called the Sun of Movement because it moves and follows its path. And as the elders continue to say, under this Sun, there will be earthquakes and hunger, and then our end shall come.

As the names of the previous Suns were taken from the date on which they were destroyed, we know that the Aztecs believed the current, Fifth Age, will end on the date of 4-Movement. That, unfortunately, only tells the day and not the year. According to Table VI in Caso's *Los Calendarios Prehispanicos,* the day 4-Movement correlates to May 10 on the Gregorian calendar. According to the prophecy, earthquakes and hunger will ravage the earth, then on that fateful day in an unknown year, the Fifth Age will come to an end.

•

The conquered provinces delivered up massive quantities of tribute. By A.D. 1519, a total of 371 towns were paying regularly to Tenochtitlán. Aside from agricultural products such as cotton, maize, cacao, and fruit; and building materials like stone and wood; a wide variety of manufactured items were also demanded. These included military uniforms and insignia; weapons; men's, women's, and children's clothing; gold, jewels, and mosaic art works; and utilitarian items like paper, reed and straw products, pottery, and boats. Labor was also provided as tribute. All of this was overseen by tax-gatherers appointed for each province and carefully recorded by scribes.

Because of this system, the Aztec ruling class and their allies grew fabulously wealthy. But the union was a turbulent one. There was, quite naturally, bitter resentment over the way the Aztecs treated everyone. Yet because of the climate of terror that had been fostered to ensure that the flow of tribute continued, the rebellions in the provinces, which the Aztecs eagerly awaited as a means to gather prisoners for their sacrificial offerings, after a while slowed to a trickle.

FLOWERY WARS

Peace created real problems for the Aztecs because their society was, after all, geared toward war. The majority of the young men—especially among the common people—attended a school known as the *telpochcalli,* where everything possible was done to prepare them for battle from earliest childhood on. The exploits of the nation's fiercest warriors were held up as models of exemplary behavior. Brainwashed with the idea that to die in war, or as a sacrifice, promised eternal happiness as a companion of the sun, the idea was held widely that to be Aztec was to fight.

Furthermore, Huitzilopochtli, who had guided them to victory after victory as the empire was assembled, had long been nourished by human blood. And he needed more. The Ocelot and Eagle warrior societies had a sacred obligation to supply sacrificial victims. But where could they be found in times of peace?

To solve this problem that threatened the very foundation of Aztec society, Tlacaelel arrived at an ingenious yet diabolical solution called the Flowery Wars. He told his brother, Moctezuma I, who had succeeded Itzcoatl, of his plan. "Our god need not depend on the occasion of an affront to go to war," said Tlacaelel according to Duran. "Rather, let a convenient market be sought where our god may go with his army to buy victims and people to eat as if he were to go to a nearby place to buy tortillas . . . whenever he wishes or feels like it. And may our people go to this place with their armies to buy with their blood, their heads, and their hearts and lives, those precious stones, jade, and brilliant and wide plumes . . . for the service of the admirable Huitzilopochtli. . . . Our god will feed himself with them as though he were eating warm tortillas, soft and tasty, straight out of the oven. . . . And this war should be of such a nature that we do not endeavor to destroy the others totally. War must always continue."

The Flowery Wars were more like deadly dances than the all-out destructive onslaughts that we associate with the word *war.* For their purpose was not to kill but capture opposing warriors to sacrifice to Huitzilopochtli. The last thing one would want to achieve, according to this reasoning, would be to totally destroy an enemy's society. If that were to occur, where would one gather the most precious of offerings?

THE GREAT TEMPLE

During the final eighty years of the empire, Tlacaelel's reformulation of the official state ideology resulted in an horrendous increase in the number of human sacrifices. The most important rituals were presided over by the emperor at the Great Temple, which was the physical and spiritual center of the Aztec universe. Estimated to have been fifteen stories in height, the Great Temple dominated the city and was enlarged and rebuilt seven times. Pyramidal in structure, it faced west and had two steep stairways of 114 steps that ran parallel to the top. At the summit, were twin temples. One was for the patron god of the Aztecs, Huitzilopochtli, and another for Tlaloc, the ancient god of rain.

A green, sacrificial stone was set in front of the idol of Huitzilopochtli. At the climax of a colorful ceremony in which elaborately costumed priests and captives dressed like gods danced to sacred songs, a captive would be laid backward over the green sacrificial stone. While held down by four attendants, the presiding priest would quickly cut through the victim's chest wall with a flint or obsidian knife, reach in with his hand, locate the still-beating heart, and rip it out. The heart would be held up as an offering to the sun, with the vapor given off regarded with special reverence. It was then placed in a vessel and burnt or eaten by the priests. Following the pattern first set by the treatment of Coyolxauhqui, Goddess of the Moon, at Coatepec Hill, the body was then thrown down the temple steps where, at the bottom, it was decapitated and dismembered. After skinning, the skull was displayed in the open air on one of seven large skull racks.

In 1487, at the rededication of the enlarged Great Temple presided over by Emperor Ahuitzotl, Duran reports that captives were mustered out before dawn and positioned in four lines that stretched from the Great Temple outward along the four causeways that led into Tenochtitlán. Each line was about three miles in length. Emperor Ahuitzotl, and his three top princely advisers, one of which was Tlacaelel, took their places and, armed with sacrificial knives, began the killing. When the lords grew tired, priests took over. The sacrifices went on for four days, from dawn to dusk, and by the time it was over, 80,400 men had been sacrificed. Blood ran down to the bottom of the Great Pyramid like a river, where priests scooped it up in gourds. Then they ran to their various temples and smeared it on the walls.

Ahuitzotl had wanted a spectacle that would impress and intimidate his guests, who included not only the leaders of the subjugated provinces, but his enemies, as well. That goal was certainly achieved. The stench of death was so overpowering, however, that residents of Tenochtitlán were sickened as a result.

Ripping out a human heart was not the only way of honoring the Mexica's bloodthirsty deities. Other methods were practiced, including being shot with arrows, burning, gladiatorial combat, and, if you were female, beheading. Drowning was a favorite method of sacrificing victims to Tlaloc. Children in particular were favored. The more the youngsters screamed and wailed, it was thought, the better were the chances of rain. Quail and other kinds of birds and animals were offered to various local deities. But in all of the most important ceremonials, human blood was required.

During the reign of Moctezuma II, a number of mass immolations were held like the one initiated by Ahuitzotl. According to Native testimony collected by Sahagun, "when they had completely ended the slaying . . . all the chiefs and lords, who were men due great reverence, were ready, and stood waiting in complete array. Moctezuma led them. He had put on the turquoise diadem, the royal diadem. . . . In either hand they grasped a paper incense bag. Thereupon they came down [from the temple], dancing rapidly. And when they had descended, then they circled [the courtyard] . . . four times. And when they had danced, then they dispersed and went away, and thereupon all entered the palace in proper order. And this was known as the Lordly Dance."

NEW FIRE CEREMONY

Every fifty-two years, a pivotal ceremonial pageant known as the Bundling of the Years, or New Fire Ceremony, was held. Based on observation of the Pleiades star group, known in Nahuatl as Tianquitzli ("marketplace"), the ceremony would commemorate its reappearance at precisely the same spot on the horizon. On that night, the cluster of stars makes a dramatic meridian transit of the heavens. The New Fire Ceremony paid homage to the supreme god Ometeotl, whom we will examine soon, while at the same time underlining the central role of the *tlatoani* as father and mother of the empire.

The ceremony was a major event not only for the society, but in each individual's life as well, since few would ever witness the great spectacle of renewal twice. In the nights leading up to the ceremony that had been awaited with great anticipation for 18,980 days, the people of Anahuac would ritually extinguish all fires, toss household statues of deities and hearthstones into lakes and streams, and sweep homes and city streets clean. Sahagun tells us that women were locked up to prevent them from being transformed into monsters, and children were kept awake so that they would not turn into mice. At the core of the ceremony was the belief that if the Pleiades did not appear, terrible monsters would be set loose to roam the earth and the end of the universe would be at hand.

The ritual began when a procession of priests and a brave captive warrior dressed "in the garb of the gods" ascended the Hill of the

Star to a ceremonial observatory overlooking Tenochtitlán. The city-dwellers, meanwhile, vowing to stay up all night, climbed onto their roofs, and anxiously observed the shrine.

Upon the summit of the hill, an assemblage of the most important astronomers, priests, and lords were gathered to await the momentous event. When the stars appeared, there were suppressed sighs of relief. Rapidly, the Pleiades would rise to its zenith at midnight, to a spot directly overhead which the Aztecs believed was the fifth cardinal point.

The night was thus considered to be divided in half and the people were reassured that the the universe would have another fifty-two years. The astronomers and daykeepers synchronized their calendars. Then, a little pile of kindling was ignited on the bare chest of the brave warrior, whom four attending priests had stretched supine over a stone. As soon as a bit of fire fell onto his chest, the presiding priest would slash open the warrior's chest with a knife, rip out his heart, and set it into the fire. In his open wound, a new fire was started.

Watching from their rooftops, the people pierced their flesh with cactus thorns and cut their ears. Then they flicked the blood with a middle finger toward the flames. The fire was then carried down the mountain by a runner to the Great Temple, where it was placed in the fire holder of Huitzilopochtli's temple. There, priests from throughout the imperial realm were gathered, and in a ceremony presided over by the *tlatoani,* they received the new fire and carried it back to the people of the empire. The last Aztec New Fire Ceremony occurred in November 1507, and was presided over by Moctezuma Xocoyotzin.

AZTEC PHILOSOPHY

Though Huitzilopochtli was the national deity, not every Aztec held him in high esteem. Many wise people and philosophers expressed their doubt openly and, casting aside myths and popular beliefs, speculated about the nature of God and what humankind's role in the scheme of things might be.

Popular religion incorporated literally hundreds of diverse regional gods, yet above all stood Ometeotl. Referred to by many names, including Lord of the Close Vicinity, Lord of the Every-where, The One Only God, and Tloque Nahauque, this ultimate, unseen deity was perceived as being beyond time, self-invented, and everlasting. Ometeotl resided in the twelfth heaven, which was uppermost in the Mexica conception of the universe. It was this god that was thought to have placed man on earth and determined the fate of each individual.

Knowing the exact time and day on which a person was born, and to a lesser extent, of other important occasions, like entering school or getting married, was critical in the all-important task of divining that person's future.

Immediately after a child was born, an astrologer-priest would be summoned and would arrive carrying the *tonalamatl,* or the "book of the days and destinies." Leafing through the crinkly pages of black and red ink, he would solemnly determine whether the infant was born on a good day or bad.

All of this harkens back to the Maya. For they were the ones who first developed sacred astrology and formulated the concept of the unseen, all-powerful god, whom they know as Hunab Ku.

Among the more pessimistic Mexica, however, the Lord of the Close Vicinity was considered to be more than the impersonal godhead whose sole role is as "giver of movement and measure." Recorded by Sahagun, the wise men explained: "Our Master, the Lord of the Close Vicinity, thinks and does what He wishes; He determines, He amuses himself. As he wishes, so will it be. In the palm of His hand He has us. . . . We shift around, like marbles we roll; He rolls us around endlessly. We are but toys to Him; He laughs at us."

So the ultimate Aztec God found human beings a joke. And, according to this school of thought, nothing we do really matters. Of course, it is not hard to understand how such a conclusion had been reached. The Aztecs placed little value on human happiness. Reality for most people was fraught with anxiety and pain, whether through endless work for oppressive tribute, capture and sacrifice on the stone, or as servants of brutal, demanding gods. Considering the amount of blood flowing in Tenochtitlán, it is easy to under-stand the pervasive sadness of the Mexica. Death came as a release. As one anonymous Aztec poet put it:

> Truly earth is not the place of reality.
> Indeed one must go elsewhere;
> beyond, happiness exists.
> Or is it that we come to earth in vain?
> Certainly some other place is the abode of life.

One's ultimate destiny after death was determined not by the manner in which one had lived life, but rather by how one died. If you died a natural death, you would travel inside the earth and suffer through the nine levels of Mictlan. After four years of wandering through this hell in the company of a small dog, you would disappear into the "place of the fleshless." Obviously, there was little incentive to die in a normal manner.

Tlalocan, an earthly paradise brimming with plenty, was thought to be the second place of the dead. You could be admitted only if you died in some way related to water, as it was believed the ancient god of rain, Tlaloc, had personally intervened to call you to his side. Unlike the rest of the dead, these corpses were buried rather than cremated.

The third place where souls went after death was heaven, where these lucky ones became companions of the sun. This glorious finale was reserved for warriors killed in battle, captives sacrificed by enemies, and women who had died in childbirth. It was considered to be the most desirable eternal resting place of all.

At the onset of old age, those of truly fanatical religious devotion would find a way to get into heaven, or at least earthly paradise, and that often meant suicide of one form or another. At the same time, many other Aztecs refused to believe that there was any afterlife at all. And so, these heretics reasoned, there was nothing left to do besides live well. This was particularly true among the noble class of astronomers, philosophers, architects, scientists, and other educated members of the wealthy ruling class. Mexican scholar Miguel Leon-Portilla has termed this the "epicurean" philosophy of life.

Partly due to the incredibly sophisticated artistic and intellectual heritage that had been inherited not just from the Toltecs, but Teotihuacan, and even further back from the Maya, Aztec culture was permeated with a keen sense of esthetics. The design and workmanship of the sacred precinct that surrounded the Great Temple, and the adjacent districts where the lords of the realm kept houses, were of astonishingly high quality. "Everything was made in masonry and well cemented, baths and walks and closets, and apartments like summer houses where they danced and sang," according to Bernal Diaz del Castillo, the great chronicler who accompanied Cortez into the city.

The climate of the time, with frequent yet not excessive rain, was perfect for horticulture. And the Spaniards were awestruck by the beauty of the gardens. "The gardens of flowers and sweet-smelling trees, and the many kinds that there were of them, and the arrangement of them and the walks, and the ponds and tanks of fresh water where the water entered at one end and flowed out of the other; and the baths . . . and the variety of small birds that nested in the branches, and the medicinal and useful herbs that were in the gardens. It was a wonder to see," wrote Bernal, adding "there were many gardeners."

The Mexicas love of beauty, though, had a desperate quality to it. Hear the words of another anonymous poet:

> For only here on earth
> shall the fragrant flowers last
> and the songs which are our bliss.
> Enjoy them now!

Flowers, along with death, were the twin obsessions of the Aztec poets; and feathers, with which the artists adorned their costume arrays, were like jewels to them. Gold and silver, though they had much of it, were less sought after than exotic feathers and gems. The guilded green plume of the quetzal bird was the most highly regarded, followed by the blue-green feathers of the xiuhtotl, the yellow feather of the parrot, translucent obsidian, garnet, turquoise, and jade.

Music, performed by trumpet, flute, whistle, and drum, was primarily used as a melodic background for singing and dancing. For it was through song and dance that the people were able to liberate themselves from their daily angst and approach the Lord of the Everywhere. Though this ultimate god cared little for those of flesh and blood, Ometeotl still was perfection. And only by singing and dancing and freeing the spirit was it possible to glimpse the bliss of God. Witness the final stanza of "A Spring Song":

> How much, alas, shall I weep on earth?
> Truly I have lived here in vain illusion;
> I saw that whatever is here on earth must end with our lives.
> May I be permitted to sing to thee?
> The Cause of All,
> there in the heaven,
> a dweller in thy mansion,
> there may my soul lift its voice and be
> seen with Thee and near Thee,
> Thou by whom we live,
> Ohuaya! Ohuaya!

Waiting for Quetzalcoatl

The beginning of the end occurred on February 8, 1517, when Spanish captain Francisco Hernandez de Cordova, commanding a company of 110 men, sailed from the Cuban port of Ajaruco on a voyage of discovery. Three weeks later, the expedition arrived off the coast of the Yucatán. After being ambushed by Mayan forces at Cape Catoche, Cordova sailed west along the coast to Campeche, where a contingent was sent ashore to refill water casks.

There, some fifty Maya soon approached and through sign language asked who the Spanish were and what they wanted. Bernal Diaz del Castillo, who was a member of Cordova's expedition, reports: "They then made signs with their hands to find out whether we came from the direction of the sunrise." The Spanish, of course, responded that that was indeed the direction from which they had come.

Cordova's men were approached again by Mayans while refilling their casks at Champotón. "Squadrons of Indians clad in cotton armour reaching to the knees, and armed with bows and arrows, lances and shields, and swords like two handed broad swords, and slings and stones and carrying feathered crests . . . came in silence straight towards us," reports Bernal. "By signs they asked whether we came from where the Sun rose, and we replied that we did."

The Natives' preoccupation with the question puzzled the Spanish. "We were at our wits end considering the matter," continues Bernal, "and wondering what the words were which the Indians called out to us."

Having apparently not given the proper response, the Spanish were attacked the next day with a rain of arrows and fire-hardened darts, and then in hand-to-hand combat, with such ferocity that forty-eight Spaniards lost their lives and everyone else in the party was wounded. Bernal was hit with three arrows, including one that pierced his ribs. The disillusioned survivors sailed back to Cuba.

Seated upon his throne upholstered with the skin of a jaguar, Moctezuma Xocoyotzin listened to reports of the battles with the bearded men who had appeared from the east. In response, he quietly ordered a watch be kept along the coast.

The following year, Captain Juan de Grijalva returned to Champotón with four ships and two hundred soldiers. During his attempt to avenge the honor of Spain, Grijalva and some sixty others were wounded, and seven other Spaniards lost their lives. But the toll among the Maya was far greater. Armed with their iron swords and muskets, the Spanish left some two hundred of the Indian wounded and dead.

The expedition sailed west and south along the coast, eventually into provinces dominated by the Aztecs. In the Province of Tabasco, the Spaniards went ashore and managed to barter a few glass beads and mirrors with the locals for gold and jewels worth sixteen thousand pesos. Grijalva's expedition reached as far west as the island of San Juan de Ulua. After being attacked by local forces at Cape Rojo, they returned to Cuba.

In his palace at Tenochtitlán, Moctezuma viewed drawings of the strangers made secretly by artists who had posed as members of the trading party. He was apprized how the strangers, while few in number, possessed sticks that fired lightning, and that for every one of the strangers that had been killed, many more Natives lost their lives. Spooked, the emperor contemplated the glass beads and mirrors, and commanded everyone to keep the affair a secret.

So it was that in the following year, on April 21, 1519, in the ominous Aztec year of One Reed, that eleven ships under the command of Hernando Cortez appeared off the eastern shore. Cortez's command included 508 soldiers armed with thirty-two

crossbows and thirteen muskets; 100 shipmasters, pilots, and sea-
men; sixteen horses; and two greyhounds. Within half an hour of
anchoring near San Juan de Ulua Island, which today is just outside
the modern port of Veracruz, two canoes full of Indians rowed out
and approached the ships.

Proceeding directly to the flagship, they indicated they wanted
to board and were granted permission. The Indians then paid their
respects to Cortez and inquired about the reason for his arrival.
Through his interpreters, including a Spaniard named Aguilar who
had been ransomed from the Maya, and an Indian woman of royal
descent named Dona Maria who had earlier been given to Cortez
as a present, up the coast, the Spaniard replied that they had come
to trade and meet new peoples. Their arrival, furthermore, should
cause the locals no uneasiness but be looked on by them as fortu-
nate. Before the Natives left, they said that if the Spanish were in
need of anything, they would supply it.

The explorers disembarked from their ships and made camp the
next day at a place called Xicalango. Careful attention was paid to
the erection of defenses. Two days later, on Easter Sunday, a special
emissary of Moctezuma, the Totonac chief Tentlil, accompanied by
a slave, announced himself from a hilltop. Entering camp, the
emissary was followed by a horde of locals bearing gifts of food.
Cortez welcomed and embraced the visitors. Then, he ordered Fray
Bortolome de Olmedo to say Mass.

Tentlil was amazed to see Cortes and the others kneeling in front
of a large, wooden cross, and asked why the Spanish humbled
themselves in front of the symbolic tree. Cortez then took the
opportunity to speak about his Catholic faith. He had heard reports
of the remains of human sacrifices witnessed by Grijalva and Cordova, and added that one of the reasons he had come was to abolish
human sacrifice. The lead emissary responded that he would relay
Cortez's words to Moctezuma.

Dinner followed, and after the table had been cleared, Cortez
told the Indians that he was a vassal of the greatest lord on earth,
who had many great princes as his vassals, and that it was at his
orders that he had come to Mexico. Cortez explained that he had
heard of Moctezuma and wanted to be friends with him. Where
could they meet to confer?

"You have only just now arrived and you already ask to speak with our prince," Tentlil replied. "Accept now this present which we give you in his name." The emissary then gave Cortez a number of beautifully worked gold objects, as well as cloth made of cotton and feathers that the Spanish remarked were "wonderful things to see." Food, including some biscuits, was also provided.

Cortez ate the biscuits and Tentlil made special note of it. For the food was a test. Tradition held that if the stranger recognized the food given him and ate it, then indeed he was Quetzalcoatl returning to Anahuac.

Cortez gave the reverent official some glass beads and begged him to send his brethren to trade, letting him know that he was particularly interested in gold. Cortez then demonstrated his power. Upon his signal, a party of horsemen galloped up. Bells had been attached to the horses' harnesses, and the resulting musical thunder provoked great wonder amongst the Mexicas. They had never seen such animals before and thought each horse and rider was a single creature. Then followed an intimidating display of firepower as the cannons were ignited, belching smoke and knocking down trees. As Cortez knew they would be, the Indians were terrified and fell as if paralyzed to the ground.

After being revived with wine, a tipsy Tentlil noticed that one of the conquistadores had a rusty helmet with gold gilding. "It was like one that they possessed which had been left to them by their ancestors of the race from which they had sprung," reports Bernal. "And that it had been placed on the head of their god—[Huitzilopochtli], and that their prince Moctezuma would like to see this helmet."

Cortez graciously gave it to them, along with more glass baubles, some Spanish biscuits, a carved armchair, and a crimson cap with a gold medal of St. George slaying a dragon. He asked Tentlil to present the gifts to Moctezuma, along with the question of where the Great Lord would wish that they should meet so that they might confer together. Shaken, the emissaries promised to return as soon as possible with a reply.

Moctezuma, meanwhile, was in torment and unable to eat or sleep while he awaited word. "What will become of us," he was repeatedly heard to moan. When his officials finally returned, he met them at the temple of Huitzilopochtli where he sacrificed several captives and sprinkled the messengers with their blood. Tentlil then told him what they had seen and heard, about the mighty guns, and the metal with which the gods clothed themselves and of which their weapons were made. They told him about the strange deer that bore them on their backs and showed Moctezuma the helmet and the biscuits.

The Great Lord examined the helmet in silence. He expressed his conviction that the foreigners indeed belonged to the race which, as his forefathers had foretold, would come to rule over the empire. And as he contemplated the unusual biscuits, his strength ebbed. He ordered that his priests carry the divine gifts from Quetzalcoatl to the city of Tollán where they were buried in his temple in a ceremony replete with solemn hymns. The glass beads, too, were interred with great pomp at the temple of Huitzilopochtli. For Moctezuma felt unworthy to possess the holy gifts.

"Thus he thought," relates Sahagun, ". . . that this was Topiltzin-Quetzalcoatl who had come to land. For it was in their hearts that he would come, that he would come to land, just to find his mat, his seat. For he had traveled there [eastward] when he departed."

But Moctezuma vacillated. Perhaps the god could be talked out of coming. Perhaps surrender and destruction could be avoided. Although Native and Spanish accounts differ, it appears that Moctezuma dispatched warriors from his fanatic Ocelot Society to greet the returning god and present him with gifts. More than a hundred Aztecs and other Native officials, led by Tentlil and a Mexica governor, Quintalbor, who bore a striking resemblance to Cortez, arrived soon thereafter in the Spanish garrison. Quintalbor looked so much like Cortez that the Spanish started speaking of "our Cortez" and "the other Cortez." Moctezuma had sent Quintalbor for psychological effect, of course, but it had no great effect on the wily Cortez.

After fumigating the Spaniard and all the soldiers near him with holy incense, the Mexicas solemnly presented Moctezuma's personal religious vestments. They dressed Cortez in one and laid out the others in rows. The arrays were used by the emperor whenever he was impersonating Quetzalcoatl, Tlaloc, or Texcatlipoca at religious rites. Each dripped with precious feathers, gold, turquoise, and shells and were of the most astonishingly beautiful designs. Cortez later sent almost all of these items back to King Charles. The works included a large golden wheel that was said to look like the sun, and was as "big as a cartwheel." Another, heavy and made of silver, was a representation of the moon. Then came a dizzying display of other treasures, such as twenty gold ducks and other animal effigies, bracelets and earrings, jeweled helmets, feathered harpoons, gem-encrusted scepters, two sacred books of red and black ink, and richly woven cotton clothing in white, tawny, and black.

Cortez and his men received the gifts with delight. The gold, they noted, was of exceptionally high quality and told them that the mines of Mexico produced very pure ore. It was, after all, for gold that they truly thirsted.

Once the Aztec dignitaries had presented Moctezuma's gifts, the leader of the group, through the interpreters, passed along a message from their Great Lord. Moctezuma Xocoyotzin asked that the visitors stay in port, consider themselves his guests, and that if anything could be done to aid them, those requests would immediately be fulfilled. As for the interview, it would be best if they should not worry about it, for there was no need for it.

Cortez responded in a courtly manner with objections. He had been charged by his king to speak with Moctezuma in person. If he failed in that task, he would be held accountable. The statement, in fact, was a bold lie that Cortez would use again and again throughout the conquest. The truth of the matter was that King Charles in Spain knew nothing of Cortez or his journey. Cortez's own superior, Diego Velázquez, who was governor of the Island of Fernandina (Cuba), only found out himself after word reached him that Cortez had disobeyed his direct orders.

Velázquez himself had petitioned King Charles for permission to lead a voyage of discovery and was merely awaiting a reply. Cortez's orders were clear-cut. He was to go in search of Grijalva's fleet, which had returned after Cortez left, and search for any shipwrecked Christians who might be held captive in the Yucatán. There was to be no colonizing or establishing of settlements.

It did not take Hernando Cortez long, though, to recognize the historic opportunity that lay before him. Educated in a semiformal fashion in the law, Cortez quickly decided that he had to find a way to reach Moctezuma's capital with his men and somehow force him to acknowledge Charles of Ghent, King of Castile and newly elected emperor of the Holy Roman Empire, as his sovereign ruler. He hoped that when he had conquered the Indian Empire and handed it to his monarch on a literal platter of gold, his insubordination would be overlooked.

Rounding up a Florentine glass cup engraved with hunting scenes, three Holland shirts, plus a few other items, Cortez beseeched Tentlil to present them to Moctezuma as gifts along with a demand that his audience be reconsidered. Tentlil promised to relay the gifts to his lord. But as for the meeting, he told Cortez that he considered the possibility remote that the Great Lord would change his mind.

Cortez watched the emissaries depart and contemplated his unique situation. He had been mulling over the strange riddle of the Indians' prophecy concerning the anticipated return of a powerful god from the east. Whatever the origin of it, Cortez quickly realized that the Mexica had been sizing him up, wondering if he might be that deity. That he learned of the prophecy would be one of his most powerful weapons as he pressed on toward his goal.

Indeed, Cortez had no idea how lucky he was. For according to the Aztec calendar, the year Ce Acatl, or One Reed, recurs only once every fifty-two years. The fact that Cortez had appeared off the Gulf Coast on the anniversary of Topiltzin-Quetzalcoatl's birth, the year in which it was prophesied he would return to strike down kings, had Moctezuma totally shaken.

In his palace at Tenochtitlán, he listened carefully to the reports of Tentlil and Quintalbor. Wrapped in his royal turquoise cloak, the Ruler of the World was attended by four councilors, including the vice-emperor, who was cloaked in elegant black and white. All were blood relations. Tentlil relayed Cortez's declarations that his lord, who remained where the sun rises, had ordered him to visit Moctezuma.

Perhaps the stranger wasn't Quetzalcoatl after all, remarked one of the councilors, but only a representative. The ramifications of that conclusion were discussed in all their permutations. Other advisers were brought in. Cortez's declaration of his intention to abolish human sacrifice sounded like Topiltzin-Quetzalcoatl. Yet even if it is the Lord of the Dawn who has returned, argued one, why must the empire be turned over to him? Did not tradition tell of another way to deal with Quetzalcoatl?

Legend of Topiltzin-Quetzalcoatl

The concept of Quetzalcoatl had its origins in the great culture of Teotihuacan, which dominated central Mexico from about A.D. 200 to 750. Quetzalcoatl was associated with the values of humility, love, mercy, and compassion, and was greatly revered by the common man. It was said that the enlightened deity had created humankind, founded agriculture, science, and the arts, and invented the sacred calendar of 120 days. Quetzalcoatl was the patron divinity of the Aztec priesthood. The highest rank one could attain, in fact, was named after him. Yet more than that, to be a Quetzalcoatl was to have achieved a state of spiritual purity, the closest one could come to the God Behind the Gods.

Yet the Quetzalcoatl that the Aztecs were preoccupied with was an actual human being. Though there are conflicting versions of his story, almost all agree that he was named Topiltzin and he was born in the year Ce Acatl. Little is known of his childhood, but it is said that as a young man he and a group of his followers returned to the Toltec capital of Tollán after unsuccessfully attempting to colonize the Puebla-Tlaxcala Valley. Trained as a warrior, the tall, athletic Topiltzin is said to have had large eyes and a fair beard. After his return, he entered the priesthood, and giving up all earthly pleasures and material things, became a contemplative and enlightened priest.

He achieved the rank of Quetzalcoatl, which made him the principle ruler of Tollán, but came into conflict with a powerful, sacrifice-happy, militaristic faction of the city's establishment led by Huemac. Several times, Huemac sent sorcerers to try and break Topiltzin-Quetzalcoatl's steadfast opposition to the practice of human sacrifice, but to no avail. Then, at the height of his influence, the high priest withdrew from society to meditate in the solitude of his temple.

Huemac then called upon the god of the underworld, Tezcatlipoca (Smoking Mirror), who was Quetzalcoatl's timeless archrival, to cast a spell over Topiltzin. Tezcatlipoca responded by formulating and executing a cunning plan to impersonate Topiltzin's servants. Under this guise, he and two of his minions infiltrated Topiltzin's inner sanctum. There, they presented the high priest with a mirror. When Topiltzin-Quetzalcoatl saw his reflection, he was shocked to see how his face had wrinkled and how his eyes had sunken with age.

Cleverly, the impersonators played upon the holy man's vanity and received permission to have a beautiful religious costume of quetzal feathers made for him. Topiltzin insisted that he had no intention of wearing the gaudy array. But when it arrived, his manipulators convinced him to try it on. When he did, he was struck by his new-found splendor. Tezcatlipoca then painted the old priest's lips red, drew little yellow squares on his forehead, and topped it with a red and blue wig. Delighted with his appearance, Topiltzin walked out of his temple for the first time in years and mingled with the people in the streets.

Public reaction was bad. They had known Topiltzin, revered him, as a humble and self-disciplined servant of god who wore plain cotton. Suddenly, in his old age, he was acting like a vain old fool.

Back in his temple, Topiltzin was persuaded by the evil magicians to eat a fiery stew of chili, tomatoes, corn, beans, and herbs, and then slake his thirst with an alcoholic beverage called pulque. Although Topiltzin had abstained from drinking for decades, he and his underlings drank five large cups, and spilled into the streets uproariously drunk.

The people of Tollán were shocked and embarrassed to see Quetzalcoatl and his retinue drunk. Their respect for the esteemed figure evaporated like dew in the sun. It is said that children laughed at him, disrespectfully, and picked at the feathers of his costume. Later that night, the holy man called for his sister, Quetzalpetlatl, and in an ultimate act of excess, made love to her.

The next morning, recognizing his depravity, he climbed into a stone casket and laid there for four days. Then, he abandoned the city. Traveling as a simple pilgrim, Topiltzin-Quetzalcoatl eventually reached Tlapallan, generally believed to be the Gulf Coast. There, according to Sahagun, he constructed a raft of serpents and sailed away, "navigating across the sea."

•

Moctezuma contemplated the tradition. He had previously de-
duced that if that god had departed for the east, any god arriving
from the east had to be Topiltzin-Quetzalcoatl. But perhaps it
would be possible to deflect him—to turn him away, in order that
the empire might be preserved. Sahagun tells us the *tlatoani* sent
his own evil magicians, soothsayers, and incense-offering priests to
cast spells over Cortez and his men so that they might sicken and
leave his shores. They blew upon the strangers, recited incantations
over them, and cast magic stones. In one of their more outlandish
acts, they presented the Spaniards with a repast of meats, sweet
potatoes, avocado, and other foods, soaked in human blood. If
Cortes was indeed a god, reasoned the Aztecs with their twisted
religious logic, they would be attracted to such fare. If not, perhaps
they would leave.

Aside from provoking nausea and disgust, however, the effect on
the Spanish was negligible. The Aztec witches soon saw that they
had no power over the foreigners. So they repaired to their emperor, defeated, and Moctezuma fell into even greater despair.
Before long, word seeped out to the general population and people
were crying in the streets, miserable over the approaching apocalypse.

When Moctezuma learned from his emissaries that the strangers
had been asking many questions about him, he was overcome by
fear and made plans to flee. He would hide from the god, simply
be unavailable to him. Why should he have to be present for such
a cataclysmic event? But when the time came for him to go, he was
unable to, for all of his energy had drained away.

Cortez, meanwhile, was dealing with the problem of how to
achieve his dreams. By sharing the wealth that had been accumulated with the members of his expedition, and permitting
them to trade on their own, he had fed their desire for gold. When
he dramatically declared that they should all return immediately to
Mexico, he provoked a negative outcry that played into his hands.
It enabled him to argue he was only going along with the wishes
of the majority, and that for the greater glory of Spain and the
Catholic faith, they had to press on.

Another contingent of astrologers and magicians soon went out from Tenochtitlán to try and turn the Spaniards back. Along the road, Sahagun tells us, they came upon a drunken man who demanded to know what they were doing. When he was told they were going to engage in a battle of magic against the Spanish, the drunk castigated them unmercifully, and told them Mexico was doomed. Then he ordered them to look back in the direction of Tenochtitlán, and it appeared to them in a vision engulfed in flames. The emperor's officials subsequently reported that the oracle was actually the god Tezcatlipoca. And everyone was shaken to their bones.

Five months after setting foot on shore, the conquistadores started on their march. Moctezuma, meanwhile, desperately sent four more emissaries laden with gifts of gold and embroidered cloth. The messengers related the Great Lord's concern over the hardships Cortez must have suffered during the long journey, and promised more gold if he promised to go home. Cortez smiled broadly. He could not turn back, he maintained. It would be a contravention of his orders and would subject him to ruin.

Instead, he beached his ships, and leaving some 150 members of his army to build a fortress at Veracruz, on approximately August 16, he led his army toward Tenochtitlán. When Moctezuma Xocoyotzin learned the results of the efforts of his representatives, he hung his head in dejection and for a long time would not speak.

The conquistadores proceeded inland to Tenochtitlán, surprised by the level of support people showed them along the way. Whenever Cortez would make a speech to the Natives about the glories of Jesus Christ, the Trinity, and his most Catholic faith, his words were dutifully reported to Moctezuma.

The Great Lord pondered the statements made by the one who arrived from the east and thought about his own religion. Topiltzin-Quetzalcoatl had railed against human sacrifice. And now more humans were being sacrificed than ever before. His advisors, Prince Cuauhtemoc among them, urged him to attack the invaders and annihilate them. But the Ruler of the World was weighted down by the augeries of doom and was frightened by the invaders' power. He vacillated between appeasement and preparation for war, unable to act decisively.

Upon reaching the frontiers of Tlaxcala, the Spanish were finally attacked and fought a fierce battle that lasted two days. Hundreds of warriors were left dead on the battlefield. The Aztecs had never been able to conquer the Tlaxcalans, and the fact that the Spanish had crushed them so completely greatly impressed Moctezuma. Pressing on, the conquistadores with their superior weaponry committed a massacre in Cholula in order, it appears, to enhance their fearsome mystique. When they reached Itztapalatengo, they were met by an elaborate entourage led by the new King of Texcoco, who accompanied the Spaniards toward Tenochtitlán.

As they neared the capital, according to Bernal, "we saw so many cities and villages built in the water and other great towns on dry land and that straight and level Causeway going towards Mexico, we were amazed and said that it was like the enchantments they tell of in the legend of Amadis, on account of the great towers and [temples] and buildings rising from the water, and all built of masonry. And some of our soldiers even asked whether the things we saw were not like a dream."

The company spent the night in a gorgeous palace at Itztapalapa, and the next morning began the final leg of their journey. As they crossed the magnificent causeway into the city, a throng of people turned out to view the gods. Once on the island, Cortez and his men were met by another party of some two hundred barefoot and solemn lords.

Finally, Moctezuma Xocoyotzin himself appeared, borne on a litter, wearing a turquoise diadem and richly embroidered robes. When he stepped to the ground, although he was the only one wearing sandals, cloths were laid in front of him so his feet would not have to touch the ground. The *tlatoani*'s four princely councilors escorted him toward Cortez. None of his subjects dared to look at him directly.

Having dismounted from his horse, Cortez exchanged greetings and gifts with Moctezuma. According to the Spaniard's second letter to King Charles, Moctezuma declared that it had long been held that Topiltzin-Quetzalcoatl or his descendants "would come and conquer this land and take us as their vassals. So because of the place from which you claim to come, namely from where the sun rises, and the things you tell us of the great lord or king who sent you here, we believe and are certain that he is our natural lord, especially as you say that he has known of us for some time. So be assured that we shall obey you and hold you as our lord in place of that great sovereign of whom you speak."

Feeding the Aztec's paranoia over the prophecy, Cortez cleverly replied that King Charles was indeed the one whom they had all been expecting. Then Moctezuma escorted his visitors to a palace next to the Great Temple that had belonged to his father. Upon their arrival, Cortez ordered two cannon to be fired and the explosions filled the Mexicans with great fear. Moctezuma then departed, promising to return soon, and every need of the Spaniards was met.

Over the next three days or so, the visitors were treated like royalty, visited by reverent Aztec officials, and waited on hand and foot. Cortez and his inner circle spent quite a lot of time in Moctezuma Xocoyotzin's presence, and he proved to be a good-natured and generous host with a princely demeanor.

By day four, however, the Spanish began to detect a subtle change in the way they were being treated. The food was not brought as quickly at mealtimes, nor in such quantity as in the first couple of days. Moreover, the attitude of a few of the servants was becoming disrespectful. As none of the Spaniards had left the palace since their arrival, on November 12, 1519, Cortez asked Moctezuma to grant him permission to explore the city. After some hesitation, the *tlatoani* agreed and sent a company of lords to escort Cortez, all of the Spanish with horses, and a detachment of foot soldiers, on their tour.

The grandeur of Tenochtitlán astounded the Spanish. One of their first stops was the great market in the suburb of Tlatelolco, which was larger and more packed with goods of every manner and description than any of them had ever seen before in their lives. Another district was reserved for the dancers, musicians, singers, and other artists who performed for Moctezuma.

Finally, Cortez's party arrived at the Great Temple of Tlatelolco, where on top at the temple of Huitzilopochtli, the Ruler of the World was sacrificing human beings to sustain the sun. Escorted by four priests and two chieftains, Cortez and a party of guards climbed to the summit. There, Moctezuma came out from the temple, and holding Cortez by the hand, pointed out the features of his beautiful city. After taking in its loveliness, Cortez asked if he could view the Aztec gods.

The Great Lord conferred with his high priests, then gave his assent. The Spanish stepped into the temple of Huitzilopochtli and found the inside covered with layers of blackened blood. The idol itself, according to Bernal, had "a very broad face and monstrous and terrible eyes" while "the whole of his body was covered with precious stones, and gold and pearls . . . and in one hand he held a bow." In a ceramic brazier, smokey with copal incense, three human hearts were sizzling. Sickened by the overpowering stench of blood, the Spanish quickly withdrew.

Through his interpreter, Cortez declared with a smirk: "I do not understand how such a great Prince and wise man as you are has not come to the conclusion, in your mind, that these idols of yours are not gods, but evil things called devils, and so that you may know it and all your priests may see it clearly, do me the favor to approve of my placing a cross here on top of this tower."

Angrily, Moctezuma told Cortez that he had insulted his gods who had provided well for his people and asked him not to say another word of dishonor against them. Recognizing his perilous position, Cortez graciously departed. While Moctezuma and his priests worshipped in their own way to assuage the sins of Cortez's impertinence, the Spanish headed back to their quarters. It is a testament to the power of prophecy that they were alive at all.

Along the way, they saw more of the city. Surrounding the sacred precinct was a ten-foot wall of carved serpents. Measuring 440 meters on each side, the wall enclosed more than seventy buildings, including administrative facilities, schools, and temples, housing for priests and nobility, a dance court, at least two ball courts, as well as other buildings that supported the rituals at the Great Temple.

Bernal describes one in which "they cooked the flesh of the unfortunate Indians who were sacrificed, which was eaten by the priests." Another was "full of skulls and large bones arranged in perfect order, which one could look at but could not count, for there were too many of them. The skulls were by themselves and the bones in separate piles. In that place there were other Idols, and in every house or [temple] or oratory that I have mentioned there were priests with long robes of black cloth. . . . The hair of these priests was very long and so matted that it could not be separated or disentangled, and most of them had their ears scarified, and their hair was clotted with blood."

Back inside their quarters, Cortez and his captains discussed strategy. They were in a dangerous spot to be sure. At any moment, Moctezuma might revoke his good will and they all would be carried off to the sacrificial stone. If they tried to leave, the road back to the Gulf Coast could prove perilous. What was needed, it was decided, was a bold stroke. Without further delay, Moctezuma should be seized.

The next morning, two Indian messengers arrived from the fortress at Veracruz with bad news. The local people were in revolt against the defenders of the fort and refused to furnish them with any more food or supplies. Realizing that their position was deteriorating rapidly, Cortez and his men settled on a plan.

Announced before their arrival, Cortez and some thirty of his men and interpreters arrived at Moctezuma's palace. After the usual salutations were traded, Cortez and his men simply took Moctezuma captive. "Come with us to our quarters," Bernal reports Cortez as saying, "where you will be as well served and attended to as though you were in your own house, but if you cry out or make any disturbance you will immediately be killed by these my Captains, whom I brought solely for this purpose."

Moctezuma was stupified and incredulous, but after half an hour of wrangling, crumbled and agreed to do as Cortez instructed. He told his guard and the lords in attendance that Huitzilopochtli had advised him to go with the Spaniards to their quarters. Once the conquistadores had escorted him there, they posted guards of their own.

If it were not for Moctezuma's overriding expectation that the age was coming to an end, the conquistadores might never have lived up to their name. He could have had the Spaniards killed at any time. Only briefly was Moctezuma under physical restraint. He was allowed to be comforted by his mistresses and served by his two wives. Twenty officials of the empire, plus his relatives the princes, naturally wanted to know the circumstances of his captivity. To that the Great Lord replied that it was nothing to be concerned about, that he was staying where he was due to his own choice, and the will of Huitzilopochtli.

The *tlatoani* delivered up a mountain of gold, silver, and gems to Cortez. He even offered his daughter in marriage. For four months the Spanish indulged themselves in luxurious sensuality as Cortez ruled the empire through Moctezuma. Then, in March 1520, reality intruded in the form of Panfilo de Narváez, who arrived off the coast near Veracruz with a Spanish army of nearly sixteen hundred men to punish Cortez for his disobedience. Leaving Moctezuma in the custody of Pedro de Alvarado and eighty men, Cortez departed Tenochtitlán to do battle with Narvaez. Through violence and an appeal to greed, plus an alliance with anti-Aztec Native peoples, Cortez defeated Narváez and disarmed his followers. But soon after his victory, he learned that the Mexica had risen up in revolt against those he had left behind in the capital.

Combining his own forces with those of Narváez that were still remaining, Cortez rushed back to Tenochtitlán with thirteen hundred soldiers, ninety-six horses, eighty musketeers, and two thousand Tlaxcala Indian warriors. On June 21, 1520, they entered the city to find everyone hiding behind locked doors. At the palace, Moctezuma came out with Pedro de Alvarado and his other guards to greet Cortez. But the Spaniard was angry over Moctezuma's secret encouragement of Narváez, and ignored the *tlatoani,* causing him to return to his quarters sad and depressed.

Cortez then destroyed the idol of Huitzilopochtli, enraging the Aztec priests. It was not long afterward that the Mexica attacked in waves. The first hail of javelins, arrows, and darts killed twelve and wounded forty-six. Brave Ocelot and Eagle warriors, leading the charges, showed extreme tenacity and endurance in vicious, hand-to-hand combat. The Spaniards superior weaponry seemed to have little effect, for the cannon and musket hardly gave them pause before the next assault. The Aztecs set fire to their sanctuaries, hurled rocks, howled at and taunted the foreigners. They called for them to release their Lord Moctezuma and told of how the Spanish would all soon be sacrificed.

In the face of impossible odds, Cortez decided to sue for peace and leave Mexico with whatever treasure they could carry. To try and force negotiations, he led Moctezuma onto the roof of his palace, where ten years before the Great Lord had seen the first ominous smoking star. When the Aztec captains saw the one once revered as a god, they ordered their warriors to be silent. Four lords edged forward to tell Moctezuma that his brother, Cuitlahuac, had been chosen as the new Tlatoani Cemanahuac. A moment later, the Great Lord was hit in the head by a stone thrown by one of his countrymen, and within minutes was dead.

•

Why did the mighty Moctezuma capitulate so easily? It must be recognized first of all that his opponent, Cortez, was a visionary strategist with a talent for diplomacy and a depth of human understanding that only the greatest military leaders have ever possessed. Obviously, the superiority of Spanish weaponry and the conquistadores' ability to massacre once-feared adversaries such as the Tlaxcalans cowed Moctezuma's naturally aggressive impulses. Under such circumstances, it is understandable why he never ordered his forces to attack the Spaniards during their long march to the capital.

But Moctezuma's actions after their arrival in Tenochtitlán are another matter entirely. After he had been taken prisoner, he told his people that it was Huitzilopochtli's will that he remain in the custody of the Spanish. It is unlikely that this was merely to save his own skin. Death during captivity, after all, ensured one eternal bliss as a companion of the sun. Was Moctezuma, who had personally dispatched innumerable victims, nothing more than a coward?

A more likely explanation revolves around his preoccupation with the prophecies of doom and the fact that he was the leader of a sick civilization. Imagine what it would do to a person to rip out hundreds if not thousands of still beating human hearts. For a priest with no hope of changing things, there was little value in questioning whether such actions were right or wrong. But for a contemplative leader of the entire system, such depravity as the Aztecs were engaged in must have weighed heavily upon him. True, Moctezuma continued to sacrifice human beings until the end. Yet like an addict who knows his behavior is killing him but is unable to stop, the Great Lord seems to have known in his heart that the strange system could not continue.

Throughout the world, the idea of a Messiah that will come to rescue the downtrodden masses from their cruel and overbearing rulers is a common theme. We shall see it in various forms throughout the course of this book. In the realm of Anahuac, that role was played by Topiltzin-Quetzalcoatl.

•

Cortez and many of his men escaped only with great effort during the night of July 10, 1520. Within a matter of five days, according to Bernal, over 930 soldiers were killed or captured then sacrificed at Cuitlahuac's coronation. Reaching the safety of the Aztec-hating Tlaxcallans, who were now allies of the Spanish, Cortez and his men rested for nine months and regrouped for a final assault.

TLATOANI CUAUHTEMOC

When Cuitlahuac died of smallpox after a reign of only eighty days, Moctezuma's nephew, twenty-six year old Cuauhtemoc, became the eleventh and last Ruler of the World. "He had the appearance of a man of quality, both in features and in body," writes Bernal. "His face was somewhat large and cheerful, with eyes more grave than gay . . . and his complexion was somewhat lighter than that usual to brown Indians."

Cuauhtemoc had initially argued for peace with the Spanish. But seeing that such a course was not possible, he gallantly organized and led the fierce resistance. When his spies informed him that Cortez was planning a counterattack, he worked tirelessly to strengthen defenses and tried to reconstitute the shattered Confederacy of Anahuac. But the Aztecs' insatiable demand for blood and hearts and tribute from their vassals proved to be a legacy impossible for young Cuauhtemoc to overcome.

With the support of ten thousand Tlaxcalan and other Indian allies, Cortez and his army, which had been reinforced from Cuba, slowly encircled the Aztec capital. The water line from Chapultepec was destroyed and all food into the city was embargoed. Despite a heroic defense, the city was taken after four months and on the afternoon of August 13, 1521, Cuauhtemoc was captured trying to flee in a boat with his family and top aides.

When the *tlatoani* was brought to Cortez, Bernal reports him as saying: "I have done what I was obliged to do in the defense of my city and my people. I can do no more. I have been brought before you by force as a prisoner. Take that dagger from your belt and kill me with it quickly." Cuauhtemoc then wept.

Cortez instead embraced him. At first, he was treated with deference. But as the conquistadores grew desperate to recover the gold they had lost during their flight from the city, they demanded that Cuauhtemoc produce two hundred ingots of gold. When Cuauhtemoc said there was no more gold to be given, Cortez resorted to Inquisition-like torture and burned his feet with boiling oil. Cuauhtemoc was left crippled as a result.

Cortez dispatched one of his captains, Cristobal de Olid, to occupy Honduras in January 1524. But upon his arrival, Olid renounced Cortez's authority. In the fall of that year, Cortez left for Honduras to put down the rebellion and took Cuauhtemoc and his cousin, the former ruler of Tacuba, with him. Along the way, both were hanged from a tree. Though Cortez claimed that he had gotten wind of a conspiracy fomented by Cuauhtemoc, Bernal reports that there was no truth to the claim. "Their death was very unjust and made a bad impression on all present," he writes.

Before he died, Cuauhtemoc is said to have uttered the following.

Prophecy of Cuauhtemoc

One day, a New Sun will arise to resurrect the glory of Anahuac.

When night fell, Cuauhtemoc's followers cut his body down from the tree. They carried his corpse for forty days through the jungle, or so it is claimed, before secretly burying him beneath a pyramid in the tiny town of Ichcateopan in the state of Guerrero. Seeing that the site was a religious mecca, but not knowing or caring about the reason why, the Spanish dismantled the pyramid and erected a Catholic church on its base in 1539.

For nearly 425 years, the supposed tomb of Cuauhtemoc was kept a secret. Then in 1949, Don Alejandro Rodriguez Chimalpopocatl—the last member of his family charged with the care of the tomb—revealed its presence to the world. The reason the veil of secrecy was finally lifted is unclear. But whatever Chimalpopocatl's motivations, the news traveled quickly throughout Mexico and caused a sensation.

The government appointed a Grand Commission to undertake the excavation. Diego Rivera, the famous Mexican artist, participated in the investigation. The conclusion, however, was that there is no scientific basis to believe that the bones found in the tomb were Cuahutemoc's. Yet many Mexicans refuse to accept that as fact. Today, the purported skeleton of Cuahutemoc is on exhibit inside the church, which has been turned into a monument honoring him as a hero for his valiant defense of the people.

Despite the controversy, Cuauhtemoc's valor in the defense of his people and his prophecy continues to live in the minds of many Mexicans. Juan Morales, born in Veracruz and of Nahua ancestry, has traveled widely throughout the country. "It's possible to interpret the prophecy to say that Cuauhtemoc is going to come again to save Mexico," said in an interview with the author. "At this point in time, many people believe that Cuauhtemoc Cardenas, the politician, is the reincarnation of the last *tlatoani.*"

Cardenas, the son of a revered former president of Mexico, ran for president himself as a candidate of the Democratic Revolution Party against Carlos Salinas de Gotari of the Institutional Revolutionary Party (PRI) in 1988. Cardenas was so popular among the voters that he officially racked up a total of 31 percent of the vote. Salinas, with only 50.36 percent, was elected with the lowest margin of victory in the more than sixty-year history of the PRI. Despite the totals, Cardenas and his supporters have charged the election was stolen. Indications are that Cardenas will run again for the presidency of Mexico in 1994.

"A lot of Indians in Mexico are following him," states Juan Morales. "The last time, when the election was stolen from him, Cardenas made the decision not to foment a revolution. It would be very easy for him to say, 'Go there!' Millions of people would follow. But the next time, if it happens again, well, we don't know what's going to happen."

CHAPTER THREE

DEGANAWIDAH: PEACEMAKER OF THE IROQUOIS

On his second assignment as a diplomat, Benjamin Franklin was sent to Albany, in the Province of New York, by King George II of Great Britain. There, along with several other royal commissioners, Franklin was to reaffirm the alliance with the Indians of the Iroquois Confederacy—or League of Six Nations—in order to undermine the influence of Britain's arch-rival France in North America. But a number of other important developments also occurred at the Albany Conference. Not the least of these was how it became evident that Franklin's theories of government had been deeply influenced by an Indian who may have been dead for some three hundred years.

The year was 1754. Franklin was forty-eight years old. His brown hair, although receding, was worn at shoulder length. His manner of dress was stylish, yet by no means ostentatious, and his posture was erect. Six years before he had turned over his printing, insurance, and other businesses to a managing partner and with the substantial income they provided him, he was able to devote himself to politics and science. In the intervening period, he had been elected to the Pennsylvania Assembly, appointed deputy postmaster general of the British colonies, and founded the American Historical Society along with several other public and private institutions in Philadelphia.

As Franklin took his seat on a wooden bench in front of Governor De Lancey's house where the conference began on June 14, he attracted considerable notice. Only the year before, he had achieved international fame when he was awarded the Copley gold medal by the Royal Society of London for his experiments with electricity.

Surrounding him and the other royal commissioners at the conference were representatives of most of the other colonies as well as some 150 Indian men, women, and children. The leader of the Indian delegation was the Iroquois *sachem,* or chief, Hendrick Peters. Hendrick at the time was about seventy years old. He was a majestic figure, a born leader, with a prominent tomahawk scar running across his left cheek. Worldly wise, as a young man Hendrick had even traveled to London.

The conference got underway according to strict and traditional Iroquois diplomatic protocol. Songs were sung, ceremonies recited, and belts of wampum were exchanged in order to underline particularly significant points. In diplomatic negotiations, the Iroquois were generally recognized as being more evolved than the Europeans in the art of "political farce and compliment." They would never interrupt a speaker and demanded the same courtesy in return. Then, to affirm even minor agreements came the ritualistic response of "*Yo-hah!*"

All of this was familiar to Franklin. Over time, he had learned a lot about the advanced social and political organization of the Six Nations. His own son, William, had participated in a treaty council with them held in Ohio in 1750. And for more than ten years, Franklin had been corresponding with Cadawallader Colden of New York, who was a recognized authority on the League. Franklin had attended his first Indian parley at Carlise in 1753 at the request of Governor Hamilton of the Province of Pennsylvania, and saw firsthand that the Iroquois preferred their way of life to that of the colonists. He saw no need to convert them to Christianity or "civilize" them. Instead, as he wrote in a letter less than three years earlier on behalf of the Pennsylvania Assembly to Governor Hamilton, it was his belief "that sincere, upright Dealing with the Indians, a friendly Treatment of them on all Occasions, and particularly in relieving their Necessities at proper times by suitable Presents, have been the best Means of securing their friendship."

By the time Franklin became personally involved with them, the once-mighty league was in a state of decline. For more than two hundred years, they had kept two of the world's greatest powers—England and France—at bay. They had managed this due to both their geographical position and their unique political unity. But as the ever-burgeoning European population encroached inch by inch upon their lands in New York, Pennsylvania, and beyond the Iroquois were being squeezed out. Generally disillusioned after decades of being tricked and swindled by both "pen and ink work" and force of arms, the Iroquois were angry by the time they arrived in Albany.

At the conference, Hendrick illustrated his anger over the way the English colonies had been treating the Iroquois by contemptuously throwing a stick over his shoulder. "You have thus thrown us behind your backs and disregarded us; whereas the French are a subtile and vigilant people, ever using their utmost endeavors to seduce us," he declared.

There was, in fact, a strong pro-French element among the League that contributed to its internal rivalries and threatened its cohesion. At the same time, the fractious colonies were anything but unified. Connecticut was squabbling with Pennsylvania over boundaries. Virginia and New Jersey refused to attend. And New York struggled in vain to maintain its leadership in Indian affairs and dominance over the Confederacy. Massachusetts, New Hampshire, Rhode Island, and Maryland all had their own schemes and axes to grind. Nevertheless, the British crown recognized that if the remaining Iroquois were to ally themselves completely with the French, westward expansion of the colonies could prove to be impossible.

Many different dates have been suggested for the founding of the Iroquois Confederacy. All, however, fall in the period from slightly before A.D. 1400 to A.D. 1600. Binding together the nations of the Mohawk, Onondaga, Seneca, Oneida, Cayuga, and Tuscarora (who were admitted as junior members in 1724), the Confederacy was a sophisticated political institution without equal in its time and utterly uncredited in our own. It was the world's first federal-style government, in which internal affairs were left to each nation, while overriding issues of "national security," as they are now called, were decided by a Grand Council. Universal suffrage, impeachment of officials, leaders as the servants of the people—all of these were working principles of the great League. And whether Franklin knew his name or not, the entire system was the creation of a man who is totally unknown today. A man whose name was Deganawidah.

•

Before we examine what happened at the Albany Conference, it is necessary first to go back even farther in time to explore what is known of the man who had such a profound effect on Ben Franklin, the man sometimes called "America's first philosopher." Known as the Peacemaker, Deganawidah is perhaps the greatest prophet ever born in the Americas. As the spokesman of a new way of thinking, he changed the way people lived in his own time and for hundreds of years thereafter. And, as we shall see, his innovations still play a major role in our world today.

Deganawidah came from the north, born among a people known today as the Hurons, near present day Kingston in the Canadian Province of Ontario. The territory of the Hurons bordered on the northern shores of Lake Ontario. It was a beautiful land; green and lush and bountiful. Yet at that time, relations among humans were stuck in a kind of hell. Savage blood feuds and warfare among the Woodland nations of the Northeast had progressed to the point where hatred and revenge enveloped society like an endless spider-web. Everyone had a grudge against someone else. And those grudges required that the pain be paid back in a cycle that led inevitably to greater pain and death. It seemed that no one could escape the vortex of violence. The people were mentally and physically exhausted.

Through oral histories that have been carefully passed down for countless generations and finally committed to paper in the nineteenth century, we know some of this great man's story. It is said that Deganawidah's mother and grandmother were poor and despised and lived alone in a small lodge by themselves on the outskirts of the Huron village. All of their relatives were dead, victims of the ongoing warfare. One day, the watchful mother became aware that her daughter would herself in due time give birth to a child, and she was bitter about it. She reproached her daughter for not marrying a man in the customary way, for now she was bringing scandal upon them both.

The daughter, however, steadfastly maintained that she had never slept with a man at any time and was, in fact, still a virgin. Naturally, her mother found the story hard to believe—her daughter's expanding belly was evidence to the contrary—and she castigated her unmercifully. But then one night she had a prophetic dream.

The Grandmother's Dream

In her dream, she was told by a divine messenger that she was doing her daughter great wrong in not believing her statement that she did not know the source of her condition. She was further told that her daughter would bear a male child, whom they must call Deganawidah. He would grow up to live among foreigners and raise up a great Tree of Peace. But he would also one day indirectly be the cause of the Huron's demise.

Upon awakening, Deganawidah's grandmother apologized to her daughter and explained her dream. Because of the prophecy about the child being indirectly the cause of the Huron's ruin, though, after much agonizing, they arrived at a terrible decision: when the baby was born, he would have to be killed.

So on the day the squalling infant entered the world, they carried him to a nearby stream, which was frozen over due to the season. After cutting a hole in the ice, they threw the child into the frigid water. Then, with heavy hearts, they returned to their lodge. When they awoke the next morning, however, they found that the child had not drowned as expected but was unharmed and lying asleep between them. Twice more they attempted infanticide in the same manner yet each time the boy turned up unharmed at dawn. Shaken, they contemplated the unnatural situation and decided that it had to be the will of the Master of Life that the boy should live. So they raised him and gave him the name Deganawidah, meaning he-who-thinks, as the dream had directed the grandmother to do. As the boy grew up, it was apparent that he was an extraordinary child, possessed of a deep and thoughtful nature.

Among the rest of the Hurons, however, the intelligent but withdrawn young man was an outcast. A primary problem was that he had no interest in making war. Seeing it all around him, Deganawidah somehow grew up to see war as little more than the quarreling of children. While other teenagers were honing their battle skills, he was developing a philosophy that would come to be known one day as The Great Law of Peace.

His outcast status, though, had other roots, as well. For although he had a lofty intellect and was quite a handsome young man, Deganawidah suffered a major disadvantage in a culture that valued a good speech. He stuttered.

When he came of age, Deganawidah left the land of the Huron and journeyed south. He crossed the waterway we now call the St. Lawrence, hiked through the Adirondack Mountains and into the land of the "flint people," or Mohawks, seeking converts to what certainly must have been a strange way of thinking. The Mohawks, a progressive yet highly aggressive forest nation, had long been at war with their brutal neighbors, the Onondagas. One of the surviving Mohawks was a man named Hiawatha.

Of the many ironies associated with the story of Deganawidah and the Iroquois Confederacy, one of the most unfortunate is the mistaken identity in the public mind of Hiawatha. Blame for this can be traced to the poetic license of the American author, Henry Wadsworth Longfellow. In writing his famous poem about the Algonquian Indians, *The Song of Hiawatha* (1855), Longfellow deliberately substituted the name Hiawatha in place of the Algonquian mythic hero Nanabozho used in an earlier draft. After that, the damage was done. Knowledge of who the real Hiawatha was has been obscured ever since.

When Deganawidah first met him, the real Hiawatha was filled with hatred for mankind. His wife and seven daughters had only recently been murdered by the odious Onondaga war chief, Ododarhoh. Pushed past the limits of sanity by the atrocity, Hiawatha was living alone deep in the forest, waylaying and devouring luckless travelers. Ceremonial cannibalism was, at that time, an integral part of warfare. A warrior victorious in battle would often eat the heart or other vital organs of a vanquished enemy in order to gain his opponent's courage. Yet Hiawatha's lust for flesh had grown into something far more horrific. When Deganawidah first laid eyes on him from the edge of the forest, the Mohawk was dragging a corpse into his lodge.

Deganawidah had heard of this cannibal beforehand from a woman named Jikonsaseh. She owned a cabin near a trail that was used as a way station by warriors as they traveled to and from frequent battles. She was, in the words of Pete Jemison, director of the Ganondagan State Historic Site in Victor, New York, "as much a part of the evil that was happening as the ones who were carrying it out, because she fed on the stories." After hearing Deganawidah's message, however, she became the first person to accept it, and is affectionately referred to by the Iroquois to this day as "the Mother of Nations."

Enlightened by Jikonsaseh, Deganawidah was not surprised when he came upon the mass murderer's shack in the woods. Deganawidah climbed onto the roof and peered through the smoke hole. Below, Hiawatha was quartering and cooking the carcass when he saw a face reflected in the water of the cooking pot. It was, in fact, Deganawidah's, but Hiawatha mistook it for his own. Hiawatha, it is said, was struck by the purity of that face and contrasted it with the character of the work in which he was engaged. "That face and this kind of business do not agree," he exclaimed and at that very moment resolved to give up eating human flesh. He carried the pot out and cast its contents away at some distance from the lodge.

When Hiawatha returned, Deganawidah climbed down from the roof and drew the Mohawk into conversation. In the course of the discussion, the prophet related his vision of peace and a new philosophy of living. That philosophy is known as *"Ne Gayaneshagowa,"* the Great Commonwealth, or Great Law of Equity and Righteousness and Well-being. It includes three double principles. The first is *Ne Skenno*—health of body and mind, peace between individuals and groups. The second, *Ne Gaiihwiyo*—righteousness in conduct, its advocacy in thought and deed; equity and justice in the adjustment of human rights. The third, *Ne Gashedenza*—maintenance of physical strength or power, and *orenda,* or magical power, of people and institutions. In more recent times, Deganawidah's philosophy has been distilled into Health and Reason (soundness of body and sanity of mind), Law (justice codified to meet particular cases), and Authority (which gives confidence that justice will prevail).

Upon hearing Deganawidah's ideas, Hiawatha underwent a truly tremendous personal transformation. His overwhelming sorrow and hate were literally swept away by the prophet's bold vision of peace. By burying the hatchet and forming a federal union of nations, Deganawidah insisted through his coarse-tongued stutter, they could bring an end to war and suffering.

Then and there, the story goes, Hiawatha made the decision to follow Deganawidah and started calling him the Peacemaker. If Deganawidah had enlisted anyone else for such an important role, his plan might never have worked. But Hiawatha was a handsome man who possessed that invaluable trait known as charisma. While the prophet at times had a hard time communicating at all, Hiawatha was capable of eloquence, wit, and persuasion. Hiawatha became Deganawidah's partner and voice. He was, in our modern vernacular, the perfect front man.

In the 1880s, Seth Newhouse, an Onondaga living on the Grand River Six Nations Reserve in Canada, prepared a version in so-called Indian-English of the story of the founding of the League and its constitution. Then in 1916, Arthur C. Parker, in the *New York State Museum Bulletin,* published an edited, English-language version of this material. Parker himself was a Seneca. His text relates how the prophet completed his ceremonial addresses and discourse on the Great Peace, then gave Hiawatha thirteen strings of shell, or wampum, and said the following:

The Great Peace

My junior brother, these thirteen strings of shell are now completed. In the future they shall be used in this way: They shall be held in the hand to remind the speaker of each part of his address. . . . My junior brother, we now shall make our laws and when all are made we shall call the organization we have formed The Great Peace. It shall be the power to abolish war and robbery between brothers and bring peace and quietness.

Hiawatha responded by saying that what Deganawidah had told him was good and that he agreed with it. Deganawidah then proposed that they compose a Song of Peace. "We shall use it on our journey to pacify Ododarhoh," he said. At that point, Hiawatha was taken aback. Ododarhoh was the monstrous chief of the Onondaga nation who was responsible for the deaths of Hiawatha's entire family.

Before they confronted Ododarhoh, they decided to approach the Mohawk, Oneida, Cayuga, and Seneca peoples. "My younger brother," said Deganawidah, "we shall now propose to the Mohawk Council the plan we have made. We shall tell our plan for a confederation and the building of a house of peace. It will be necessary for us to know [the council's] opinion and have its consent to proceed." Hiawatha's ties to the Mohawks eased the implementation of this part of Deganawidah's strategy, for his late wife was the daughter of a Mohawk chief.

Through Hiawatha, Deganawidah told the Mohawks that "he had been sent by the Master of Life from whom we are all descended to establish the Great Peace. . . . He spoke about establishing a union of all the nations. He told them that all the chiefs must be virtuous men and be very patient."

In response, one of the Mohawk leaders declared that all Deganawidah said was "surely true and we are not able to contradict it." What they wanted, however, was proof that the young revolutionary before them had indeed been sent by the Master of Life. Deganawidah agreed to furnish that proof. One of the powers that the Master of Life had given him was dominion over his own death. To prove it, he proposed that he climb to the top of a tall pine tree overhanging the swift Mohawk River and that they chop down the tree. The test was accepted. It was done and a multitude saw him disappear. They thought he had surely drowned.

When night came and Deganawidah still had not appeared, the people were sure that he had died and were satisfied that his claims were false. But the next morning some warriors saw smoke arising from an empty cabin. They approached cautiously. Peering in the side of the wall where the bark was loosened they saw Deganawidah. He was not a ghost; of that they were sure. He was alive as any of them and cooking his morning meal. The watchers ran back to the village to report their discovery. Before the day was out, everyone was convinced that Deganawidah was who he claimed to be.

The Mohawk elders suggested that the plan for a union of tribes be presented to their enemies, the Oneida, or "People of the Stone," to see if they would also consider it. When their chief, Odatshedeh, had been asked, he said, "I will consider this plan and answer you tomorrow." Tomorrow, in the vocabulary of the time, meant one year. After that period had past, the answer came from the Oneida Council. They would join the confederation.

Over a five-year period, due in large part to everyone's weariness of war, the Mohawk, Oneida, Cayuga, and Seneca nations were won over by Deganawidah's vision of a Great Commonwealth. Finally, the only impediment to the realization of the prophet's vision were the Onondaga and their evil war chief, Ododarhoh. Spies had returned with reports that "Ododarhoh has seven crooked parts, his hair is infested with snakes, and he is a cannibal." It was obvious to everyone that the League would never work without the Onondagas, who were centrally located between the other nations.

Deganawidah then addressed the council of the four nations. "I am Deganawidah," he said. "And with me is my younger brother. We two now lay before you the laws by which to frame the [union]. The emblems of the chief rulers shall be the antlers of deer. The titles shall be vested in certain women and the names shall be held in their maternal families forever." The laws were then recited and confirmed by Hiawatha. Deganawidah then sang the song used when conferring titles, and taught the people the Song of Peace and other songs. It is said that many people came to listen and learn and that the *orenda,* or holy magic, helped carry the Great Peace ahead of them on the wind. Then they all marched on to Onondaga.

When the expedition reached the frontiers of Onondagan territory, a fire was lit, which was a customary warning. Word had spread ahead of the group, however. News of the impending union of the four previously hostile nations had penetrated into Onondagan territory and had been met with great interest. The Onondagan people and their chiefs came out to greet Deganawidah, Hiawatha, and the crowd. Combining forces, the throng is then said to have marched to the fireside of Ododarhoh.

Deganawidah walked to the door of Ododarhoh's lodge and performed a great miracle of healing. The anxious chatter of the enveloping crowd faded to silence as he sang the Song of Peace.

Soon the monster emerged. Listening to the sweet sound of the prophet's flawed voice, Ododarhoh's expression deflated by degrees from anger to sadness. When he finished his song, Deganawidah walked up to Ododarhoh and with a face full of pity, reached out to him. Ododarhoh let the prophet's hand pass over his face. Through friendly persuasion, Deganawidah metaphorically combed the snakes— the evil and insane thoughts—out of the war chief's hair until his mind regained its health.

Transformed, Ododarhoh declared himself one of Deganawidah's disciples, and the entire Onondaga nation, amazed at their leader's stunning reformation, followed him into the Great Peace. The prophet proclaimed him keeper of the new Confederacy's fire which, he said, would burn always at Onondaga. That position of "firekeeper," comparable to that of president of the U.S. Senate, made Ododarhoh one of the most powerful people in the new Iroquois nation.

Stuttering Deganawidah, the Huron outcast, was no mere dreamer. He had proven to be a political genius. Because of him, the League of Five Nations was created. And just as today people of the fifty states are citizens of the federal republic of the United States of America, so were the Seneca, Mohawk, Onondaga, Oneida, and Cayuga welded into citizens of the League.

They called themselves People of the Longhouse, a name that referred to their handsome communal dwellings. These longhouses had entrances at either end and were constructed of logs, sheathed in elm bark, and roofed with bent saplings and boughs. Several families occupied each of these extended houses, sharing one of several fire pits and each others' lives.

Because the League itself was basically a collection of villages running from east to west along a well-worn forest path, the longhouse became an important symbol of Iroquois culture. The Mohawk were keepers of the eastern door. The Seneca stood guard in the west.

At the ceremony marking the birth of the Confederacy, the prophet put it all into perspective. With the citizens of the new nation gathered around him in a clearing in the cool, clean forest, here, in part, is what he said.

The White Roots of Peace

I am Deganawidah and with the Five Nations' confederate lords I plant the Tree of the Great Peace. I plant it in your territory, Ododarhoh and the Onondaga Nation, in the territory of you who are firekeepers.

I name this tree the Tree of the Great Long Leaves. Under the shade of this Tree of the Great Peace we spread the soft, white feather down of the globe thistle as seats for you, Ododarhoh and your cousin lords. . . . There shall you sit and watch the council fire of the Confederacy of the Five Nations.

Roots have spread out from the Tree of the Great Peace . . . and the name of these roots is the Great White Roots of Peace. If any man of any nation outside of the Five Nations shall show a desire to obey the laws of the Great Peace . . . they may trace the roots to their source . . . and they shall be welcomed to take shelter beneath the Tree of the Long Leaves.

The smoke from the confederate council fire shall ever ascend and shall pierce the sky so that all nations may discover the central council fire of the Great Peace.

I, Deganawidah, and the confederate lords now uproot the tallest pine tree and into the cavity thereby made we cast all weapons of war. Into the depths of the earth, down into the deep under-earth currents of water flowing into unknown regions, we cast all weapons of strife. We bury them from sight forever and plant again the tree. Thus shall all Great Peace be established and hostilities shall no longer be known between the Five Nations but only peace to a united people.

In the government Deganawidah created, each of the five nations debated proposals first at the local level. Once the village chief had ascertained the views of the majority of men and women, the proposal would be debated by all of the chiefs. Once a consensus was reached at this, what might be called the state level, the question could be put before the federal level, or Grand Council of the League.

Matters of overriding foreign policy, including declarations of war, were reserved solely for the federal Grand Council. The council deliberated upon important matters in accordance with established rules and principles of procedure and was guided by precedent. Federal chiefs were divided into three groups according to clan. When an issue was presented to the council, one side considered it first and then passed it "across the fire" to the second side for discussion. If a consensus was reached, they referred the matter to the firekeeper for confirmation.

As firekeeper, the Onondagas called the meetings, prepared the agendas, and provided the moderator. If the other nations agreed on a measure, the Onondagans were obliged by the Great Peace to confirm the decision. If they disagreed, they were empowered with a veto and could send the measure back for reconsideration. If the same decision was rendered again, however, the Onondagas had no other choice but to certify it.

The council usually met in the summer in the presence of both men and women. Procedures were established in case it should be called into session at other times. To guard against unscrupulous demagogues, Deganawidah built in a number of safeguards. One was the rule that public discussion of an important proposal could not take place the same day it was received in council. Time had to be allowed for study. If the subject under consideration was especially controversial, it would be discussed thoroughly in a committee made up of a representative of each nation. Speakers were never to be interrupted and relied on ethical proof to persuade others to accept their point of view. Furthermore, they frequently employed such oratorical methods as cause and effect, reductio ad absurdum, turning the tables, and refutation by presenting additional evidence contrary to that presented by the opposition. Once an oration was concluded, a small period of silence was alloted in case any important, forgotten points were remembered. And in order to guard against the kind of overreaction that springs from exhaustion, discussion in the federal council was not permitted to continue past sunset.

The lands of each of the Five Nations, and every nation that was incorporated into it afterward, became the sovereign territory of the union. This was symbolized by a common dish on which was laid a beaver tail. "It is forbidden that there be any knife in this dish which we have put before ourselves, lest there be blood in the dish from some cut of this knife," said the Peacemaker. "Let us rather use our hands only."

In order to bind the people of the League together more tightly, Deganawidah constructed a system of clans that overlapped each of the Five Nation's boundaries. Each clan was headed by a revered, older woman. Named Bear, Wolf, Hawk, Turtle, and the like, these clans helped to break down age-old rivalries. Forty-nine chiefly titles were also created, representing most of the clans, and were filled only by men. Iroquois society was built upon these maternal families. Each clan was comprised of a woman and all of her children and the descendents of her daughters. Her husband was a member of his own mother's clan and her sons' children members of their wives' clan. The farmland that produced corn, beans, squashes, berries, nuts, and roots were owned communally by the women.

Indeed, when it came to the role of women in the new society, Deganawidah was once again centuries ahead of his time. One of the most important powers he gave them was the right to vote. In what other contemporary society did women have this right? They were even entitled to cast the votes of their infants. In counsels, women could propose subjects for discussion and were empowered to nominate chiefs and other *sachem.* After the nominees were confirmed, assuming they were, and installed by officers of the federal council, they could be impeached and deposed by a matron of the clan.

Here is how that worked. The head matron would first visit the errant official in person and warn him to reform and return to the path of righteousness and duty. If he failed to heed this warning, she would seek out her brother or eldest son, as a representative of the men of her clan, and together they would go to give the erring chief a second warning. If he still would not reform his behavior, the matron visited the chief warrior of the clan. Then together these three would inform the wayward leader that he must appear on a given day at the tribal council. On that day, the chief warrior would ask him whether he would or would not conform to the expressed wish of his clan. If he refused to reform he was deposed at once. The chief warrior then took back the symbolic horns of leadership.

Adoption of captive foreigners to replace family members killed in war was another important feature of Iroquois life and this melting pot affected the demographics of the League. But it was not only other Indians who were adopted; Europeans joined as well. Frenchmen, in particular, were susceptible to "the savage life" once they had tasted it. Again, illustrating the power of women in the new society, both captives and defectors were adopted or killed through the decision of the presiding matron of the clan.

Iroquois statesmen were advised by Deganawidah to have skin "seven thumbs thick" in order to remain oblivious to gossip and criticism. To retain his office, a chief had to have the welfare of the people uppermost in his mind and keep the approval of the public at large. Indeed, the League's decisions were actually enforced by public compliance, which was secured by appeals to public opinion.

Along with impeachment due to irresponsibility in office, mental incapacitation could also bring about dismissal. If that became the case, there was an elaborate and solemn ceremony for removing the *sachem*'s title and investing it upon someone new.

The names of the original forty-nine chiefs have been passed down through the generations as federal titles and serve as living reminders of the story of the birth of the Confederacy. Since then, there has always been a Hiawatha, an Ododarhoh, and the rest. But there has never been another Deganawidah. No one else could ever take his place.

Despite his remarkable achievement, Deganawidah never lost sight of his reverence for the earth. As related by Paul A. W. Wallace in *The White Roots of Peace,* Deganawidah instructed the federal chiefs that whenever "they shall assemble for the purpose of holding a council . . . the Onondaga Lords shall make an address and return thanks to the earth where men dwell, to the streams of water, the pools, the springs, and the lakes, to the maize and the fruits, to the medicinal herbs and trees, to the forest trees for their usefulness, to the animals that serve as food and give their pelts for clothing, to the great winds and the lesser winds, to the Thunderers, to the Sun, the mighty warrior, to the Moon, to the messengers of the Creator who reveal his wishes, and to the Great Creator who dwells in the heavens above, who gives all things useful to man, and who is the source and the ruler of health and life."

Once his vision was fulfilled, Deganawidah disappeared. He is said to have paddled westward in a canoe made of white stone.

While his followers watched from the shore, the great prophet disappeared into the setting sun. How or when he died is unknown but it is said that his body is buried somewhere near Lake Onondaga. According to Iroquois tradition, only five years had passed since Deganawidah had left the Hurons to begin his ministry of peace. That would have made him about twenty-three years old.

Among Deganawidah's great teachings is the haunting prophecy of the White, Red, and Black Serpents passed down to us by Mad Bear Anderson. Powerful in its symbolism, the prophecy exalts serpents as bringers of knowledge and the power that goes with it. With that knowledge comes death of the old and ultimate resurrection.

Prophecy of the White, Red, and Black Serpents

When Deganawidah was leaving the Indians in the Bay of Quinte in Ontario, he told the Indian people that they would face a time of great suffering. They would distrust their leaders and the principles of peace of the League, and a great white serpent was to come upon the Iroquois, and that for a time it would intermingle with the Indian people and would be accepted by the Indians, who would treat the serpent as a friend. This serpent would in time become so powerful that it would attempt to destroy the Indian, and the serpent is described as choking the life's blood out of the Indian people. Deganawidah told the Indians that they would be in such a terrible state at this point that all hope would seem to be lost, and he told them that when things looked their darkest a red serpent would come from the north and approach the white serpent, which would be terrified, and upon seeing the red serpent he would release the Indian, who would fall to the ground almost like a helpless child, and the white serpent would turn all its attention to the red serpent. The bewilderment would cause the white serpent to accept the red serpent momentarily. The white serpent would be stunned and take part of the red serpent and accept him. Then there is a heated argument and a fight. And then the Indian revives and crawls toward the land of the hilly country, and then he would assemble his people together, and they would renew their faith and the principles of peace that Deganawidah had established. There would at the same time exist among the Indians a great love and forgiveness for his brother, and in this gathering would come streams from all over—

not only the Iroquois but from all over—and they would gather in this hilly country, and they would renew their friendship. And Deganawidah said they would remain neutral in this fight between the white serpent and the red serpent.

At the time they were watching the two serpents locked in this battle, a great message would come to them, which would make them ever so humble, and when they become that humble, they will be waiting for a young leader, an Indian boy, possibly in his teens, who would be a choice seer. Nobody knows who he is or where he comes from, but he will be given great power, and would be heard by thousands, and he would give them the guidance and the hope to refrain from going back to their land and he would be the accepted leader. And Deganawidah said that they will gather in the land of the hilly country, beneath the branches of an elm tree, and they should burn tobacco and call upon Deganawidah by name when we are facing our darkest hours, and he will return. Deganawidah said that as the choice seer speaks to the Indians that number as the blades of grass and he would be heard by all at the same time, and as the Indians are gathered watching the fight, they notice from the south a black serpent coming from the sea, and he is described as dripping with salt water, and as he stands there, he rests for a spell to get his breath, all the time watching to the north to the land where the white serpent and the red serpent are fighting. Deganawidah said that the battle between the white and the red serpents opened real slow but would then become so violent that the mountains would crack and the rivers would boil and the fish would turn up on their bellies. He said that there would be no leaves on the trees in that area. There would be no grass, and that strange bugs and beetles would crawl from the ground and attack both serpents, and he said that a great heat would cause the stench of death to sicken both serpents. And then, as the boy seer is watching this fight, the red serpent reaches around the back of the white serpent and pulls from him a hair which is carried toward the south by a great wind into the waiting hands of the black serpent, and as the black serpent studies this hair, it suddenly turns into a woman, a white woman who tells him things that he knows to be true but he wants to hear them again. When this white woman finishes telling these things, he takes her and gently places her on a rock with great love and respect, and then he becomes infuriated at what he has heard, so he makes a beeline for the north, and he enters the battle between the red and white serpents with such speed and anger that he defeats the two serpents, who have already been battle-weary.

When he finishes, he stands on the chest of the white serpent, and he boasts and puts his chest out like he's the conqueror, and he looks for another serpent to conquer. He looks to the land of the hilly country and then he sees the Indian standing with his arms folded and looking ever so nobly so that he knows that this Indian is not the one that we should fight. The next direction that he will face will be eastward and at that time he will be momentarily blinded by a light that is many times brighter than the sun. The light will be coming from the east to the west over the water, and when the black serpent regains his sight, he becomes terrified and makes a beeline for the sea. He dips into the sea and swims away in a southerly direction, and shall never again be seen by the Indians. The white serpent revives, and he, too, sees this light, and he makes a feeble attempt to gather himself and go toward that light. A portion of the white serpent refuses to remain but instead makes its way toward the land of the hilly country, and there he will join the Indian People with a great love like that of a lost brother. The rest of the white serpent would go to the sea and dip into the sea and would be lost out of sight for a spell. Then suddenly the white serpent would appear again on the top of the water and he would be slowly swimming toward the light. Deganawidah said that the white serpent would never again be a troublesome spot for the Indian people. The red serpent would revive and he would shiver with great fear when he sees that light. He would crawl to the north and leave a bloody shaky trail northward, and he would never be seen again by the Indians. Deganawidah said as this light approaches that he would be that light, and he would return to his Indian people, and when he returns, the Indian people would be a greater nation than they ever were before.

This chilling prophecy seems to speak about the events of the last few centuries. Taken literally, we might interpret it as describing the vanquishing of the Indian people by the white man and their subsequent death through assimilation of his ways. In time, this White Serpent turns his attention to the Red Serpent, which in the twentieth century could mean the Red Scare or Communism. The ensuing battle is so violent that the mountains shake and the rivers boil. This could be a metaphor to describe nuclear testing and the industrial pollution that has turned so many rivers into cauldrons of chemicals incapable of supporting life. And could the "great heat [that] would cause the stench of death" be a prophecy of global warming?

The section describing how the Black Serpent from the south receives great truths from a goddess spirit and defeats the two battle-weary serpents of the north might be interpreted as predicting a resurrection of Black people and culture. This serpent leads the flight from the burning light that glows in the East, a symbol of new beginnings for the Indian. Once again, they find happiness in mutual love and respect for one another, thus heralding the second coming of the Peacemaker.

But this is a literal interpretation and a facile one at that. There are other considerations.

In religions throughout the world and across time, serpents have represented wisdom and rebirth. The colors White, Red, and Black are also the sacred colors of the Great Goddess, Mother Earth herself. Red symbolizes the water elements as well as our own emotions and is recognized at the southern end of the sacred circle used in many Native American ceremonies. White is associated with the North and the workings of the mind. As the cold white snows of the North bring purity, so shall they bring clear thinking. Black is the color of the earth and the West, where the sun sets and dark night takes its place. In the sacred circle, black, like the serpent itself, symbolizes that which must die in order for resurrection to take place.

Thus the Black Serpent dies to make way for the Second Coming of the Peacemaker. The Red Serpent, spilling its bloody guts of emotional pain and heartbreak finds its way to the cool North. The White Serpent of intellectual knowledge splinters itself to partially remain with the Indian people, the rest of it disappearing into the Eastern lights.

On a number of different levels, the divination speaks to the future of the Indian people and the entire world as we face our most challenging period of survival.

The prophet died but his ideas lived on. For generations, the verses from the Song of Peace, also called The Six Songs, were sung by citizens of the League in thanksgiving for what Deganawidah and his disciple, Hiawatha, had accomplished.

The Song of Peace

Hai! Hai! Hai!
Once more we come to greet and thank the League;
Once more to greet and thank the nations' Peace.
Hai, hai, hai, hai, hai!

Hai! Hai! Hai!
Once more we come to greet and thank the Kindred;
Once more to greet and thank the dead chief's Kindred;
Hai, hai, hai, hai, hai!

Hai! Hai! Hai!
Once more we come to greet and thank the Warriors;
Once more to greet and thank the nations' Manhood.
Hai, hai, hai, hai, hai!

Hai! Hai! Hai!
Once more we come to greet and thank the Women;
Once more to greet and thank the mourning Women.
Hai, hai, hai, hai, hai!

Hai! Hai! Hai! that which our Forefathers accomplished!
Hai! Hai! Hai! the Law our Forefathers established!
Oh listen to us, listen, continue to hear us, our Grandsires!
Oh listen to us, listen, continue to hear us, our Grandsires!

Although the Iroquois had no alphabet, Deganawidah's code, or constitution, was not completely unwritten. It and other important texts were recorded on wampum belts and strings made of shell. Cadawallader Colden observed how this worked. The *sachem* "has a bundle of small sticks in his hand," he wrote in *The History of the Five Nations.* As soon as the speaker has finished any one article of his speech, this *sachem* gives a stick to another *sachem,* who is particularly to remember that article; and so when another article is finished, he gives a stick to another to take care of that other [article], and so [forth]. In like manner when the speaker answers, each of these [*sachems*] has the particular care of the answer resolved on to each article, and prompts the orator, when his memory fails him, in the article committed to his charge."

Once or twice a year, the Iroquois *sachem* would select an up-and-coming young man and take him to a meadow. There, they would teach the young man the meaning of the wampum. In this way, the

Code of Deganawidah was passed down through the generations. Hiawatha is generally credited with the invention of this memory-aid system, which was also used to record the minutes of important meetings.

Although there were struggles between the individual nations, Deganawidah's dream of peace was maintained for generations among the Five Nations in their forest realm. It was in many ways an idyllic world. The women grew the crops, as it was thought their fertility in childbearing transferred magically to the corn, beans, seeds, berries, maple sugar, herbs, and tobacco. The men on the other hand traveled constantly in pursuit of trade, diplomacy, and war. As the Peacemaker had envisioned, the Iroquois found great strength and prosperity in their union. Citizens of the League were safe under the symbolic boughs of the Tree of Great Long Leaves.

Those outside the union, however, were considered fair game. Like all great powers, the League exhibited a superior attitude toward other nations. Those who came in conflict with them would be asked politely three times to join the Great Peace. Father Le Jeune, writing in the *Jesuit Relations,* documented an attempt to fashion a treaty with the French in 1642. "Listen to me!" a *sachem* yelled from a canoe in midstream. "I come to treat for peace with all the nations in these parts . . . the land shall be beautiful, the river shall have no more waves, one may go everywhere without fear!" If after three times the foreigners still refused to join, the Iroquois were entitled to attack.

Early in the seventeenth century, Samuel de Champlain arrived to develop New France. He sailed up the St. Lawrence River, exploring and trading furs, and then made a fateful mistake by joining Huron and Algonquian warriors in a battle against their archenemies, the Iroquois, at Ticonderoga. The name *Iroquois* is, in fact, a French slur, bastardized from an Algonquian word meaning "venomous snakes." Champlain is said to have personally killed two Mohawk war chiefs. The mighty Iroquois braves fled, terrified by the Europeans' firearms.

The French would come to regret Champlain's actions. His involvement ignited more than one hundred years of enmity by the Iroquois. Emissaries from the Five Nations soon learned that the Dutch were willing to trade anything for furs. Even rifles. The

Iroquois quickly incorporated those weapons into their war machine and became more fearsome than ever.

During this period, the French and English began a heated competition in North America for furs. The entire seventeenth century
encompassed the struggle for control of this lucrative trade. Native
peoples were drawn into the colonial economies by the Europeans'
willingness to trade such items as copper kettles, steel knives, and
cotton cloth for pelts. The beaver was particularly prized. While the
forests overflowed with them, a relative peace reigned. But when
the beaver, mink, and fox began to be depleted, the competition
grew increasingly violent.

The Indians richest in furs were the Huron. They traded corn
and tobacco to more northerly tribes for beaver pelts. In 1646, they
are reported to have sailed eighty canoe-loads into Montreal. The
Iroquois's lands, on the other hand, had grown barren. Would the
Huron be willing to share their wealth? *Sachem* diplomats from the
Five Nations were dispatched, but negotiations proved fruitless.

Then, on a cold morning in March 1649, the prophetic dream
of Deganawidah's grandmother finally came true. More than a
thousand Iroquois warriors armed with some four hundred guns
attacked the sleeping Huron villages at dawn. Whole settlements
were obliterated. Hundreds were killed. Two Jesuit missionaries
were tortured. Scores more of the Huron were taken into captivity
and forced to become Iroquois or die. Long after Deganawidah's
grandmother had her dream predicting the destruction of her people, it had come to pass. And her grandson, due to his role in
forging the Five Nations, had—as prophesied—indirectly played a
part.

The Iroquois went on to destroy the Erie or Cat People, the
Neutrals, and other nearby nations, and eventually ranged as far as
present-day Illinois to the west, Maine to the east, and Tennessee
in the south. It was from these campaigns, popularly known as the
Beaver Wars, that the Iroquois achieved their reputation for ruth-
less savagery in war.

But this reputation is not entirely deserved. Like others who
wrote in the seventeenth and eighteenth centuries, Louis H. Mor-
gan, in his classic work of American anthropology, *League of the
Ho-dé-no-sau-nee, or Iroquois* (1851), claimed that warriors of the

League were so feared that other tribes would flee upon a mere rumor of Iroquois approach. But at least one modern-day scholar has proven this to be more myth than reality. Through his research conducted for the Newberry Library Center for the History of the American Indian, Francis Jennings has documented that many tribes fought back against the Iroquois, and often quite successfully. "It was sagacity rather than ferocity that elevated the Iroquois to leadership among the tribes allied to Great Britain," writes Jennings in *The Ambiguous Iroquois Empire.* "Other tribesmen were their peers in courage and fierceness . . . [but the Iroquois] achieved their greatest successes by a judicious combination of war and negotiation. . . . The instrument of negotiation was the treaty council."

•

Just how much of the story of Deganawidah and the founding of the League was known to Benjamin Franklin, we will never know. No reference to the Peacemaker is in any of Franklin's writings. He may have heard of him, however. The Iroquois referred to their founder frequently on ceremonial occasions. The Wampum Code of the Confederacy, for example, which was often recited during solemn negotiations, contained the phrase, "I am Deganawidah, and with the Five Nations Confederate Lords, I plant the Tree of the Great Peace." Such history was usually related in Mohawk. Although Franklin was not conversant in that language, at the Albany Conference during those summer months in 1754 there were at least three interpreters who were.

If we cast off the blinders of our traditional European bias and examine Franklin's words and deeds at Albany, it is clear that the man often incorrectly called "America's first philosopher" understood and respected Iroquois ideas. On June 28, 1754, he presented his "Short Hints toward a Scheme for a General Union of the British Colonies on the Continent" to the delegates of the conference. It contained what establishment historians like Catherine Drinker Bowen have termed "a shock and a surprise to the world even after the Revolution." What was that shock? It was pretty close to a duplicate of the federal form of government that had been used by the League for perhaps three hundred and fifty years.

"One General Government," declared Franklin, to "be formed in America, including all the said Colonies, within and under which Government, each Colony may retain its present Constitution." He proposed a single-chamber "Grand Council" of representatives with members from each province to be presided over by an officer with veto power. No mention was made of a Supreme Court. Decisions made by this Grand Council were not to interfere with the governments of the individual colonies, "who are to be left to their own laws."

Franklin did not go so far as to suggest the colonial union provide women the right to vote. Nor did he propose a mechanism for impeachment of officials. These would come much later. But as Franklin biographer Carl Van Doren has written, "He admired the Iroquois confederation, and plainly had it in mind in his earliest discussion of the need of union among the colonies."

Ten years before the Albany Conference, Richard Peters, one of the other three royally appointed commissioners had attended a treaty council with the Iroquois at Lancaster, Pennsylvania. Two hundred and forty-five chiefs, warriors, women, and children showed up to parley with the governor of the Province of Pennsylvania and the commissioners of Virginia and Maryland, among others. They stayed for about two weeks in order to discuss the squatter invasions of Indian lands, the English-Iroquois alliance against the French, and other problems involved in "polishing the covenant chain."

The Iroquois were led by Canassatego, an Onondaga *sachem* who was Hendrick's predecessor as elected speaker of the League's Grand Council. Canassatego was exceptionally tall and still athletic at sixty years old. He had a booming voice and possessed a charisma similar to that of the great Hiawatha. Cadawallader Colden, present in the role of a commissioner from New York, later remarked that Canassatego reminded him of the great men of Greece and Rome. Another commissioner, Witham Marshe, wrote that Canassatego carried off "all honors in oratory, logical argument, and adroit negotiation."

At the end of that treaty council on July 4, 1744, Canassatego rose to his feet to address the colonists with the following prophetic advice.

Canassetego's Advice

> We have one thing further to say, and that is, we heartily recommend union and a good agreement between you our Brethern. Never disagree, but preserve a strict friendship for one another, and thereby you, as well as we, will become the stronger.
>
> Our wise forefathers established union and amity between the Five Nations; this has made us formidable; this has given us great weight and authority with our neighboring nations.
>
> We are a powerful Confederacy; and, by your observing the same methods our wise forefathers have taken, you will acquire fresh strength and power. Therefore, whatever befalls you, never fall out with one another.

Franklin, of course, knew of this advice. Aside from printing much of the paper money and official proclamations of Pennsylvania, he also printed the transcripts of the treaty councils. When the interpreter's record of the Lancaster Conference was sent to him, he was so impressed that he printed two hundred extra copies.

Ten years later to the day after Canassatego gave his stirring advice, Franklin signed the Plan of Union in Albany. He made a speech to the delegates in which he pointed out "the strength of the League which has bound our friends the Iroquois together in a common tie which no crisis, however grave, since its foundation has managed to disrupt."

After the Iroquois had departed, the colonial delegates to the conference went over the Plan of Union clause by clause. Franklin redrafted it according to their input and it was voted upon and approved. The plan was by no means an early Declaration of Independence. Franklin intended that his plan be voted on by the British Parliament and that the mother country itself be its "final guarantor." By drawing the squabbling colonies together under a single North American government that reported to England, Franklin and others felt that a stronger face could be presented to the treacherous French.

But the Albany Plan of Union was ahead of its time. It was ultimately ignored by New York, rejected by Massachusetts, and voted down by the Pennsylvania Assembly on the last day of its session while Franklin was away from Philadelphia. The idea of a federal union, though, as we know, took on a life of its own. As for the crown's original intent of satisfying Indian grievances at Albany, in light of the flagrant land swindles that were arranged there, the conference actually aggravated them.

Over the past two centuries, as the white man systematically exterminated the red man, it has been easier for Americans to focus on the "savagery" of the Iroquois and other native peoples than on the achievements of Deganawidah. By denigrating or ignoring the intellectual achievements of the Native American, genocide was easier to carry out.

Native Americans were considered to be equals by thoughtful European-Americans until about the beginning of the nineteenth century. And not just by Benjamin Franklin. When English explorer Henry Hudson opened North America to the British in 1610, he brought back tales of wonder. Just as American corn, tobacco, furs, and people flowed from the New World to the Old, so did ideas. Encounters with strange peoples and tales of unusual customs were in the holds of those rickety wooden ships. Thinking men and women in Europe stood amazed.

In 1690, the English philosopher John Locke, sometimes called the intellectual ruler of the eighteenth century, published his *Two Treatises on Civil Government.* His book was a radical attack on the theory of the divine right of kings. Locke declared that men in their natural condition are in a state of freedom. The logical conclusion, according to the influential Locke, was that no man has any more rights than another. All men are equal.

Across the channel in France, reports of Native American societies traveled home through the writings of Jesuit missionaries and stories of fur traders and explorers. In 1750, Jean-Jacques Rousseau published his *Discourse On the Arts and Sciences* and in 1753 *Discourse on the Inequalities of Men,* essays that catapulted him to sudden fame. In those works, he maintained that the tribal period is mankind's happiest and that only men who have retained their primitive simplicity have stayed virtuous and strong. From this, talk of the "Noble Savage" arose.

Who were those that had retained their simplicity and remained strong? Where had the Europeans gotten these ideas? From the New World, of course. As Benjamin Franklin himself said, "Liberty best thrives in the woods." Aside from the ideals detailed above, the Iroquois Confederacy was a society without jails, where the leaders were the servants of their people and unlawful entry into private homes was forbidden. These were revolutionary notions to Europeans emerging from feudalism, and evidence of a culture in many ways more highly advanced than their own.

Indeed if you compare the ideas of Locke, the widely heralded English Enlightenment philosopher, and Deganawidah, the unknown Native American sage, you find two major differences. First, as Iroquois scholar Donald Grinde, Jr., has put it, "The words of Deganawidah express the same ideas as those of John Locke, with at least one critical distinction. Locke's ideas were not accepted in Europe in the late 1600s, while the Iroquois had lived in such a democratic state for centuries." A second distinction is that when it comes to their attitudes toward the earth, the Englishman, in comparison to the founder of the league, is far less evolved.

Twenty years after Franklin presented his Albany Plan of Union, the colonies stood on the threshold of rebellion. They were enraged by the crown's Stamp Act and other taxation issues. Is it surprising then that when rebellious colonists dumped tea into Boston Harbor they dressed up as proud and independent Mohawks—the living symbols of freedom?

Fighting broke out at Lexington and Concord the next year. Representatives of the informally united colonies met in August in Philadelphia with the representatives of the Six Nations. They asked that the Iroquois ally themselves with the United States or at least remain neutral during the coming war for independence. Then they made known their gratitude. "Our business with you," a commissioner declared, "is to inform you [that] the advice that was given about thirty years ago . . . sunk deep into our hearts. Our forefathers rejoiced to hear Canassatego speak these words."

The Iroquois were flattered. And somewhere Deganawidah must have been smiling, too. On July 4, 1776, *thirty-two years to the day* after Canassatego proffered his advice, the colonies took their famous stand. Benjamin Franklin and our other founding fathers signed the Declaration of Independence from Great Britain.

But then some of the Iroquois had second thoughts. The United States would be a much more formidable adversary than thirteen quarrelsome and independent units ruled by a power across the Atlantic. British agents worked overtime to convince the League that an alliance with the Americans would not be in their interest. Subsequently, all but two of the Six Nations—the Oneida and Tuscarora—made the mistake of joining the British during the Revolutionary War. In response, George Washington in 1779 sent General Sullivan to attack the Confederacy. Sullivan reportedly burned forty villages, destroyed 160,000 bushels of corn, and generally left the earth scorched.

Iroquoian refugees fled to what is now Oklahoma, Wisconsin, and Canada. Others stayed behind to pick up the pieces but the power of the great League had been crushed once and for all.

People of the Six Nations still reside on seven reserves in Canada, one in Wisconsin, one in Oklahoma and in New York upon the Ganienkeh, Oneida, Onondaga, Tonawanda, Tuscarora, Cattarauqus, Allegheny, and Akwasasne reservations. The Six Nations or Handenosaunee, issues its own passports, though it is only a shadow of what it once was. Increasingly violent internal squabbles over big-time gambling on the reservation only underscore how the Peacemaker has been forgotten by many of his own people.

Why has Deganawidah been so ignored? How is it that his iconoclastic ideas have been attributed to so many others? A number of factors obviously conspired to keep it that way. Only now, at the close of the twentieth century, has the dominant Anglo culture begun to probe the significant histories of Americans who lived in this land before Columbus. Only now, after almost two centuries, are we returning to the idea that Native Americans were and are our intellectual equals. And in some ways our superiors.

Many of us like to think of the United States as unique in the world—a melting pot. A society unlike any other. But like all conquerors, ours is the privilege to rewrite history. Although he has been ignored, there is no doubt that Deganawidah's ideas contributed in a major way to what our nation and the world is today. It is time to correct the history books. This great Native American sage deserves a place in our pantheon of heroes. May Deganawidah never be forgotten again.

CHAPTER FOUR

WOVOKA:
PAIUTE GHOST DANCER

My children, my children,
Look! the earth is about to move,
Look! the earth is about to move.
My father tells me so,
My father tells me so.

—Arapaho Ghost Dance Song

In a windswept cemetery in the tiny, Paiute Indian hamlet of Shurtz, Nevada, lies the grave of a man whom tens of thousands once believed to be the Son of God. A wooden marker declares the plot to be the last resting place of Jack Wilson. But that was only one of his names. During his lifetime, he was also called Wopokahte, Cowejo, Quoitze Owe, Big Rumbling Belly, and Jesus Christ. The name that he is most widely known by, however, is Wovoka.

Born around 1858, Wovoka died on September 20, 1932. His long life spanned a period of American history that saw the closing of the frontier and the subjugation of the western tribes. In a matter of a few generations, once proud peoples found themselves enmeshed in a catastrophe of staggering proportions as almost everything they held true was turned upside down and destroyed.

So it came to pass that in the midst of their suffering, Wovoka "went up to heaven and saw God." When he returned, he prophesied the end of the white race and reestablishment of an Indian paradise on a rejuvenated earth, all to be brought about by a sacred, five-day-long ceremony that came to be called the Ghost Dance.

Wovoka's message of hope spread like wildfire among the demoralized tribes. But like a rumor, it grew increasingly distorted with each retelling. By the time the fervor reached its climax less than three years later, Wovoka had elevated himself from prophet to Son of God. And the Ghost Dance became the spark that ignited the Last Indian War.

•

Wovoka was born in an oval-shaped hut, known as a *wikiup,* near the Walker River in the Mason Valley of western Nevada. Some thirty miles in length, Mason Valley is a flat expanse carpeted with mountain grasses and dotted with sagebrush, juniper, and scrub pine. The lowlands that teem with rabbit and deer are walled in by towering, pine-skirted mountains, and roofed by a sky of the purest blue. It is one of those places on earth that seems to have been set aside for dreamers.

The Paiutes had lived in the valley for countless generations when the first white settlers began to appear in the 1860s. In 1863, the Wilson brothers—David, William, and George—arrived to lay claim to the land that Wovoka's family and others had long occupied. The Wilsons started a cattle ranch and the Indians on it simply became a part of their holdings.

Wovoka was the eldest of three brothers. Nothing is known of his mother, but his father, Tavibo, played an important role in shaping Wovoka's future. Tavibo was a holy man and follower of the Paiute prophet Wodziwob, originator of an earlier Ghost Dance that surfaced in Mason Valley in 1870. Wovoka was in his early teens at the time. The Ghost Dance of 1870 featured many of the same elements that Wovoka would later incorporate into his own doctrine, including the return of the dead and the regeneration of the "worn out" earth. This pre-Wovoka Ghost Dance flowered among the decimated tribes in Nevada, northern California, and southern Oregon before inexplicably dying out. Exactly what happened to Wodziwob is unclear. At least one scholar asserts that he died around 1872, leaving the movement leaderless.

When Wovoka was about fourteen, he was unofficially adopted by the Wilsons. According to Paul Bailey, Wovoka's sole biographer and source of much of the information on the prophet's early life, the Wilsons "taught him how to brand a calf, how to pitch hay, how to clean a stable, and how to handle a plow. They took him out of rabbit skins, and into white man's jeans." They also "taught him to sit on a chair when in their house, and not to squat on his hams on the floor." Just as his learning at the feet of his holy man father would play an important role in the development of Wovoka's thinking, so would his white man's education among the Wilsons.

The Paiutes, at that time, were a sullen lot, permeated with hatred toward those who had stolen their lands. Wovoka, though, was different. According to William Wilson's daughter, Beth, he appeared to envy the white man. And he was very willing to work.

Wovoka developed a close friendship with David Wilson's son, Bill. Despite their obvious differences, the two boys were of the same age, and together, they toiled on the ranch under the hot Nevada sun. Bill was a curious lad. He questioned Wovoka closely about the Paiute way and Wovoka shared many stories with him.

One was about the last big battle between Paiutes and whites that took place in April 1860, near Pyramid Lake. The trouble started when a group of white miners kidnapped and raped a couple of Indian women. With help from friends, their husbands rescued the women without exacting revenge. The miners, however, whipped their compatriots into a frenzy over this act of Indian defiance and a large number of them marched toward Pyramid Lake to teach the "savages" a lesson. But the Paiutes were forewarned. They ambushed the miners and defeated them, armed almost entirely with bows and arrows. Nearly fifty of the miners were killed.

Although the Paiutes had won the battle, Wovoka realized that they had not won the war. On a personal level, he knew that no matter how "white" he became in terms of manners and customs, he would always be a red man. Bill Wilson, though, was naive and had a hard time accepting the bigotry around him. He believed in brotherhood as Jesus taught it. To prove their oneness, he suggested they become blood brothers. So with a penknife, they drew blood from their wrists and rubbed them together in a solemn ceremony of kinship by the river. Though surrounded by events tantamount to Indian genocide, these two young men shared a rare moment of hope. It was something Wovoka would always remember. And it would have its rewards.

Wovoka was eventually invited to dine at the Wilson's table at mealtimes while the other Paiute ranch hands ate at a crude trough out back. It was during dinner that his adoptive family concluded that since he was learning how to be a white man, he should also have a white man's name. So they gave him the name Jack Wilson.

The Wilsons were a devoutly Christian clan. Every night after dinner, David Wilson would take the leather-bound Bible down from a shelf and read to his family. It was at these nightly readings that Wovoka, or "Jack" as he was called, learned about Jesus Christ. He learned of the many miracles, of Jesus' love, how he was nailed to the cross by his hands and feet, and how he died, went to heaven for three days, and returned to earth. Perhaps most importantly, he learned that Jesus was sent to earth by God to save all mankind. And that his way is what we all must aspire to.

But while "Jack" lived as a white man during the day and was provided with a small cabin, at night "Wovoka" often slept on the ground in a *wikiup* on the banks of the Walker River. He had always been spiritually introspective, having been schooled in the mysteries by his father, Tavibo. Now with one foot in the white world and the other in the Indian, what he learned about Jesus filled him with wonder. What would it be like to be Jesus? To perform miracles? To preach a message of peace and enlightenment? To save his troubled people? Surely this would be a holy path.

Inevitably, Wovoka and Bill Wilson's bond of blood began to thin as they reached their late teens. It was, after all, one thing for Bill to tell his family he thought of "Jack" as his brother. But it was something altogether different to try to explain it to girls. To most whites, an Indian was an Indian, no matter how much he tried to dress and act otherwise. Wovoka had, for a time, believed Bill's declarations of equality. But ultimately he had to face up to the fact that he would always be different in the eyes of most whites.

Around the age of seventeen, Wovoka broke off his relationship with the Wilsons. This was a period of soul-searching for the young man, who had grown into an imposing figure with a height of six feet and broad, heavy features. At times he felt consumed by an overpowering hatred of the white race. His people's loss of traditional hunting grounds had led to hunger and disorientation. Relocation of much of the tribe onto the Walker River and Pyramid Lake reservations left them demoralized. Once dignified braves were reduced to drunks, selling their women to the whites as whores. And then there were the white man's diseases. When he was a boy, two years of epidemics had wiped out about one-tenth of the Paiute population. Wovoka's heart ached for the sad state of his fellow natives.

Bailey tells us that Wovoka, unable to bear the situation any longer, took to the road and traveled through Nevada and neighboring California. In the summer, he hired on as a farm laborer and joined other Paiutes in picking hops in the fields of California, Oregon, and Washington State. In what little free time they had, the Indian farm workers would lose themselves in gambling, horse racing, drinking, and whoring. But such vices held no interest for the young philosopher.

Instead, he sought to learn from the Native Americans whom he met along the way. Wovoka felt an urgent need to understand their concerns and found out that they were not so different from his own. Language obstacles were overcome by a comaraderie of shared oppression and the healthy Paiute's disarming good nature.

During one of these visits, Wovoka came in contact with the followers of John Slocum. Slocum, a Squaxon Indian from Washington State whose native name was Squ-sacht-un, claimed to have walked and talked with God in heaven. Borrowing rituals from the Catholic faith, adding a dash of Presbyterian austerity, and mixing in traditional Native American practices of the Plateau, Slocum's Shaker Religion appeared around 1880 and came to have a great effect in southwest Washington and northwest Oregon.

Although there is no evidence that Wovoka ever took part in any of this strange new religion's public worship services, apparently he did study it closely and saw the regenerating effect it had on participants. Slocum believed in God and Jesus Christ as the savior of mankind. But he also felt that the Bible and its prophecies were too old and irrelevant to be of value to Indians. In Shaker ceremonies, the faithful crossed themselves like Catholics and, once imbued with "spirit," literally shook and twitched and fell into trances induced through swaying candles, chanting, and the monotonous ringing of a bell. Those that succumbed would often awaken days later. Wovoka was fascinated by the new religion's appeal.

When he had gotten his fill of traveling, Wovoka returned to Mason Valley where he, at about the age of twenty, married a young Paiute woman. He gave his bride the name Mary, though it is unclear whether it was in homage to David Wilson's wife, Mary, or to Jesus' mother. Eventually, the couple would have three daughters and a son who died at an early age.

David Wilson gladly hired him again to work on the ranch and it did not take Wovoka long to reestablish his reputation as a reliable worker among the white community of Mason Valley. Soon, he became a procurer of laborers for area ranchers. Wovoka encouraged the Paiutes to dress like the whites and adopt their ways. Many accepted his advice and most showed him great respect. After all, he was the son of Tavibo the medicine man. They had long expected great things of him.

Not long after he returned to Mason Valley, his fellow tribesmen began to bring their sick to his *wikiup* and ask him to heal them. But Wovoka was adamant about not wanting to be a medicine man. If he failed in his role as healer, if a few patients died under his care, he might just as quickly find his own life in jeopardy. So he turned the sick away.

But while physical illness was one thing, sickness of the spirit was another. Wovoka had made a decision to minister to his people. But what he had in mind was something far greater than a mere medicine man. He wanted to be like Jesus. A doer of miracles. A seer into the future. A communicant with God. For what Wovoka sought was nothing less than the regeneration of his people's broken spirit.

But how to start? How does one become a prophet? Tavibo had prepared him in a minor way to be a miracle worker by teaching him hand tricks with disappearing coins and others with feathers and hats. But these tools were of little use in light of the enormity of the task at hand. Then why not a bigger miracle? Even Jesus, he reasoned, performed wondrous acts to get the people's attention in order to teach them the path.

To lay his claim, Wovoka began with a small act of *doo-mur-eye,* or wizardry, in midsummer. He let it be known among the Paiutes that he had had a vision of the future. At noon on a certain upcoming day in July, he declared, ice would float down the Walker River despite the searing temperatures of the season.

Wovoka's prophecy spread quickly among the Paiutes. Both skeptics and those inclined to believe Tavibo's son eagerly awaited the magical day; each for their own reasons. At the appointed hour, a crowd assembled on a bridge that spanned the waterway. The prophet rode up in a horse-drawn wagon, climbed down, and ceremoniously took his place upon the bridge. All eyes were upon him as he began to chant. Only the sound of the wind, the rushing river, and Wovoka's voice broke the silence.

Time passed with no sight of the ice. Disbelievers began to heckle him. "You see," they cried. "We told you, Quoitze Owe is a fraud."

Wovoka scanned the river nervously while he kept up the chant. The hot summer sun was relentless and the crowd became fidgety. Catcalls and laughter punctuated the air. Wovoka had gambled heavily upon the "miracle" and his reputation hung in the balance. Then just as some in the crowd began to drift away, a glimmer of sparkling sunlight was reflected from the river. There it was! Chunks of ice for all to see, just as he had predicted! The skeptics fell silent as an awe-inspired murmur rippled through the crowd. Wovoka was indeed capable of strong medicine.

What no one knew at the time, however, was that Wovoka had help with his "miracle." It came from none other than his old friend Bill Wilson. In a log shed on their ranch, the Wilsons stored winter ice from the lake, packed in sawdust, for use throughout the year. To assist their old buddy in his chosen profession, Bill and his brothers dumped a wagonload of the ice into the Walker River. This is how Wovoka's first act of prophecy came to be.

Although his motivations were good, this simple act of dishonesty was the first step down a slippery slope of ever-greater deceit. Like a landslide that begins with a pebble, Wovoka's deceptions would grow until there could be no other end than catastrophe.

Naturally, those Paiutes who saw through Wovoka's miracle

tried to tell the less-sophisticated members of their tribe that they had been tricked. So, in order to dispell the doubt, Wovoka brought forth another ice miracle. This time he announced that he would call ice down from the sky and everyone should gather at a certain spot near the Walker River to witness the blessed event. When the day arrived, Wovoka laid a blanket underneath an old cottonwood tree, sat down, and once again began to chant. After several hours, it happened again. A twenty-five-pound chunk of ice crashed to the ground next to him and splintered into pieces! A washtub was brought forth and the ice set inside. As it melted into water, it was religiously drunk.

Edward Dyer, a Yerington, Nevada storekeeper who would come to act as a letter writer and interpreter for the prophet, later explained what had really happened. During the night before the second miracle was scheduled to occur, Wovoka had hoisted the ice chunk up into the dense foliage of the cottonwood, knowing that the summer sun would eventually cause it to slip from its perch. Dyer maintained that Wovoka was ashamed of such manipulations but believed them to be means to a greater end—to raise the Paiutes out of their spiritual cellar. Yet Wovoka clearly enjoyed the attention such deceptions brought to him.

The wizardry worked for a while. His reputation as a seer with a direct line to "the Old Man," as he sometimes referred to God, was secure. His strong work ethic served as a model to other Natives, as well, and generated white respect throughout the valley. But still it was not enough.

When he was about twenty-seven years old, Wovoka resurrected Wodziwob's Ghost Dance. In a cleared spot near the river, he taught its compelling steps. Scarcely lifting his left foot from the ground, Wovoka would advance it a step, with the right foot following into its spot, in unison with a song he sang. His followers learned quickly. The dancers formed a ring and slowly it revolved.

For two years, he led periodic dances of relatively short duration. Majestic in bearing, he conveyed a sense of serene pride and self-worth. Yet despite Wovoka's efforts, the dismal situation of the Paiutes did not change in any fundamental way. Indians still sought whiskey and prostituted their wives. They were still treated as peons by the white landlords. His people were lost, wandering aimlessly through a spiritual hell in a land that once was theirs, but where now all the rules had been changed. And Wovoka felt their pain deeply.

In the winter of 1888, Wovoka accepted another job from David Wilson, chopping wood in the mountains at Pine Grove. Jack, as the Wilsons called him, had long been known to be good with an ax. One of his nicknames, in fact, was "the Cutter." So Wovoka loaded his wife and kids into a wagon and headed into the mountains.

Not long after he started work, he became ill with a high fever. Mary took him home to watch over him and laid him on a pallet inside their *wikiup.* As he failed to improve, she worried that her husband was slipping away for good. A neighboring white rancher visited frequently and "ministered" to him. Then, on January 1, 1889, while Wovoka was unconscious, one of the most awe-inspiring occurrences of the natural world took place. There was a total eclipse of the sun.

The Paiutes in Mason Valley, in the Walker River and Pyramid Lake reservations, like many Indians throughout the West, were terrified by the sudden "death of the sun." In their religion, the sun is a powerful living being. The darkness was thought to have been caused by a supernatural monster which was devouring the sun. Throughout the Nevada Galilee, Indians banged on pots and pans, fired guns into the air, shouted and wailed, and made whatever loud noise they could to scare the monster off. So much had been stolen from them in the preceeding fifty years. Now they feared they had even been robbed of the eternal light of the sun. For almost an hour the eclipse went on before finally a crescent appeared, then grew, and slowly the munificent sun reemerged, dominant once again.

Wovoka lay in a death trance for days after the eclipse and word spread that the holy man was in another world. People gathered around the *wikiup.* Some of them insisted on testing his seemingly lifeless flesh with fire and a knife. But nothing evoked a response. Wovoka just lay silent and unmoving in a most unusual sleep. Then one day his color slowly began returning to normal. For a long time there was no other outward change. Finally, his eyes fluttered open and he spoke in a quiet voice: "I have been to heaven and talked with God." Not long afterward, Wovoka elaborated on his trip to his sober followers.

Prophecy of a New Indian Age

When I was in the other world with the Old Man, I saw all the people who have died. But they were not sad. They were happy while engaged in their old-time occupations and dancing, gambling, and playing ball. It was a pleasant land, level, without rocks or mountains, green all the time, and rich with an abundance of game and fish. Everyone was forever young.

After showing me all of heaven, God told me to go back to earth and tell his people you must be good and love one another, have no quarreling, and live in peace with the whites; that you must work, and not lie or steal; and that you must put an end to the practice of war.

If you faithfully obey your instructions from on high, you will at last be reunited with your friends in a renewed world where there would be no more death or sickness or old age. First, though, the earth must die. Indians should not be afraid, however. For it will come alive again, just like the sun died and came alive again. In the hour of tribulation, a tremendous earthquake will shake the ground. Indians must gather on high ground. A mighty flood shall follow. The water and mud will sweep the white race and all Indian skeptics away to their deaths. Then the dead Indian ancestors will return, as will the vanished buffalo and other game, and everything on earth will once again be an Indian paradise.

Wovoka later explained to ethnologist James Mooney that he had been appointed the "Old Man's deputy" to "take charge of affairs in the West, while [President] Harrison would attend to matters in the East, and He, God, would look after the world above." In order to hasten the renewal of the earth and all the fantastic events that would accompany it, God decreed that the Indians must perform the Ghost Dance at three-month intervals, for five consecutive days each time. By doing so, they would also "secure happiness."

Strange as it may sound to contemporary ears, Wovoka's revelation awoke a spiritual fervor in the weary Paiutes. Like other Native people that would be receptive to his doctrine, the Paiutes were at their nadir spiritually and were extremely receptive to the idea of celestial intervention. Quite simply, it was the last, best hope of regaining their pride and independence.

The vision itself was a bridge linking two worlds, a brilliant combination of Christian and Native American theology. Had it been offered at another time or place, it might never have hit the chord it did. But the moment proved auspicious. Wovoka's entire life until this point had been a struggle to find a way for his people to live honorably in both cultures. Through his startling vision, it appeared that he had finally found the means.

The first Ghost Dance at the Walker Lake Reservation was held in late January 1889, about a mile above the railroad bridge near the agency. Considering the new role that the expanded dance had been given in provoking the new Indian Age, the participants undertook it earnestly and with special reverence.

Not long afterward, Wovoka sent a letter to the agent at Pyramid Lake and requested that it be forwarded to Washington. In the letter, he stated that if the government would "acknowledge him as a prophet" he would in return "cause lots of rain to fall" so that the Indians would never lose a crop to drought again. He would also keep people informed of the latest news from heaven. The agent chose to ignore him, however, and the letter was never forwarded.

Native Americans, on the other hand, took him very seriously. News that a prophet had appeared in Mason Valley spread quickly, first to the neighboring Utes, Washo, and Western Shoshone in Nevada, and Pit River Indians in northeastern California. Then, early in the spring, Native travelers from all sorts of tribes west of the Rockies began showing up at the Ghost Dances. Usually traveling in secret, the Indian seekers tried to avoid arousing interest from the agents of the Federal Bureau of Indian Affairs.

Among the first of the investigators to arrive from outside the area was a northern Arapaho from Wyoming named Nakash, or "Sage," who showed up with several Shoshone from Idaho. The Arapaho are typically a contemplative and highly spiritual people. In contrast to the more skeptical Cheyenne, for example, next to whom they have lived for generations, the Arapaho devoted themselves to questions of religious mystery and were constantly speculating about the unseen world. After closely scrutinizing the self-proclaimed prophet, Nakash and the Shoshone were, in effect, ordained as priests through the ceremony of "giving the feather." Then, clutching the sacred crow and eagle feathers like scepters, the initiates returned home and started Ghost Dances among their own peoples. From them, word of the miraculous events in Nevada began to spread eastward. And as the numbers of visitors grew, Wovoka underwent a startling transformation.

Christianity, the Shakers, and Tavibo's traditional teachings all had an important influence on the philosophy Wovoka had been melding together in his mind. Yet there was another school of thought that also had a heavy influence on him. Although it is not known precisely when or where, sometime before Wovoka reached the age of thirty, he came in contact with the ideas of the Mormon church. Whether or not missionaries from the Church of Jesus Christ of Latter-Day Saints were actively proselytizing in Mason Valley in the 1880s has not been firmly established due to the apparent reticence of Mormon officials to release pertinent records. Nevertheless, it is known that by this time the church had made impressive inroads among Native Americans in eastern Nevada. In large part, this was due to the kindness displayed toward them by Mormons, who believed Indians to be the Lamanites, descendants of the House of Israel.

Joseph Smith, the great prophet of the Mormon church, responding to questions put to him in 1842 by the editor of a newspaper in Chicago, explained the root of this belief. He claimed that on September 21, 1823, while in New York, an Angel of God appeared to him and declared he had been chosen to be an "instrument in the hands of God. . . . The preparatory work for the second coming of the Messiah was speedily to commence. . . . I was also told where there were deposited some plates on which were engraven an abridgement of the records of the ancient prophets that had existed on this continent."

Smith went on to explain that "on the morning of the 22nd of September, A.D. 1827, the Angel of the Lord delivered the records into my hands. These records were engraven on plates which had the appearance of gold. Each plate was six inches wide and eight long, and not quite so thick as common tin. They were filled with engravings in Egyptian characters." He also claimed to have been given a "curious instrument, which the ancients called 'Urim and Thummim,' which consisted of two transparent stones set in the rim of a bow fastened to a breastplate." With this instrument and with God's "gift and power," Smith translated the tablets.

The strange records told how "America in Ancient times had been inhabited by two distinct races of people. The first were called Jaredites. . . . The second race came directly from the city of Jerusalem about six hundred years before Christ. They were principally Israelites of the descendants of Joseph. The Jardeites were destroyed about the time the Israelites came from Jerusalem. . . . The principal nation of the second race fell in battle towards the close of the fourth century. The remnants are the Indians that now inhabit this country."

Smith, who would be shot to death in 1844 by a mob while incarcerated in the Carthage, Illinois jail, translated the full text of the plates, which became the Book of Mormon. The church subsequently maintained that the Indian people were suffering because they had lost their way. But if they lived by the Mormon Gospel, they might be "redeemed and become again a white and delightsome people."

Although Wovoka never learned to read or write, his wife, Mary, could. As they sat in their *wikiup* on the banks of the Walker River, she would occasionally read aloud books and other publications that interested him. Whether it was from Mary, a missionary, or some other unknown source, Wovoka seized upon a prophecy in widespread circulation throughout the Mormon church concerning the Second Coming of Christ. The prophecy originated in February 1843 when a delegation of young men from New York visited Joseph Smith at his residence in Nauvoo, Illinois. They were bothered with questions about the timing of Jesus' return and solicited Smith's views. Smith explained that many things would need to take place before Christ came again. But once, when he was praying very earnestly, God told him.

Prophecy of the Return of Christ

Joseph, my son, if thou livest until thou art eighty-five years old, thou shalt see the face of the Son of Man.

Later, Smith maintained that he was unable "to decide whether this coming referred to the millennium or to some previous appearing, or whether he should die and thus see the face of Christ."

In the decades following his revelation, however, there was a substantial group within the Mormon church that had no trouble deciding. Known as the Millennialists, they fervently believed that Jesus Christ would again walk upon the earth in the year 1890. That was the year that Smith, had he not been martyred, would have been eighty-five; his birthdate was December 23.

As more and more Native Americans journeyed to see Wovoka and hear firsthand of his meeting with God, he could see in their eyes and hear from their lips that they saw him as their savior. From that point, it was not that great a leap for him to declare himself not just the "Old Man's deputy" but the Old Man's son. After all, since he wanted to be like Jesus, why not just be Jesus? People desperately wanted to believe. Since he had fooled them before, it was not that hard to do it again.

Still, some had doubts. Josephus, a captain of the Paiute Indian police, was one of them. Josephus had heard that Wovoka claimed that while he was in heaven God had given him control over the elements through five holy songs. The first song would bring on a mist or cloud, the second a snowfall, the third a gentle shower, the fourth a hard rain or storm, and the fifth song would clear the air. The area had been experiencing a severe drought, so Josephus decided to test the new Messiah by asking him for his help.

Josephus rode his horse to Wovoka's *wikiup,* arriving late in the evening. Mary admitted him into an adjacent hut often used by visitors and provided him food and drink while he waited. After some time, Wovoka entered and the policeman examined him silently. The prophet's dark brown hair was cut off squarely at the bottom of his ears and there was a purposeful cast to his features as his keen eyes probed the policeman's face. Wovoka sat down and Josephus explained the importance of his mission. Wovoka bowed his head. All this time, he had not spoken a word. After some time, he went off to bed. Then early the next morning, he came in to where Josephus was staying and said, "You can go home and on the morning of the third day you and all the people will have plenty of water."

Impressed by Wovoka's demeanor yet still quite skeptical, Josephus galloped home. He related the prophecy to his people and to several whites, as well. Then sure enough, shortly after he arrived home, it began to rain. On the morning of the third day, Josephus got up at daylight to find the Walker River overflowing its banks.

Local whites did their best to explain that the sudden downpour had nothing to do with Jack Wilson. But Josephus and other Indians were convinced of the opposite. "Now, I am a strong believer in the unnatural powers of the New Christ," he later declared.

By the summer of 1889, rumors that a redeemer had appeared among the Indians of the West reached the southern Arapaho and Cheyenne in Oklahoma through letters written by graduates of the government's Indian schools. Similar stories had filtered to the Crows and the Bannocks of the Fort Hall Reservation in Idaho, as well as to the Cheyenne and Sioux to the east of the Rocky Mountains in Montana and the Dakotas.

The news hit the prairie tribes at the lowest point in their existence. Never before had their populations been as small and as threatened. The greatest single factor leading to their diminished state was the virtual elimination of the buffalo. At the beginning of the century, an estimated forty million roamed the plains. But after the 1868 treaty between the Sioux and the U.S. government confined the tribe to a single, great reservation, traditional hunting grounds were opened to settlers and hunters slaughtered the buffalo in astonishing numbers. Discovery of gold within the reservation's sacred Black Hills led to a further influx of whites, many of whom were murderers and thieves. In response, angry Sioux braves and their Cheyenne allies went on the warpath, resulting in the massacre of General Custer's Seventh Cavalry at the Battle of Little Big Horn. But the victory was short-lived. A new agreement in 1876 forced the Sioux to give up one-third of their previously "guaranteed" reservation, including the Black Hills. Meanwhile, the killing of the buffalo continued unabated. By the end of the 1880s, the total number of buffalo had been reduced to a devastating 1,091.

It is hard to overstate the magnitude of this calamity from the point of view of the prairie nations. Food, tents, and bedding were all the direct result of buffalo hunting. As articles of barter, the furs and pelts had made it easy for the Indians to procure whatever constituted the necessities, the comforts, and even the luxuries of life. For nearly two hundred years, the Sioux, who were the most populous of the plains tribes, were the lords of an immense territory sprawling from Minnesota to the Rocky Mountains and from Yellowstone to the Platte River. Within a generation, they were expected to abandon the freedom of the chase and the boundless plain to become farmers in a land largely unsuited for such use.

When some did begrudgingly take up the plow, the results were, to put it mildly, disappointing. In 1889, the Sioux were required to attend a special council with the U.S. government appointed Sioux Commission. As the council's work dragged on for months, the absence from the fields took its toll. The result was widespread crop failure.

Many Sioux were further disillusioned by the deal being offered to them by the commission to break up the Great Sioux Reservation into five separate, smaller reservations. Aside from a miserly amount of money, the commission was promising increased educational appropriations, prompt availability of interest on a permanent $3 million Sioux trust fund, legislation for apportioning the permanent fund and its interest among the new reservations according to population, and an appropriation to compensate the Cheyenne River and Standing Rock Indians for ponies seized by the army in 1876. The commission was also promising that the rations the Sioux had become dependent upon for their very survival would not be cut. Many Indians, however, were haunted by previously unfulfilled treaties and government obligations. The belief was widespread that the only promise the government intended to keep was the promise to take their land.

In such a pervasively apprehensive atmosphere, rumors of an Indian "Messiah" were taken seriously. In July 1889, Elaine Goodale, a teacher at Pine Ridge, South Dakota, was on an antelope hunt with a party of Ogalalas Sioux. On July 23, she wrote in her diary: "Chasing Crane, on his way home from Rosebud, is welcomed with supper and a smoke. God, he says, has appeared to the Crows! In the midst of a council he came from nowhere and announced himself as the Savior who came upon earth once and was killed by the white men. He had been grieved by the crying of parents for their dead children, and would let the sky down upon the earth and destroy the disobedient."

Similar stories continued to accumulate until the fall of 1889 when Sioux at Pine Ridge, Rosebud, and Cheyenne River met in separate councils to discuss the situation. Unable to determine the veracity of the reports, they selected delegates to travel west and find out the truth. Short Bull, Kicking Bear, and nine other representatives were chosen for the important mission.

In November, the delegation set out in secret and journeyed westward to the Wind River Reservation in Wyoming. There, five Shoshones, three Northern Cheyennes, and an Arapaho from Oklahoma joined them. Boarding a passenger train, the party traveled on to the Fort Hall Agency in Idaho, where it was further enlarged by five Bannocks and Western Shoshones.

While at Fort Hall, the Indian agent summoned several of the emissaries, including a Cheyenne named Porcupine, to inquire where they were going.

"I told him I was just traveling to meet other Indians and see other countries," reported Porcupine later to a military officer at his home agency at Tongue River in Montana. "My people were at peace with the whites, and I thought I could travel anywhere I wished. He asked me why I did not have a pass. I said because my agent would not give me one. He said he was glad to see me anyhow, and that the whites and Indians were all friends. Then he asked me where I wanted a pass to. I told him I wanted to go further and some Bannocks and Shoshones wanted to go along. He gave passes—five of them—to the chiefs of the three parties."

Via the Union Pacific Railroad, the group traveled on to Salt Lake City, Utah, then continued their journey by rail over the Rockies into Nevada. Throughout their adventures in Mormon country, Porcupine was taken aback by the kind manner in which he and the others were treated.

"They treated me well on the cars, without pay. They gave me food without charge, and I found that this was a habit among them toward their neighbors. I thought it strange that the people there should have been so good, so different from those here," he recounted later to the officer.

When the delegation finally arrived at the Ghost Dance camp

near Walker Lake, they found a great throng assembled. No less than sixteen prominent tribes were represented including, besides those already named, Gros Ventres, Snakes, and Piegans.

"There were more different languages than I ever heard before and I did not understand any of them," related Porcupine. There were also a large number of Mormons who believed Wovoka to be the fulfillment of Joseph Smith's prophecy. "The whites and Indians danced together. . . . I and my people have been living in ignorance until I went and found out the truth. All the whites and Indians are brothers, I was told there. I never knew this before."

After several days of waiting, Porcupine and his compatriots journeyed to a place on the Walker River Reservation where they were told they would finally meet the Messiah. A space had been cleared of grass and hundreds waited anxiously all day.

Again in the words of Porcupine: "Just after dark some of the Indians told me that the Christ was arrived. I looked around to find him, and finally saw him sitting on one side of the ring. . . . They made a big fire to throw light on him. I never looked around, but went forward, and when I saw him I bent my head. I had always thought the Great Father was a white man, but this man looked like an Indian. He sat there a long time and nobody went up to speak to him. He sat with his head bowed all the time. After awhile he rose and said he was very glad to see his children. 'I have sent for you and am glad to see you. I am going to talk to you after awhile about your relatives who are dead and gone. My children, I want you to listen to all I have to say to you. I will teach you, too, how to dance a dance, and I want you to dance it. Get ready for your dance and then, when the dance is over, I will talk to you.' He was dressed in a white coat with stripes. The rest of his dress was a white man's except that he had on a pair of moccasins. Then he commenced our dance, everybody joining in, the Christ singing while we danced. We danced till late in the night, when he told us we had danced enough."

Later, Wovoka went into a trance and upon awakening addressed those assembled. "I am the man who made everything you see around you," he proclaimed with a straight face. "I am not lying to you, my children. I made this earth and everything on it. I have been to heaven and seen your dead friends and have seen my own father and mother. In the beginning, after God made the earth, they sent me back to teach the people, and when I came back on earth the people were afraid of me and treated me badly. This is what they did to me."

Wovoka folded back the cuffs of his sleeves and removed his moccasins to reveal scars that appeared to have been caused by nails in the same places where nails had penetrated Jesus' hands and feet when he had been hung on the cross.

"I did not try to defend myself," Wovoka said. "I found my children were bad, so I went back to heaven and left them. I told them that in so many hundred years I would come back to see my children. At the end of this time I was sent back to try to teach them. My father told me the earth was getting old and worn out and the people getting bad, and that I was to renew everything as it used to be and make it better."

According to the Sioux delegates, Wovoka conjured up a vision in which they saw an ocean, and beyond it a land where all the nations of Indians could be seen coming home. But as they looked, the vision faded away. Wovoka said that the time had not yet arrived.

Porcupine's version was slightly different. Wovoka, he claimed, "told us that all our dead were to be resurrected; that they were all to come back to earth, and that, as the earth was too small for them and us, he would do away with heaven and make the earth itself large enough to contain us all; that we must tell all the people we met about these things. He spoke to us about fighting, and said that was bad and we must keep from it; that the earth was to be all good hereafter, and we must all be friends with one another. He said that in the fall of the year the youth of all good people would be renewed, so that nobody would be more than forty years old, and that if they behaved themselves well after this the youth of everyone would be renewed in the spring. He said if we were all good he would send people among us who could heal all our wounds and sickness by mere touch and that we would live forever. He told us not to quarrel or fight or strike each other, or shoot one another; that the whites and Indians were to be all one people. He said if any man disobeyed what he ordered his tribe would be wiped from the face of the earth; that we must believe everything he said, and we must not doubt him or say he lied; that if we did, he would know it; that he would know our thoughts and actions no matter what part of the world we might be."

Did Wovoka really believe that he was Jesus? Judging by his cynical scarring of his hands and feet as well as subsequent deceptions, the answer is no. Yet his thinking was muddled. On the one hand, he was preaching a very shrewd message by telling those assembled that whomever followed his teachings were brothers be they Indian or white; and that those who did not believe would be wiped off the face of the earth. Don't fight with the rest of the white people, he exhorted, let God punish them. If that had been the extent of his message, we could simply declare him a faith healer who lied without shame and manipulated people for his own aggrandizement while giving them hope for a better world to come.

But Wovoka's message did not end there. Instead, he predicted specific things would happen at specific times—not in the distant future—but within the next eighteen months! In the fall of 1890, he declared, the youth of good people would be renewed so that no one would be older than forty. And by the spring of 1891, a mighty flood would sweep white and Indian skeptics alike away to their deaths. Herein lies the riddle. Why would someone interested in preserving and enhancing his power set such dates? Did all the attention cause him to go temporarily insane? Or did he slip by suggesting approximate dates for the fulfillment of his prophecies and then find himself painted into a corner? Whatever the reasons, it is clear that once the ball got rolling, he did nothing to slow it down. Instead, time and time again he sought to solidify his position.

Take, for example, how Wovoka dealt with the continuing problem of skeptics. He could lecture reverent supplicants who approached with averted eyes about his conversations with the Old Man, ad infinitum. He could mesmerize with his prophecies of the future, hypnotize with a feather, and cause some to recount glorious visits to the other world. But even after summoning all of his charisma and talent, there were those who simply did not believe that the Indian standing before them was the Son of God.

To solve the problem Wovoka turned once again to an act of

doo-mur-eye. For this ultimate test, though, he knew no ice, no trance, no simple act of magic would do. He needed nothing less than to prove his dominion over death. After quiet reflection, he settled on a plan that borrowed an idea once again from the Mormons. Unfortunately, this plan would eventually have dire ramifications.

As mentioned previously, the Church of Jesus Christ of Latter-Day Saints had made enormous strides in converting large numbers of Paiutes in eastern Nevada to Mormonism. Many had gone on to become elders initiated into the deeper mysteries of the faith. One of the privileges of achieving that rank is wearing a holy undergarment, or Endowment Robe, emblazoned with sacred symbols that are reputed to protect the wearer from Satan and physical harm.

When and where Wovoka learned about the Endowment Robe is unknown. Likely, it was from one of the white or red-skinned Mormon Millennialists who danced at Walker Lake and saw Wovoka as the fulfillment of Joseph Smith's prophecy. That there were a lot of them cannot be doubted. A curious pamphlet published anonymously in Salt Lake City in 1892 asserts that the Messiah had indeed appeared at Walker Lake in March 1890. Titled *The Mormons Have Stepped Down and Out of Celestial Government—The American Indians Have Stepped Up and Into Celestial Government,* the pamphlet declared that in that month, "Twelve disciples were ordained, not by angels or men, but by the Messiah, in the presence of hundreds, representing scores of tribes or nations, who saw his face, [and] heard and understood his voice."

Whenever Wovoka learned of the magic underwear, it is clear that he had it in mind when he created what would come to be known as the Ghost Shirt.

He first wore one in front of an assembly at night that included the emissaries from the Sioux and Cheyenne. It must have been an awe-inspiring sight to see the man who claimed to be Jesus, illuminated by fire, walk solemnly to a blanket wearing nothing but a long, white shirt painted in red ocher with symbols of the eagle, sun, and moon. But when Wovoka's brother, standing only ten paces away, raised a shotgun and pointed it at his chest, many gasped in terror. The trigger was pulled—the shotgun exploded! Wovoka bent over as if struck by the blast, and buckshot spilled onto the blanket. But there was no blood. Screams and then a murmur of excitement swept through the crowd as the prophet stood upright for all to see that he was unharmed.

As a demonstration of his dominion over death, it was grand theater. The shirt was undamaged. The shotgun, of course, had been rigged and the buckshot dropped from his hand at the precise moment. About a year later, when questioned about the incident by army scout A. I. Chapman, Wovoka would reply nervously, "That was a joke." Nothing more than *doo-mur-eye.* But for those who saw it, it was convincing nonetheless.

Wovoka did not anticipate that the shirt would soon gain a reputation as a powerful protective shield. He also obviously did not have a handle on the impact his actions were having on his brethren. For the Ghost Dance movement, spreading rapidly across the West, showed signs of desperate and growing hysteria.

In March of 1890, Porcupine and his Cheyenne companions returned to the Tongue River Agency in Montana. A council was called and Porcupine spoke for five days in succession about the divine message and the wonders the delegation had witnessed.

Notions of meeting dead relatives and the return of the Son of God to help the Indians had been current among the tribe for five or six years. It began when a Cheyenne boy went out to wail, as was the custom, over a deceased relative. The boy was said to have fallen into a trance in which he dreamed he had wandered into a camp where everyone was happily enjoying plenty of buffalo meat, which was drying on racks and cooking over the fire. Later in the dream, the boy saw a "luminous figure" who declared himself to be the Son of God, who had been crucified by the whites. Before the boy woke up, the figure opened his robe to show his wounds.

Porcupine's confirmation of the boy's vision deeply moved the Cheyenne. Shortly afterward, the Ghost Dance was initiated among the tribe.

The report the Sioux emissaries gave to their people in April 1890 differed from Porcupine's in at least one respect. All agreed that there was a man who lived near the base of the Sierras who claimed to be the Son of God who had once been killed by the whites, and who bore scars of crucifixion. But the Sioux desperately wanted revenge for the white's mistreatment of them. So their interpretation dwelled on Wovoka's prediction that God would wipe the whites off the face of the earth, resurrect the Indian dead, bring back the buffalo and other game, and restore the Indian to his rightful place of supremacy.

Wondrous miracles were also reported. It was claimed that Wovoka—whom they referred to as the Wanekia—could make animals talk and that he came down from heaven in a cloud. He had advised the delegates that on their journey home, if they killed a buffalo they should cut off its head, tail, and feet and leave them on the ground. The buffalo would then come back to life. During their return trip, they actually encountered some of the by-then-rare creatures and acted as instructed. Miraculously, the buffalo came to life and had wandered off as prophesied. Prior to their departure, the Messiah had also told them that if they became tired, they should call on him and he would shorten their journey. When they did, they woke up the next morning and found themselves "a great distance from where we stopped."

Before they had a chance to discuss these matters in council, Colonel Gallagher, the agent at Pine Ridge, had three of the delegates arrested. They were jailed for two days but refused to answer questions. Gallagher thought he had smothered the growing "nonsense." But soon afterward Kicking Bear returned from a visit to the northern Arapaho in Wyoming with the news that they were already dancing, and could see and talk with their dead relatives while in the trance.

The Messiah Craze, as the whites would come to refer to it, could no longer be contained. Red Cloud, the great chief of the Ogalala Sioux, declared himself a believer and told his people to do as the Wanekia had commanded. Another council was called on White Clay Creek, a few miles from the Pine Ridge Agency, and with the recent delegates acting as priests, the Ghost Dance was inaugurated among the Sioux.

Defiance of the agent at Pine Ridge was fueled in part by events that had taken place during the time the delegation was gone. By a clever strategy of divide and conquer, the Sioux Commission had manipulated a majority into agreeing to the government's demands. As stated in the report of the Sioux Commission dated December 24, 1889, the Indians were assured "that signing would not affect their rations, and that they would continue to receive them as provided in former treaties. Without our assurances to this effect it would have been impossible to have secured their consent to the cession of their lands."

Yet only two weeks after the Sioux Commission had departed for Washington, beef rations at Rosebud were reduced by two million pounds, at Pine Ridge by one million, and at the other agencies by proportional amounts. That this was due to an economy move dictated by Congress rather than the commission was a distinction lost on the Sioux.

Perhaps the cruelest blow of all, however, came on February 10, 1890, when President Benjamin Harrison threw open the ceded Sioux territories to settlement. Contrary to promises made by the commission, no surveys had been made of the precise boundaries of the new reservations, nor had any provision been made for Indians living on the lands ceded to "homestead." The president recommended that legislation to deal with these matters be enacted quickly.

Although the Senate passed a bill rectifying the situation on April 26, the House of Representatives took no immediate action. The house also delayed passage of the regular Indian Appropriation Act for so long that clothing and other supplies did not reach the Sioux until late that winter. The cold and hunger they were forced to endure only aggravated epidemics of measles, influenza, and whooping cough. At Pine Ridge alone, where the total population was estimated at 5,550, the death rate rose to 45 a month. Life had become a living hell.

Once again, the Sioux were tricked by the diabolical white man. So they turned with heartfelt hope to the promise offered by Wovoka's Ghost Dance. They danced with all their strength to "shake the dead" and hasten the new world.

One of those dancers was a thirty-year-old named Black Elk. At the tender age of thirteen, he had fought alongside Crazy Horse at the Battle of Little Big Horn. More recently, he had been traveling with Buffalo Bill's Wild West Show in Europe. According to David Humphreys Miller, who interviewed Black Elk years later while doing research for his book, *Ghost Dance,* the young warrior had a vision of the Ghost Shirts while dancing. After the dance, Black

Elk described his vision to Kicking Bear, who recalled that during his visit to Nevada, he had seen Wovoka wearing the same type of garment. Kicking Bear then related the dramatic tale of Wovoka being shot with the shotgun. That was all the confirmation Black Elk needed.

"All the next day," writes Miller, "Black Elk set himself to the task of making 'ghost shirts' like those he had seen in his vision. There was no doubt in his mind after listening to Kicking Bear that the garments would be bulletproof. Of their power to guard the wearer against any danger he was certain."

On June 20, 1890, Mrs. Z. A. Parker, a teacher at Pine Ridge, observed a dance of between three hundred and four hundred Sioux at White Clay Creek. She wrote down her observations in an article that was subsequently printed in several publications. The dance she witnessed was the first in which Ghost Shirts and Dresses were worn by the Sioux, as the white cotton garments "were all new." They were covered with "figures of birds, bows and arrows, sun, moon, and stars, and everything they saw in nature . . . a number had stuffed birds, squirrel heads, etc., tied in their long hair. The faces of all were painted red with a black half-moon on the forehead or on one cheek."

She describes the dance as follows: "One stood directly behind another, each with his hands on his neighbor's shoulders. After walking about a few times, chanting, 'Father, I come,' they stopped marching, but remained in the circle, and set up the most fearful, heart-piercing wails I ever heard—crying, moaning, groaning, and shrieking out their grief, and naming over their departed friends and relatives, at the same time taking up handfuls of dust at their feet, washing their hands in it, and throwing it over their heads. Finally, they raised their eyes to heaven, their hands clasped high above their heads, and stood straight and perfectly still, invoking the power of the Great Spirit to allow them to see and talk with their people who had died. . . .

"And now the most intense excitement began. They would go as fast as they could, their hands moving from side to side, their bodies swaying, their arms, with hands gripped tightly in their neighbors', swinging back and forth with all their might. The ground had been worked and worn by many feet, until the fine, flour-like dust lay light and loose and to the depth of two or three inches. The wind, which had increased, would sometimes take it up, enveloping the dancers and hiding them from view. In the ring were men, women, and children; the strong and the robust, the weak, consumptive, and those near to death's door. They believed those who were sick would be cured by joining in the dancing and losing consciousness. From the beginning they chanted, to a monotonous tune, the words—'Father, I come; Mother, I come; Brother, I come; Father, give us back our arrows.'

"All of which they would repeat over and over again until first one and then another would break from the ring and stagger away and fall down. . . . No one ever disturbed those who fell or took any notice of them except to keep the crowd away.

"They kept up dancing until fully 100 persons were lying unconscious. Then they stopped and seated themselves in a circle, and as each one recovered from his trance he was brought to the center of the ring to relate his experience."

To the Sioux, Arapaho, and other prairie tribes, it was known as the Spirit or Ghost Dance. But others in the thirty to thirty-five tribes that would come to practice it referred to it by other names. To the Paiute, it was Dance in a circle. The Shoshone called it Everybody Dragging, the Comanche, The Father's Dance; and the Caddo, The Prayer of All to the Father. Among the Kiowa, it was the Dance with Clasped Hands, and the fervor that it ended in, "Dance craziness."

As important as the steps themselves were the songs that accompanied the dances. These were constantly evolving, as nearly every trance produced a new song that reflected someone's experience in the spirit world. The new songs then supplanted the old ones. Only a few especially powerful songs lived on in the repertoire. The deeply spiritual Arapaho in particular crafted beautiful, moving songs that reflected the painful dilemma they found themselves in. Their songs were also often sung by the Sioux. As they would shuffle in a circle, beseeching God to intervene on their behalf, they would sing mournfully:

> Father, have pity on me,
> Father, have pity on me;

I am crying for thirst,
I am crying for thirst;
All is gone—I have nothing to eat,
All is gone—I have nothing to eat.

In late May 1890, Charles L. Hyde, a citizen in the frontier town of Pierre, South Dakota wrote a letter to the War Department. Hyde's letter warned of information he had gleaned from a half-blood schoolboy who was in communication with Sioux relatives about secret planning for breakout from the reservation. The letter was forwarded to the commissioner of Indian affairs, who requested that Sioux reservation agents investigate. Unanimously, they replied that there were no grounds for apprehension. True, there was some excitement about a self-proclaimed Messiah's prophecy of a new world. But it would all fizzle out when his predictions failed to materialize.

At about the same time, the department learned of the pilgrimage the previous winter by the delegation from the prairie tribes. Major Henry Carroll, commanding officer at Camp Crook, Tongue River, Montana was dispatched with a detachment of men who took Porcupine into custody. Carroll forced a statement out of him that was transmitted to Washington.

The upper plains, meanwhile, were in the grip of drought, and Sioux attempts at farming again ended in disaster. The dances, which at first were staged only periodically, soon became the sole focus for thousands. Many abandoned their cabins to dance around the clock. Exhausted to the point of delirium, dancers experienced fantastic visions of the other world which were reported to the medicine men and shouted to the crowds.

Agent Gallagher at Pine Ridge soon changed his earlier assessment and became alarmed. All the "civilizing" work that had been done to help the "primitives" was in jeopardy. After first sending out the Indian police with orders to put a halt to the dancing, and learning that they had been ignored, he took matters into his own hands. On August 22, he led twenty police to the dance grounds at White Clay Creek. Alerted before his arrival, the dancers had taken cover in a nearby grove of trees. As Gallagher reported later to the commissioner of Indian affairs, "several of the bucks, however, were standing around in the neighborhood of where the dance had been held. These men were stripped for fight, having removed their leggins and such other superfluous apparel as is usually worn by them and stood with Winchesters in their hands and a good storing of cartridges belted around their waists prepared to do or die in defense of the new faith." Although Gallagher managed to avoid bloodshed, he was unable to put an end to the dancing, which resumed in front of him and his men.

A similar confrontation took place on the Rosebud Reservation, where after several warnings, Short Bull defiantly continued the dance among the Brules. As one of the original emissaries, he had become swept up in the power of the movement. On October 31, he delivered an ominous sermon about the coming new world.

Short Bull's Prophecy

I have told you that this would come to pass in two seasons. But since the whites are interfering so much, I will advance the time from what my Father above told me. . . . We must dance the balance of this moon, at the end of which time the earth will shiver very hard. Whenever this thing occurs, I will start the wind to blow. We are the ones who will then see our fathers, mothers, and everybody. We, the tribe of Indians, are the ones who are living a sacred life. . . . If the soldiers surround you four deep, three of you, on whom I have put holy shirts, will sing a song, which I have taught you, around them, when some of them will drop dead. Then the rest will start to run, but their horses will sink into the earth. The riders will jump from their horses, but they will sink into the earth also. Then you can do as you desire with them. Now, you must know this, that all the soldiers and that race will be dead. There will be only five thousand of them left living on the earth.

Two weeks prior to that speech, Kicking Bear, who was one of the most incendiary of Wovoka's apostles and a member of the previous winter's pilgrimage, arrived at the Standing Rock Reservation at the invitation of the great Sioux medicine man, Sitting Bull. Sitting Bull was fifty-five years old at the time. He had become famous through his participation at the Battle of Little Big Horn and exile in Canada. Upon returning to U.S. territory, he was restricted in his movements by the authorities and had been unable to study the new religion. But once Kicking Bear revealed the Wanekia's doctrine to him, Sitting Bull supervised and encouraged the Ghost Dance among the Hunkpapas.

At the Cheyenne River Agency, Perain P. Palmer, a new Republican appointee without experience in Indian affairs, attempted to break up dances being held at the Miniconjou camps of Big Foot and Hump. Palmer told them that the Department of the Interior was very displeased with their behavior. The Miniconjou replied that they were displeased by the department and would dance.

Due in part to the insufficient rations of beef and growing dissatisfaction at Pine Ridge, Gallagher resigned in October as agent. Then in one of the most unfortunate appointments in history, he was succeeded by Daniel F. Royer, a physician, banker, and two-term Republican member of the territorial legislature from Alpena, South Dakota. Incapable of effectively dealing with the crisis he found himself in, within a week Royer had allowed half a dozen braves to release a prisoner named Little from the agency jail. From then on, it only got worse. The Sioux derisively named the new agent "Young-man-afraid-of-Indians." By October 12, Royer reported to his superiors that the Indians were totally beyond the control of the police and asked for the help of the military. On November 15, he telegraphed: "Indians are dancing in the snow and are wild and crazy. . . . We need protection and we need it now!"

The next day, Standing Rock's Agent McLaughlin, who was thoroughly contemptuous of Sitting Bull after seven years of struggling with him for dominance, visited the chief's camp at Grand River. He found several hundred Sioux engaged in a wild Ghost Dance in which Sitting Bull was interpreting a young girl's visit to her dead relatives in the other world. Wisely, McLaughlin decided not to interrupt and spent the night in the nearby cabin of a policeman. The next day, however, he confronted the old chief as he emerged from a sweat bath and attempted to reason with him about the absurdity of the Ghost Dance. Sitting Bull, however, who to many was the living symbol of the old Indian freedom, remained defiant. He suggested that he and the agent both travel to Walker Lake and decide what was true and what was not after meeting the Messiah themselves. McLaughlin refused.

News reports of the Ghost Dance, meanwhile, were being spread throughout the nation by a horde of both accredited and volunteer correspondents. At one point there were no fewer than twenty-five of these so-called journalists at Pine Ridge alone. The volunteers, known as "space writers," were paid by the amount of words, and their sensational approach to the "impending hostilities" foreshadowed the yellow journalism that would at the end of the decade help push the nation into the Spanish-American War. The staff correspondents, unfortunately, were often no more accurate nor enlightening. Not one was enterprising enough to travel to Nevada and investigate the religion at its source.

Most whites were simply unwilling to recognize that there might be a difference between a war dance and a religious dance. And they did not care that the Native Americans might have legitimate grievances. As a result, mass hysteria swept across the land.

Throughout November and December, the *Nebraska State Journal* ran stories with such headlines as "Dark Is the Outlook," "Spies Bring in Startling Reports," and "Bound to Be Trouble." The *Omaha World Herald* and *Chicago Inter-Ocean* demanded immediate military action to justify their predictions of imminent warfare. In the East, citizens woke up to read news dispatches with such terrifying headlines as "Indians Are Dancing," "Indians Buy Guns and Ammunition," "Redskins Prepare for War."

Even the venerable *New York Times* was caught up in the hype. A dispatch dated November 29, 1889, and headlined "Rosebuds Ready to Fight," declared "Their war dance began yesterday morning. . . . The Indians danced in a circle. They were stripped to their breech clothes and were painted for war. . . . Couriers report that the Rosebuds kept up the dance all night. At times it assumed the character of the so-called ghost dance, with the Indians in their fringed cotton shirts and dress; then it became the famous war dance of the Sioux, with the bucks almost naked and painted from their breasts to the tops of their heads."

Living as he was in the rural isolation of west-central Nevada, it is impossible to evaluate how much Wovoka knew about what was happening among the Sioux. If Mary or someone else had gotten a hold of a newspaper with a story on the situation, it probably would have been several weeks old. And even if he was aware, what could he do? One hundred years ago, communications were a far cry from what they are today. He would have been essentially helpless to stop the spiraling chain of events that would soon lead to disaster.

At the same time, the Mormon church was in turmoil. This was due not only to Joseph Smith's famous prophecy regarding the Second Coming, but also to the pressure being exerted on the Mormon hierarchy by the federal government to renounce polygamy as a precondition to Utah's statehood. On October 6, 1890, the church issued an official declaration known as the Woodruff Manifesto that renounced the practice of polygamy. An unintended result was that a lot of conservative Mormons criticized the church for abandoning its traditional teachings. They joined the Millennialist camp not only because many Indians kept more than one wife, but also because it was a long-standing tenet of the faith that establishment of the city of Zion would be accomplished by the redeemed Indian people.

Indeed, the belief that Christ had appeared on earth as an Indian was so widespread that Mormon president Wilford Woodruff, George Q. Cannon, and other prominent Mormon leaders took to the pulpit during the October 1890 church conference in Salt Lake City to repudiate it. Woodruff went so far as to claim he "had a great many visits with the Prophet Joseph Smith since his death" and that Smith had told him that Christ's return was still in the future. Great numbers of Mormons nonetheless continued to anticipate that the Millennium would begin on December 23, the anniversary of Joseph Smith's birth.

On November 13, President Harrison ordered the secretary of war to assume military responsibility to prevent an outbreak from the Sioux reservations. A week later the first troops arrived at Pine Ridge under the overall command of General Nelson A. Miles. The appearance of troops on the reservation caused the Sioux to panic, and some three thousand led by Short Bull, Kicking Bear, and others fled from Rosebud and Pine Ridge to the Badlands. The reservations, meanwhile, were placed under the control of the military.

At daybreak on Monday, December 15, 1890, forty-three Indian police and volunteers led by Lieutenant Bull Head surrounded the two log cabins at Sitting Bull's compound. The old medicine man was found asleep on the floor of the larger cabin. Informed that he was under arrest, he sent one of his wives to the other cabin for some clothes. While dressing, he verbally abused the police. In the meantime, about 150 of his followers congregated outside. When the police brought him out, Sitting Bull called upon them to rescue him. In response, Catch-the-Bear raised his rifle and shot Lieutenant Bull Head, who, although mortally wounded, immediately killed Sitting Bull. A bloody fight ensued in which six policemen and eight "hostiles," including Sitting Bull's seventeen-year-old son, lost their lives.

Soon Kicking Bear, Short Bull, and their followers who had been hiding out in the Badlands recognized the futility of their actions and made arrangements to turn themselves in. Big Foot and his band, meanwhile, were still desperately trying to reach what was thought to be the relative safety of that area when they were intercepted on December 28 by the Seventh Cavalry led by Major Whitside. Whitside demanded unconditional surrender. Big Foot, who was ill with pneumonia, agreed and the Indians camped in freezing weather, as instructed, at Wounded Knee Creek.

The next morning, the warriors were ordered to come out of their tipis and turn over their guns. The cavalry had been reinforced with more troops from the Seventh under the command of Colonel Forsyth for a total force of 470 men against Big Foot's 106 warriors. After the Indians produced only two old guns, a detachment of soldiers were sent in to search the tipis. In doing so, they overturned beds, roughed up the families of the warriors, and angered everyone.

While the soldiers were searching for weapons, Yellow Bird, a medicine man, urged the warriors to resist, telling them that the Ghost Shirts which nearly all wore would protect them against the soldier's bullets. Suddenly, he stooped down and threw a handful of dust in the air. Whether this was a gesture of contempt or a signal to attack will never be known. A moment later, though, a young Indian raised a rifle from beneath his blanket and shot at the troops. The soldiers responded with a deadly barrage. Other warriors pulled concealed revolvers, knives, and war clubs from their belts. A bloody battle ensued.

Minutes later, an estimated two hundred Indian men, women,

and children lay dead or wounded on the frozen ground. Many
were blown apart by the cavalry's four Hotchkiss guns that poured
in two-pound explosive shells at the rate of fifty per minute. Sixty
soldiers were also killed or wounded, a fact that enraged many
cavalry soldiers. Few had forgotten the last major battle between
the Seventh and the Sioux, fourteen years before, that resulted in
Custer's massacre at Little Big Horn. Barbarously, they hunted
down the survivors of the initial encounter. Bodies of women and
children were later found partially buried in snow up to two miles
away. Three days later, a long trench was dug and the frozen
corpses of some three hundred Indian men, women, and children,
stripped of their Ghost Shirts, were thrown in naked and buried
without ceremony. After a few more minor skirmishes, what has
come to be called the Last Indian War was over.

Although mortally wounded, Wovoka's dream of a new Indian
Age lingered on after the massacre at Wounded Knee. Among the
Sioux, to be sure, faith in the Wanekia was immediately crushed by
the military's bloody suppression. When one of the women shot at
Wounded Knee was told by a surgeon that her Ghost Shirt had to
be removed in order to treat her wound, she replied: "Yes, take
it off. They told me a bullet would not go through. Now I don't
want it anymore."

Among the Mormons, President Woodruff ordered his missionaries to suspend their work in those areas where the Ghost Dance
was taking place. The heartbroken Millennialists, having seen the
date of the anticipated New Age come and go, were forced to come
to grips with the fact that the Second Coming had been delayed.

Many Indian believers, however, were unwilling to give up the
hope that the Ghost Dance represented. They blamed the Sioux for
twisting the original peaceful premise of the dance into something
warlike and hateful. As the universally recognized time of spring
1891 for the fulfillment of Wovoka's prophecy came and went,
allowances were made. The date slipped to sometime in the future.

Delegations continued to stream into Nevada to see the Messiah
and hear his message of peace. In August 1891, a large delegation
of Cheyenne and Arapaho from Oklahoma arrived and took part
in a dance. When some asked Wovoka for proof of his supernatural
powers, he sat down on the ground with the doubters arranged in

front of him. Holding his hat upside down in front of them, he quickly passed some eagle feathers over it. An Arapaho named Black Coyote later stated that when he looked into Wovoka's hat, he "saw the whole world."

During their visit, Wovoka also dictated a statement which was written down in broken English by one of the Arapaho, and rewritten by a school-age daughter of one of the delegates upon his return home. The message instructed his followers to "come again in three months, some from each tribe [in the Indian Territory] . . . when your friends die you must not cry. You must not hurt anybody or do harm to anyone. You must not fight. Do right always. It will give you satisfaction in life. . . .

"Do not tell the white people about this," Wovoka went on to say. "Jesus is now upon the earth. He appears like a cloud. The dead are all alive again. I do not know when they will be here; maybe this fall or in the spring. When the time comes there will be no more sickness and everyone will be young again.

"Do not refuse to work for the whites and do not make any trouble with them until you leave them. When the earth shakes do not be afraid. It will not hurt you.

"I want you to dance every six weeks. Make a feast at the dance and have food that everybody may eat. Then bathe in the water. That is all. You will receive good words again from me some time. Do not tell lies."

In January 1892, James Mooney, an ethnologist employed by the Smithsonian Institution, visited Wovoka in Nevada. He had been sent by the government to study the phenomena of the Ghost Dance and had observed or participated in a number of them among the tribes of the Indian Territory of Oklahoma. Mooney was led to Wovoka in a horse-drawn wagon by the Paiute's uncle and Ed Dyer. They found him near Pine Grove, hunting jack rabbits with a shotgun.

Wovoka was well-dressed in white man's clothes, a broad-brimmed white felt hat, and a good pair of boots. He took Mooney's hand with a strong, hearty grasp, and his uncle explained the purpose of the stranger's visit. Wovoka said that the whites had lied about him and he did not like to talk to them. Some of the Indians had disobeyed his instructions and trouble had come of it.

But since Mooney had been sent by Washington, he would talk to him after he was done hunting.

That evening, around a blazing fire of sagebrush inside his *wikiup,* Wovoka talked to Mooney about what had gone wrong. Hurt by events, he was becoming disenchanted too. He disclaimed any responsibility for the Ghost Shirt. He denied ever claiming to be Jesus, the Son of God. He said he had never traveled from Mason Valley. Obviously, he was worried about being blamed for a movement that had gotten out of hand. And as he had lied on a grand scale before, his denials came easily. He repudiated all notions of hostility toward the whites and maintained that his religion was one of peace. He had been to heaven, he maintained, and had received a divine revelation.

After his meeting with Wovoka, Mooney traveled by train to the Indian Territory of Oklahoma where he was greeted as a saint by Wovoka's followers. Then in June of 1892, two-and-a-half years after the tragedy at Wounded Knee, he visited the Arapaho on the Wind River Reservation in Wyoming. The agent in charge there assured Mooney that his Indians had abandoned the Ghost Dance. Mooney, however, insisted on visiting the Arapaho in their camp. "We started," he writes, "and had gone but a short distance when we heard from a neighboring hill the familiar measured cadence of the ghost songs. On turning with a questioning look to my interpreter—who was himself a half-blood—he quietly said: 'Yes, they are dancing the Ghost Dance. That's something I have never reported, and I never will. It is their religion and they have a right to do it.'"

Gradually, though, the religious fervor began to wane and Wovoka encouraged it. The results of his years of accumulated deceit had finally hit home and he was ashamed of what he had done. In October of that same year, another delegation of Arapaho and Cheyenne visited him and returned home with a very discouraging report. Wovoka had told them that he was tired of so many visitors and wanted the dancing to stop. Although many devotees refused at first to accept the message as genuine, the ultimate effect was depressing.

In the years that followed, Wovoka received hundreds of letters from his faithful followers. Many sent money and asked for sacred objects, like feathers and red ocher paint, and anything he had touched or owned. In time, he overcame his feelings of remorse and established a booming business for his hats, which he sold for the then-large price of twenty dollars apiece. Among the majority of the Paiutes, though, he was still considered a holy man and was often given gifts of fish and game. Sometime before 1920, he traveled to Idaho, Wyoming, and Oklahoma where he was honored by Native Americans who presented him with presents that he treasured until his death in 1932.

The Ghost Dance continued to be practiced secretly by the Shoshone of the Wind River Reservation in Wyoming well into the 1950s, when the dances were conducted by medicine man Tudy Roberts. Its connection to Wovoka, though, had been forgotten. The religion that once burned so brightly dimmed and faded out. In the early 1980s, ethnomusicologist Judith Vander uncovered a cache of 147 Ghost Dance Songs that had been preserved by an elderly Shoshone medicine woman, Emily Hill. Hill apparently was the last remaining Shoshone, perhaps the last person in America, to believe in the dream of the Ghost Dance.

•

There is no doubt that Wovoka's initial motivations were good. He deeply felt his people's misery and for years searched for a way to lift their spirits and provide them with hope for the future. He understood that Native Americans had to adapt to the white man's world. That is underlined by the way he dressed, how hard he worked among the whites of Mason Valley, and the example he set for his people. After emerging from his delirium and telling of his talk with God, he preached a way of life that was as pure and simple and good as Buddha or Christ. "You must not fight. Do no harm to any one. Do not tell lies." By practicing the Ghost Dance and adhering to its code of ethics, his followers would "secure happiness." "Do right always," he admonished. "It will give you satisfaction in life."

But like many leaders who begin with the finest of motivations, as he became more powerful and well-known he lost his bearings. His little white lies became big, ugly black lies and he no longer practiced what he preached. As his love of personal glory took control, ever greater fabrications were required to keep the new faith from collapsing. He was carried away by the adulation of the masses and fell into the same trap that snares so many religious celebrities in our own time. Uneducated in a formal sense, he clearly sought the storm. That it turned out to be a destructive force greater than he could have ever imagined is the ultimate tragedy. How different it all might be if he had never claimed to be Jesus Christ.

Perhaps Wovoka's biggest mistake, though, was one that successful prophets always avoid. He set a date for the apocalypse. Christianity has endured nearly two thousand years based on the promise that its Messiah would return "soon." Were Wovoka to have left the date open and remained a prophet rather than the Son of God, the Ghost Dance, with its vision of a brighter tomorrow, might still very well be a vital force in the world today.

CHAPTER FIVE

WHITE SHELL WOMAN: BELOVED OF THE NAVAJO

The colors of the earth are what a visitor remembers most. Red hills, blue mountains, others with streaks of purple and white; the earth studded with pale green steppe grasses and spindly cypress. As a denizen of the city drove north into the historic heart of the Navajo nation in northeastern Arizona, alongside the Lukachukai Mountains that glowed like a red wall topped with a quilt of pine and granite, he drank in the colors.

The two-lane highway dipped but ran straight as an arrow to the horizon where it merged with the awe-inspiring shapes of lower Monument Valley. Signs of human habitation were few and far between. Several miles past the Thriftway gas station and minimart rose a lone windmill. At the next dirt road, he turned off the highway.

About a hundred and fifty yards in stood a small stucco house. Two wooden hogans laid beyond. As his car bounced along the rutted, dirt lane, a woman emerged from the house and strode toward the older hogan with a dirt roof. Without looking back, she stepped inside.

She waited for her visitor on a bench opposite the door, looking much like a stern queen on her throne. By the dim light that filtered in through the open doorway, the stranger saw that she was a full-blooded Navajo in her fifties. A bit stout, she wore a handmade dress of her own design yet crafted in a traditional Navajo style. Red with black "dark cloud" borders, the dress had silver diamond shapes on the shoulders. Around her neck hung a squash blossom necklace of silver and turquoise. On her feet were moccasins and around her legs, white buckskin leggings. Short, black hair, streaked with gray, framed her face. Most striking, however, were her probing, brown eyes and the proud way she held her head.

Her name is Annie Kahn and she is a Navajo medicine woman. Kahn, however, is her "in-law" or married name. And "medicine woman" is a Paleface designation. "We don't call ourselves medicine people," she explains. "We refer to ourselves as Earth People or Children of the Earth."

Not long after her guest's arrival, she led him out through the hogan's open doorway, which faces east. She walked toward the sacred mountains she called *Li bahni a'hi'* and *Ch'ooshgai,* known to some as the Goods of Great Value Range, to others still as the Lukachukais. Descended from a long line of earth people, her family had lived on that same piece land for uncounted generations. "Everything one wants to know is in these mountains," she said. "To test our beliefs, they remain quiet. They're so old. They've witnessed so much."

Solemnly, she walked onto a promontory point and stood overlooking a broad ravine. In her hands, she held two sacred feathers. The bite of the winter wind was tempered by the sunshine as she chanted her prayer in Navajo to *tadiddiin,* whom we know as the sun.

> In Blessingway, I walk in beauty
> I seek an understanding between the two worlds of western society
>   and the Indian
> My intentions are good
> I say this with my entire being
> Beauty before me
> Behind me
> Below me
> Above me
> All around me
> In beauty, I have spoken.

From a small, buckskin pouch, she removed pinches of holy corn pollen and sprinkled it toward the east. Then she gestured as though drawing the sun toward her four times, before turning "sunways"—east to south to west—and returning to her hogan.

•

Two major religious traditions underlie all Native North American cultures. One stems from the great Mayan agricultural civilization. The other is linked to northern Asia, and the brave hunters and gatherers that crossed the Bering land bridge. One of these tribes of people are known as the Athapascans. Living in a region stretching from northwestern Canada through central Alaska, bands of Athapascan Indians began migrating south over a period of time five hundred to eight hundred years ago. The Athapascan culture was primitive and centered around hunting and gathering food. Their brief religious rituals revolved around trying to ensure a successful outcome for the hunt. In the history of North America, these people earned a name for themselves as great colonizers. Tracing tribal languages, scholars have demonstrated that Athapascans mixed in with tribes in British Columbia; the Sahaptin of Oregon; and the Yurok of California to name only a few. Probably the greatest wave of Athapascan immigrants, however, took the long trek along the virgin foothills of the Rocky Mountains, while others meandered through the western deserts, finally settling in an area known today as the Four Corners of Arizona, New Mexico, Colorado, and Utah. The people who settled in this vast area were known as the Dineh. In the Navajo language, that means "The People."

In the Four Corners region, they came into contact with the Pueblo people already inhabiting the area. Descendants of the Anasazi, one of ancient America's most advanced civilizations, the Pueblos lived in compact, mesa-top towns in houses constructed of stone or clay. Highly adept at weaving and pottery making, with a corn-based economy, all the Pueblos then practiced an ornate religion whose annual cycle of colorful ceremonies were timed through close observation of the sun.

Whether through trade, intermarriage, benevolent teachers, or the kidnapping of instructors, over time the Dineh learned from their neighbors. One of the hallmarks of the Navajo over the centuries has been their remarkable ability to absorb new ideas into their culture and adapt to changing times. Sheltered in the arid canyons south of the San Juan River, they quickly mastered the arts of growing corn and weaving blankets. Some took up residence in the Anasazi apartment buildings in Chaco Canyon, abandoned since approximately A.D. 1150. The oldest, authenticated Navajo hut so far discovered was found in Gobernador Canyon, which also leads to the San Juan. The ruin has been dated, through dendrochronology, or tree-ring dating, to A.D. 1541.

Ironically, 1541 was also the date of the Spaniard Coronado's pioneering expedition into the Southwest. It took more than fifty years, however, for the Spanish to establish themselves in the area. It was not until 1598 that Don Juan de Onate rode up from Mexico with a tremendous caravan that included four thousand sheep and three hundred horses. Aside from founding Santa Fe, the expedition also provided the Dineh with their first look at the strange creatures that would come to play such an important role in their future. Gradually, through barter or theft, the Dineh began accumulating their own sheep and horses, and took to galloping like the wind between their sacred mountains.

The world abruptly changed, though, when in 1680 the Pueblos rose up in an organized rebellion and sent the hated Castillians back across the Rio Grande River. Twelve years later, the Spanish colonizers returned with a vengeance. Pueblo refugees were given sanctuary among the Dineh in their canyons' hideaways. For more than fifty years, the Navajos and the Pueblos were essentially merged. Pueblo priests, practicing their profoundly philosophical rituals, lasting up to sixteen days, had a big influence on their hosts.

Gradually, the refugees began to filter back home. Some made an accommodation with the Spanish and some did not. By the end of the 1770s, when the last of the Pueblo exiles had returned to their mesas, the Dineh became nationalistic over their lands, tribal bloodlines, and culture. During this period, Dineh theologians took the framework of Pueblo religion, mixed in myths and legends from their Athapascan ancestors, as well as new material, and built what scholar Ruth Underhill has termed "a structure Wagnerian in its grandeur."

NAVAJO SPIRITUALITY

The Navajo language contains no word that means "religion." The practice of their spirituality is so intricately woven into their lives that there is no separation between the two. To be alive is spiritual expression. There are no priests, religious societies, or religious calendars. Instead, a complex system of ceremonials, or "sings," are conducted by medicine men or women.

There are two basic types. The first is chantways accompanied by rattle playing. These ceremonials revolve around one or more "patients" whose "illness" is the reason the ritual is held. Such illnesses are not limited to physical sickness or disease, but also include psychological problems—mental illness—caused by excessive behavior such as alcoholism or compulsive gambling, or contact with evil forces such as ghosts, witches, or the dead.

"The purpose of these sings," says Annie, "is to convince the patient that he or she can emerge as a rejuvenated being. It's like using jumper cables on a car that won't start. Only here, it's the patient who's jumped."

Part of the patient's costume is a pair of moccasins. A insignificant detail until one understands that the moccasin was the Athapascans' footwear of choice. Pueblo people wore sandals made of yucca fiber or went barefoot. Here then, in their use of the moccasin, is direct evidence of Athapascan ideas interwoven into the fabric of the Navajo spirituality. Certainly there are many more that we do not recognize and will never know. The number of sings performed has also lessened with time. The late scholar Leland C. Wyman once estimated that of the approximately twenty-three chantways that existed in the past, only eight are still performed today with any frequency.

The second type of ceremonial is those in which a rattle is not used. These include the most important of all Navajo sings, the Blessingway. Blessingway rites usually involve a first night of songs that begin at sundown, then a ritual bath in yucca suds, prayers, and more songs the next day, followed by an additional all-night sing. Blessingways are performed to ensure a favorable outcome in all phases of life, including such occasions as the consecration of a new house, the installation of tribal officers, or a wedding. All other ceremonies branch from the Blessingway.

The medicine men and women who conduct ceremonials are called "singers," because every important act in each of the ceremonials is accompanied by a special chant. These singers are employed by the family of the patient for a fee that ranges from one hundred dollars to several thousand dollars, depending on whether the sing is of two-nights, five-nights, or nine-nights duration. Due to the incredible complexity of each ceremonial's use of herbal medicine, songs, prayers, sand paintings, and other ritual acts, most singers specialize in only a few.

"We really don't have any power at all to heal anybody," Annie says. "It's the natural power that the earth has that heals."

The ceremonial sings are supplemented by a large body of oral literature passed down from one generation to the next. Many of these myths and legends explain how the various chants and rituals came into being.

EMERGENCE MYTH

Navajo traditionalists, naturally, relate a story of their origin that differs greatly from that of anthropologists. What follows is a summary of what is, in effect, the Navajo Genesis. This by no means approaches a complete rendition of all of the Navajo's myths and legends. That would requires a series of volumes and is offered elsewhere. The following selections are recounted not only to provide some insight into traditional Navajo culture but also to establish a context in which the prophecies can be understood.

•

Before the world we now live in, there were four other worlds. As a Medicine Man named Sandoval once put it, the First World was black as black wool. Humans were not in their current forms, but rather were present as both male and female beings who were to become man and woman. The creatures of the First World are thought of as the Mist People. They had no definite form but evolved into the men, beasts, birds, and reptiles of this world. It was in this world that First Woman and First Man began living together in their protohuman forms. The First World was small in size and soon became crowded. The Mist People quarreled and fought among themselves, and in all ways made living unpleasant.

Having reached their limit, First Man and First Woman led the others up from the World of Darkness and Dampness to the Second or Blue World. Here, they found innumerable kinds of blue birds as well as the Swallow People. Feeling intruded upon, the Swallow People made life miserable for the newcomers. Fighting and killing took hold. So once again, First Man and First Woman led the others and escaped through an opening in the sky into the Third or Yellow World.

Separation of the Sexes

All was good and plentiful in the Yellow World, at least at first. The people already inhabiting it were kind and generous to the new arrivals. Everyone, including First Man, worked in the fields. They planted the seeds, and their harvest was great. But then one day, First Man came home and found his wife with Turquoise Boy. Unrepentant, First Woman told her husband that as she made her own fire, planted and cared for her own yellow corn, and ground it into meal, what she did was none of his business.

First Man was angered by her attitude. So with advice from Coyote, he led all the male beings across the river, leaving all the females on the other side. When they looked back, the men saw that First Woman and the female beings of every species were laughing and behaving very wickedly.

For a while, the women liked being alone. They cleared and planted a small field and reaped a harvest. On the other side of the river, meanwhile, First Man and the other males also planted their seeds and had a good harvest. Four seasons passed. The men continued to have plenty and were happy. But the women became lazy and hungry. Soon only weeds grew on their land. The women wanted fresh meat but were unable to supply their needs. Plagued by doubt about the separation of the sexes, some women tried to rejoin the men but drowned in the river.

As the surviving women had no way to satisfy their passions, First Woman suggested alternatives. Hence, some took to using long, narrow rocks. Others used the feathers of the turkey. Still others satisfied themselves with animals and strange plants. Such unholy unions gave birth to monsters and giants whom, as we shall see later on in our story, came to roam the earth, devouring people.

On the opposite side of the river, the men were also lonely. Some, driven mad with desire, ended up killing female mountain sheep, lions, and antelope. When First Man learned of this, he was enraged. He warned the men that all would be killed—that they were indulging in dangerous practices. Stubbornly, some ignored his injunction and the sun struck them down with weapons of lightning. The collective misery of the people grew even greater.

"Now we can see for ourselves what comes from our wrong doing," declared one of the headman. He suggested that the women be brought across the river so that everyone could live together once again. "Because of what we've been through, we will know how to act in the future."

First Man considered the headman's suggestion and agreed. An expedition was launched and soon male and female were reunited once again. First Woman said that she could see her mistakes, and believed that with her husband's help she would henceforth lead a good life. And with that as their common declaration, all the male and female beings paired up and moved in with each other again.

All was beautiful until a great sheet of water was sighted approaching from the east. A flood was coming! The earth was sinking! Resilient First Man then climbed up through the inside of a big, male reed that pierced the sky, and let the people of the Third World into the Fourth, which was white.

First Man emerged into the Fourth World and found a small, barren landscape. The ground was soaked, making the sowing of seeds impossible. Unimpressed, not wanting to dawdle, he planted a big female reed which grew with remarkable rapidity. Soon it pierced the sky and First Man led everyone into the Fifth World, called by some the Many Colored or Changeable Earth.

They emerged in the middle of a lake surrounded by four sacred mountains. Like sentinels, one stood in each of the cardinal directions. As the area separating them was too vast, all of them could not be seen from a single place on land. Yet ever since then they have formed the boundaries of the Navajo's mental map of their homeland. Tsinnajinnie, or Mount Blanca in Colorado's Sangre de Cristo Range, is in the east. Tso d'tzil, or Mount Taylor, looms in the south. In the west, there is Doko'slid, or Humphrey's Peak, the tallest of Arizona's San Francisco Mountains. And in the north there rises Dibensta, known today as Mount Hesperus, of Colorado's La Plata.

Living in these mountains are the Holy People. Central to Navajo spirituality, the Holy People not "holy" in the sense of being pure and good but rather in possessing the power of gods. With the exception of the White Shell Woman, who is discussed below, the Holy People are undependable. Many of their actions are actually detrimental to human welfare and they often must be coerced into helping out.

According to some medicine men, there are two worlds above this one. The first is the World of the Spirits of Living Things. The second is the Place of Melting into One.

White Shell Woman

Seeking a home, First Man and First Woman went to live at the base of a mountain near present-day Farmington, New Mexico, called Chol'i'i, or Gobernador Knob. After they had been there for quite a while, First Man noticed the mountain was enveloped by a strange fog. Curious, he climbed the peak the next day to investigate but found nothing out of the ordinary. That night, however, both he and his wife saw the fog surrounding the mountaintop. Yet when First Man climbed the peak again the following day, again he found nothing. The third night, it happened again. But this time, the fog was thicker than ever. The next morning, First Man climbed the mountain and found it still suspended in the air. From the center of the fog, he heard a baby crying. Suddenly, lightning flashed from the baby and First Man saw her on her cradleboard. In awe, he picked her up and carried her home to his wife.

The magic child would grow into the most important of the Navajo Holy People and the only one that is consistently benevolent in her attitude toward the people. To Annie, her name is White Shell Woman, although she is more widely known elsewhere as Changing Woman.

"White Shell Woman is our prophet," Annie says. "First Man and First Woman were her foster parents. They knew that their adopted daughter was exceptional and endowed with great gifts."

Under the guidance of Talking God and other Holy People,

White Shell Woman developed quickly. After three days, she was able to sit up. After four, she was walking. After thirteen days, she had her first menstruation and a ceremony, the Kinaalda', or Walked Into Beauty, was born. As related by medicine man Slim Curly in Leland C. Wyman's *Blessingway,* not long after her first Kinaalda' the Holy People gathered and sang the first Blessingway ceremonial over her. Talking God sang the twelve Hogan Songs, and the other Holy People sang their songs, as well. Then they placed White Shell Woman in charge of the Blessingway, and everything on the earth's surface, including reproduction, vegetation, and all fabrics and jewels.

Soon the holy girl began longing for a mate. As Sandoval relates, every morning when the sun rose, White Shell Woman laid on her back outside in the warming air until noon, her head to the west and her feet to the east. From noon on she went to the spring. There, she laid under a ledge and allowed spring water to drip over her body. This took place each day for four days.

Soon thereafter, the maiden was gathering ripening seeds at the foot of the mesa when she heard something behind her. Looking around she saw a great white horse with black eyes. He had a long white mane, and he pranced above the ground—not on the earth itself. She saw that the bridle was white too, and that the saddle was white. And there was a young man sitting on the horse. The young man's moccasins and leggings and clothing were all white. All was as for a bride. The holy rider who was the sun come to earth spoke: "You lay towards me each morning until noon. I am he whom you faced. When I am half over the earth you go to the spring. Your wish could not have two meanings." He went on to tell her that First Man should build her a brush hogan. Inside, they were to set a white bead basket containing a meal of seeds that she had gathered. Then, using pollen that had been sprinkled over a pair of blue birds, he instructed them to draw a line from east to west across the basket on top of the meal. Another line was to be drawn south to north, and third drawn around the outer edge of the basket. "You and your father must sit there late into the night," said the holy rider. "He will then go home to his wife and you must stay there alone."

With her father's help, White Shell Woman did as instructed.

After the first two nights, the meals in the eastern and southern sections of the basket were gone. After the third night, White Shell Woman told her father, "The meal toward the west is gone. And I thought that someone touched me last night." On the morning after the fourth night, the maiden told her parents, "The meal toward the north is gone and I thought that I was moved by someone."

Life returned to normal after that and for four days there was no sign of the luminous being. But then the young woman became aware of a curious feeling and said to her mother, "Something moves within me." First Woman answered: "Daughter, that must be your baby." And she was right. Five days later, White Shell Woman gave birth to twin boys.

The Twins

Not much is told about the Twins until their fifteenth day. By that time, the children, who would go on to become the war gods of the Navajo, were young men. First Man made bows and arrows for his two grandsons. Being of an adventurous bent, the young men found one day that they had wandered far from home; there they glimpsed a few of the monsters then ravaging the land. They also encountered Dotso, the Great Fly. Dotso let the twins in on a secret. "Your father," he told them, "is the Sun."

Surprised at the news, the Twins returned home and informed First Man and First Woman that they had decided to visit their father.

After numerous adventures, the Twins were transported by rainbows far, far to the east where they were admitted into a great house made of turquoise. While they were waiting, the Sun returned home on a magnificent turquoise horse. At first, the Sun was reluctant to believe the twins were his offspring. He was, it turned out, quite a notorious womanizer. So he put the boys through a series of tests, and as they passed every one, he was finally convinced.

To welcome his offspring, the Sun offered the Twins a choice of animals or jewels as gifts. But the young men declined every offer. They were interested, they explained, in a weapon that hung on the outer wall of the Sun's house. The weapon looked like a bow and arrows, but the Twins knew in reality it was lightning. Concerned, the Sun asked them what they would do with such a weapon. The boys told their father about the suffering on earth, caused by monsters who were eating people every day. These monsters were the ones created during the separation of the sexes.

"It is not safe for the people of the earth to possess this weapon," the Sun explained to the Twins. "Yet since you are my sons, you may use it for a while. For it is certain that the people on the earth will destroy themselves if they are allowed to keep it," he said. Then he lifted the weapon and spoke, "Now let us go to the top of the middle of the earth where there is an opening in the sky."

Once there, he handed Elder Brother the *atsinyiltl'ishk'aa'*, or the lightning that strikes crooked. Then he turned over to Younger Brother the *atso'yilghalk'a'*, or the lightning that flashes straight. And they were lowered with their weapons to the center of the world.

Slaying the Monsters

Yeitso, the Giant, lived at Tosido, Hot Springs, and the Twins went there and waited for him to come for water. They saw him come over the hill from the south and go down to the spring, drink, then spit the water back. "What are the two beautiful things that I see? And how shall I kill them?" The Twins called back: "What beautiful Big Thing is walking about? And how shall we kill it?" Then Yeitso the Giant threw his four knives. But each time the Twins were able to move out of the way. When their turn came there was a great, blinding flash of lightning. It struck the Giant, but he stood there. Then they threw back the Giant's four knives, each of which hit him, and he fell with a terrible noise.

The Twins cut off his scalp and headed for home. Upon their arrival, First Man, First Woman, and White Shell Woman were very frightened. They had squeezed themselves against the wall for they thought that some monsters had arrived to kill them. They did not recognize the Twins for they had been transformed in the house of the Sun. They were now tall, handsome young men with long hair and beautiful beads and clothing. The Twins called out: "Mother do not be frightened, we, your sons, are here." They called out to their grandfather and grandmother adding: "We have been to our father's home."

The three, still frightened, came forward, for the Twins shone with beauty. The Twins said: "We have killed the Giant, Yeitso." First Man said: "No one can kill the Giant." They said: "But we have the Giant's scalp hanging on the pole outside." First Woman went outside and, taking down the Giant's scalp, chanted and danced and then hung the scalp on the pole again.

It was decided that Younger Brother would remain behind to make medicine to safeguard his brother's journey. When everything was arranged, Elder Brother went out to hunt more monsters. The creatures he sought had supernatural strength from the rainbow and the lightning, and they were very powerful. But before he left, Elder Brother said: "To all the ends of the earth there is no such place as dangerous."

Elder Brother journeyed north of the La Plata Mountains, to a place called *Tsebit'a'i,* A Tall Rock With Wings, where his grandmother told him the Giant Birds lived. Soon, his suspicions of being watched were confirmed when he saw a black speck over the mountains. It was one of the Giant Birds. It swooped after him like a hawk after a chicken. Elder Brother lay, face down, flat on the ground. The bird swooped, missed, then circled around again and caught Elder Brother in his talons.

The Giant Bird carried him over a high peak, and over a great smooth rock and there he dropped him. But Elder Brother landed safely with the help of his sacred feathers and elk horn. The Giant Bird called his two young children and he told them to go and eat. But they quickly returned.

"He is alive, father," said the young birds. But the Giant Bird told them to hush and go eat, then flew off for another load.

When the Giant Bird returned with his mate, Elder Brother took aim and shot his lightning arrows. Both birds tumbled over with a great roar which was heard at a considerable distance.

The two young birds began to cry, but Elder Brother said to them: "I shall not harm you. You will be saved. Sit here before me," he said. They did so. "From this day on you will not think as your father thought," Elder Brother told the young birds. The thoughts of your mother have also departed from you. You will forget all that has happened to you, and the spirits of your father and mother will not enter you again. The tribe which is called Dineh shall use you. They shall use your claws, your feathers, your bill, your eyes, and your bile. Then he raised up the first bird, and then the second, and told them to go. The first became the eagle. And the second is the owl.

The next monster Elder Brother set out to slay was a beautiful and dangerous young woman known as Overwhelming Vagina. Her sex organ gained its power from the night and the blue haze and the twilight and the black sunbeam. She was a wild young woman who thought only of one thing and was very dangerous because she would seduce young men and crush their genitals.

Elder Brother had been told by his mother and grandmother that she was to be found at *Tselichii'dah'azkani,* or Red Mesa. So he made his plan, and fashioned four sticks, each shaped as a man's penis. He covered the fourth stick with a poisonous, sour juice and went forth to find the woman monster. He reached the place where his mother told him he would find her, and he saw her fresh tracks. He was following them when all of a sudden he heard a noise behind him and looking back he saw a beautiful maiden coming toward him.

"Where are you from, may I ask?" she said. "Oh," he said, "I just happened along." Coming nearer she said: "You must be my husband. The two of us can live together." Elder Brother said: "I have never touched a woman." But she told him that she knew all, that he did not have to worry. He insisted that if they were to lay together, they must both close their eyes, and she was willing. When he used the first of his sticks it was cut in two. He used the second and it was also cut in two. He used the third and it was cut in two. But when he used the fourth, she was dead.

Elder Brother went on to kill the Giant Elk, the Rolling Rock, the Twelve Antelope, the Cannibal Kicker, the Slashing Reeds, and Evil Eyes. Then he went to a place called *Tqo tzosko,* Water in the Narrow Canyon, to battle the Swallow People. There were thousands and thousands of Swallow People and he killed them right and left. He killed and killed, and he worked his way to the mouth of Mancos Canyon. Then he began running. He was tired and there were still thousands to be killed. At home, Younger Brother worked his medicine and suddenly a big, black cloud shot out of the sky over the place where Elder Brother was resting. At that moment, a great storm broke with thunder, lightning, rain, and hail, killing the remaining Swallow People.

Elder Brother went on to kill all the monsters except four that proved impossible to slay—Poverty, Old Age, Filth, and Death. He was given the name of Monster Slayer by Holy People. Then he and Younger Brother, renamed Born for Water, returned their weapons of lightning to the Sun.

Prophecy of the Monsters' Return

> It was prophesied that the monsters the twins had killed would come back. These zombies, or *Yei'iitsolbahi'*, will have no shame whatsoever. They will make everything difficult. They will try to put out your fire. We were told, "when you want to build a fire, a Yei'iitsolbahi' will pee on it."

Have the monsters returned? Many Navajos believe they have. They are the alcoholics, drug addicts, and mass murderers that plague our time. Recently, at a Squaw Dance ceremonial, Annie observed a drunken Navajo unzip his pants, turn to the fire, and pee on it. She said to herself, "Here is the fulfillment of the prophecy. The Earth and Sky are my witness. That actually happened on earth."

Belying the simplicity of one drunk's act are powerful symbols for humanity's unending drama. Over time and geography, culture to culture, from Prometheus-the-Fire-Giver to the Navajo *Yei'iitsolbahi'* who will put out fires, fire represents knowledge and progress. To have our fire taken away is a de-evolutionary act. That is, if our path to knowledge is taken away by alcoholic people we basically become stupid. Alcoholics, drug addicts, and murderers in this way can be interpreted as modern-day monsters. They impede our progress, suck away our life force, cause our societies to regress. Put another way, they put out our fires.

As the influence of traditional culture has diminished on many reservations, in too many cases alcohol has filled the void. Uncontrolled alcoholism has been termed by Michael Dorris, in his disturbing book, *The Broken Cord,* as the ultimate genocide of Native America. Spawned by poverty, hopelessness, and despair, alcohol abuse threatens to disable what is left of the Indian tribes. On some reservations one-quarter of all children have been mentally and physically impaired to some degree by Fetal Alcohol syndrome, a disastrous malady that occurs when a woman drinks while pregnant. When these infants grow into adults, they are often unable to take care of themselves or follow even simple instructions.

Of course, these monsters are also present in society at large. Do we have the weapons to combat them? Or will the gods resort again to the bolts of lightning that flash crooked and straight?

Creation of the Navajo

When the Sun came to collect his weapons from the Twins, he made it known that he wanted White Shell Woman to come and live as his wife in a beautiful home that he would build for her in the West. White Shell Woman agreed. And after a solemn ceremony attended by twelve male beings, twelve female beings, Four Rain Clouds, Four Vapors, and all the flowers of the earth, she left for her new home.

Her new residence was grand, built of white shell and floating, on a plain of white shell, over the Pacific. But the Sun was constantly on the move. The wife saw too little of her husband.

White Shell Woman was not dependent upon the Sun, however. She had power of her own. It was derived from her relationship with the Most High Power, the Great Spirit. It is toward the Spirit that she goes and becomes young again, and by whose power she knows all things. So, being lonely, White Shell Woman created her own people. They would carry on the lore that she would teach them. They would respect and hold holy the prayers and the chants that she would provide for them.

To carry out her intentions, she took a white bead stone and ground it to powder. Then she sprinkled the powder on her breasts and between her shoulders, over her chest and onto her back. When it became moist from her sweat, she rolled it between her fingers and into the palm of her hand. From time to time a little ball dropped to the ground. She wrapped these droplets in black clouds and they arose as people. These people were the Dineh.

Leaders arose among them as they lived on the ocean's shore. One day they were summoned to the home of White Shell Woman. When they entered, they saw a very old woman sitting inside. The woman got up and hobbled into the east room, carrying a white shell walking stick in her hand. When she returned, she was only a little past middle age. She walked into the south room, carrying a turquoise walking stick in her hand. Later, she came out a young woman, without a walking stick. She went into the west room and returned a beautiful maiden. She went into the north room, and returned a girl. It is because of these metamorphoses that the goddess is also known as Changing Woman.

"My grandchildren," she told the leaders. "I did not create you to live near me. Instead, you shall live between the four sacred mountains, in a land known as the Dinehtah. I will give you the seeds of different plants for your food, and I will give you pretty flowers to seed over the whole country. I will also give you rain. Whatever I do will be for your own good." The leaders of the Dineh learned her instructions and her prophecies about the future. Not long afterward, along with Twelve Holy People, White Shell Woman sent the Dineh on their wanderings.

Prophecy of the Mother's Circle Instruction

> Because our mother gave us birth and our father didn't, we are more with our mother than our father. Our mother's society is the first circle. There's another circle that you're "born for." This is our father's circle. The Instruction tells us that when the world no longer respects the Mother's Circle, then that truly will be the end of everything.

This prophecy has a double meaning. On the one hand, it refers to the conditions that would lead to the end of Navajo culture as we know it. In few other Native American societies do women traditionally occupy as powerful a position as among the Navajo. The clan system is to this day matrilineal. Property and family name are passed down through the mother. When couples got married, they went to live with the wife's parents. If the wife wanted a divorce, all she would have to do is place her husband's belongings outside the door.

Woman's exalted position flowed from the preeminent role that White Shell Woman played in Navajo spirituality. She is the giver of life, the nurturer, and the bearer of great gifts. White Shell Woman is closely associated with the earth and goes through her changes every year in concert with the seasons.

Through the years, the position of Navajo women has deteriorated as fewer people adhered to strict traditional beliefs. As the dominant patriarchal values of American society become even more prevalent, the old ways are increasingly ignored by the young. This is why some Navajos believe that the Mother's Circle is already broken, or about to fall apart. The Mother's Circle is her family, and when the family disintegrates, so does society.

"A circle is the highest form of unity. So when the Mother's Circle is no longer respected, civilization will be at an end," Annie says, adding: "We're almost there."

There is a broader meaning to the Prophecy of the Mother's Circle Instruction, as well. Aside from the immediate, nuclear family of mother, father, and children, there is a second family to which we all belong. Annie explains it this way: "Earth Mother, Father Sky, and the Dawn is Grandfather. I am a member of this family. I care for this whole family. Once I have said, "the Earth is my mother," I am Earth's child. I take responsibility for all people.

"When my parents died, I didn't feel alone because I still had Mother Earth and Father Sky," she said in a sweet, quiet voice. "People in the cities especially haven't recognized water, the earth, the mountains as part of our lives. But they are.

"Now it's very clear that the birds cannot fly up into the sky like they used to. There's too much noise, too much dirty air, and it's too hard for them to breathe. Eventually, we won't have all those beautiful ones with us. That will be the fulfillment of the prophecy. If we cannot see the true beauty in the earth, then we won't have the beauty for our children. There's an end if we don't take care of the earth. In the beginning, there were fewer people and the land was healthy and beautiful. Now there's too many people and not enough clean water and air. It's a man-made jungle, whereas before it was a paradise. I don't see that people today appreciate natural beauty.

"My clan is Two Waters Coming Together," she continues. "We take care of water, for we consider it sacred, and part of the Earth Mother. I come from water. I go to a spring feeling water is sacred. My clan believes that water is medicine. That water is life. And we pray with water.

"But where will we get clean water for my grandchildren? To me, that's a sign of the end of the world. I see the end of the world unless we change. Earth has so much patience with her children. But she can't take it anymore!" says the child of the earth.

•

Several months later, the visitor returned with more questions. Annie ushered him into her hogan and built a fire in the wood-burning stove that stood in the center of the room. Several small rugs covered patches of the earthen floor and were surrounded by a cot, a few wooden chairs, and a homemade table. Along one wall was a bookcase loaded with college texts and books on Native American topics that she and her six children had gathered over the years. On top of the bookcase was a color photograph of an elderly Navajo couple.

"Those are my parents," Annie explained matter-of-factly. Her mother, father, and maternal grandmother were medicine people and it was from them that she learned the medicine way. Her training began soon after birth. Although she most often called upon to act as a teacher, or explainer of ceremonies, she is also well-versed in the practice of traditional medicine through the use of herbs and the sweat lodge. Mental health professionals from the Indian Health Service and private physicians have consulted with her on intractable cases and achieved impressive results.

Annie attributes a lot of who she is to her grandmother. "She was the one who made me go to school and learn English. She did that because she was worried about your people—the ones that did not speak Navajo. My grandmother was born at Fort Sumner," Annie adds, referring to that wrenching period in the tribe's history a century and a quarter ago. "My great-grandmother and great-aunt are buried there."

THE LONG WALK

The causes of the Navajos' imprisonment are debated among the people to this day. By the beginning of the 1700s, the Dineh had emerged from their sanctuaries in the canyons far different from the bedraggled immigrants they had once been. Mounted on horseback, with their wealth in sheep trailing behind, they crossed the Lukachukais and surged into the relatively barren lands to the West. Due to the difficulty of farming in a region with such unreliable rainfall, and a traditional practice of abandoning any dwelling in which a death had occurred, the Dineh had little interest in building permanent towns. Instead, they roamed in groups of two or three families called "outfits," and lived in easily transportable shelters constructed of evergreen boughs. In the winter, they would graze their sheep in the lowlands. When summer arrived, their flocks were shepherded into the hills.

The arid landscape offered up a hard-fought bounty. Many young warriors, as wild and free as the ponies they rode, saw plundering the Hopi pueblos as an easier way of making a living. Their nomadic life style afforded the Dineh the opportunity to become raiders par excellence. Thundering up on their swift steeds, quick as the breeze they would carry off horses, sheep, food, and most valuable of all, captives for the slave trade. Slavery, although ruled illegal by Royal Decree in 1532, had been condoned in the New World since the earliest days of the Spanish occupation. A slave was referred to on accounting records as "a piece." Since the Spanish constantly suffered from a chronic shortage of labor, slavery was a profitable business for all concerned except the slaves themselves. The Dineh were not the only Indians involved in such practices, of course. The Utes and Comanches in the north, their distant cousins the Apaches in the south, as well as the Spanish and New Mexicans in the east, were all caught up in the barbaric compact.

But the people had Monster Slayer, their war god, to inspire them, and for generations they were fighters second to none. They fought the Spanish, and then the Mexicans, to a standstill. After Mexico declared war on the United States in 1846, and General Kearney's Army of the West took possession of the great swath of land stretching from the New Mexico Territory west to California, the Americans, too, were intimidated by the tribe that had earned the name the Lords of the Land. Seventeen years would come and go before U.S. officials resolved to put an end to Navajo marauding once and for all.

In June of 1863, just east of Arizona's Canyon de Chelley, in the heart of Navajo country, the military commander of the region, General Carleton, issued a proclamation from Fort Defiance ordering all Navajos to surrender to government authorities by July 20th. After that date, those who had not turned themselves in would be hunted down and shot. To lead its military campaign, the government selected a mountain man by the name of Kit Carson, who was, at the time, a colonel in the New Mexico Volunteers. There were never more than six or seven hundred volunteers under his command. Many were his neighbors from Taos. But it quickly became apparent that his advantage lay with his Hopi, Zuni, and Ute allies and their thorough knowledge of the rocky, backcountry canyons and peaks.

Not recognizing the depth of the U.S. military's resolve, the order to surrender was ignored. Former Navajo Tribal Council member Howard W. Gordon, in *Stories From The Long Walk,* maintains the entire problem was caused by Navajo gangsters. Their leader was a warrior named Double Face, a stubborn thief who robbed and killed Americans crossing overland to California. After a raid, Double Face would steadfastly maintain his innocence and love of peace. Most Navajo people were opposed to his violence, claims Gordon. Quietly living as farmers and shepherds, they were sucked unjustly into the maelstrom they had wanted to avoid.

Conducting a scorched earth campaign that preceded General Sherman's march through Georgia by over a year, Carson's forces waged economic warfare. The Volunteers destroyed hogans, burned crops and orchards, and confiscated livestock throughout the winter. Thousands of hungry Navajos surrendered and were confined temporarily at Fort Defiance. In March, the first column of twenty-four hundred were escorted to Fort Sumner. It was an eighteen-day forced march during which many died. In one case, say the Navajo, a pregnant woman fell behind, unable to go on, but the march did not stop. A cavalry officer broke away. A short time later, from behind there was a gunshot, followed by the officer galloping up to rejoin the ranks. The woman was never seen again. Similar executions were frequent among the old and infirm who could not keep up. Finally the exiles arrived at a barren expanse of land bordering the Little Pecos River in southeastern New Mexico. Called Bosque Redondo, or Round Grove, after the cottonwood trees that provided the only shade besides the adobe barracks, this would be home for the next four years until the Navajo were finally allowed to return home. When they did, they were not the same.

"A way of life ended on the Long Walk," says Annie gravely. "The chiefs had a vision of four suns that rose in a single day. They didn't tell everyone. Just each other. Not everyone saw the four suns rise. But the chiefs who did said, 'This indeed is the time of the end.' They didn't know if they would ever return to their homes. Everything was lost. It was the end. But they knew the people's suffering was for a reason.

"At Bosque Redondo, everything changed," she says. "Our diet changed when we were given white flour and coffee. We got cotton clothes and no longer had to weave. People even began speaking bits of English. Then it couldn't be stopped. The wagon came, and then the plow. We were captured and made over. And that was the end of the Dineh. Now in place of them are the Navajo. We are another world. The man-made world. And we're having a hard time of it."

THE FIRE DANCE

One Saturday evening, Annie escorted several Palefaces to a Fire Dance near Red Mesa. Known also as the Corral or Feather Way, the all-night "no-sleep" ceremony was the culmination of a "nine-night scene," or nine-night long ceremonial. The medicine woman stated that the dance contained a prophecy about a great leader who will arise in the East. Yet her explanations about it only deepened her companions' wonder over its full meaning.

A light rain was falling as the caravan of vehicles turned off the highway into a damp field that served as the parking lot. Unde-tered, they threaded their way through the sea of several hundred pickups and four-wheel drives and parked. The group walked into the dance site. There, floodlights illuminated a circular area in which several hundred Navajo milled about good-naturedly in the drizzle. Set up along two sides of the open space were makeshift shops selling mutton stew, fry bread, and other delicacies. Everywhere, there were grandmothers and babies, families and friends, and all were gathered waiting expectantly for the sing to begin.

In the center was a stack of firewood surrounded by a corral made of evergreen boughs piled about three feet high. On the eastern side of this Dark Circle of Boughs was an opening. Inside the northern and southern sections were eight or ten smaller stacks of firewood. At the western end of the circle, in place of a hogan, a shelter of plastic sheeting had been erected over a wooden frame to protect the medicine man, his assistants, and two young female patients from the intermittent rain.

"There are about twelve medicine people altogether working with the head medicine man," Annie explained. "Each is paid about three hundred dollars, depending upon what they're asked to do. The patients must provide four baskets of herbs and other materials to be used in the ceremony."

The Fire Dance is a curing ceremonial and focuses around one or more ill patients. Father Berard Haile, a lifelong student of the Navajo, explained the story behind the ceremonial in his book, *The Navajo Fire Dance*. It concerns "the marriage of two sisters to men whom they flee because they were deceived." The episodes reenacted throughout the night relate to the young women's struggle against Bear Man. The "no-sleep" begins when the fire is spread to the stacks of firewood in the corral. Then, there ensues a series of twelve dances, each little ceremonies in their own right, that last until dawn.

"There is a distinct conviction that the patient will benefit from every ceremonial which enters the corral," writes Haile. "It matters little whether they and their singers put on a large or a small display. The important point is that they sing their songs while they are performing. The combined efforts of all these ceremonials makes them a single unit to the extent that the patient need not have these ceremonials performed for him again."

But did Haile understand the ultimate meaning of the Fire Dance? The dancers in the circle were clad in a combination of traditional costumes and shirts and blue jeans. The consistent rhythms of the drums accompanied by the dancers' chanting voices produced a mesmerizing effect. As the first group of dancers performed in the sacred spot, Annie said the expensive ritual helped more than just the two young women inside the medicine shelter.

"The patients are representative of all humanity," the Child of the Earth quietly intoned.

After about a half an hour, the Fire Dancers exited the corral. A while later, a second set of performers entered and circled the bonfire four times. Known as the arrow swallowers, that is just what they did, in mock pain, before gliding out of the corral for good.

The night wore on, testing the endurance of the Palefaces. A group of dancers would file in, chanting a ritual song, perform their ceremony, and leave. A group of Holy People called the Yeibichais were followed by ceremonies such as the Whirling Tail Feathers, another using a Bullroarer, the "Pole That Does Things," and more by still other groups exhibiting their own special ritual acts. Chants were sung and oral traditions recited by the singer. Stories about Weasel Man and the Young Woman's flight from Old Man Bear. Time passed.

When dawn was close at hand, the last group of dancers entered the corral and acted out the final chapter of Bear Man's defeat. Once the patients were sanctified by the dancers, spruce twigs were pressed in a ritual manner onto different parts of the patients' bodies. The corral was then cut on the west, south, and north sides so as to be open to the four directions. The dawn songs followed. Annie had said that it was during the dawn songs that the Fire Dance makes its prophecy.

> He is coming
> He is coming
> He is coming from the East
> He is coming with power.

More than twenty-five years earlier, Annie had discussed this same chant with a writer who interpreted it to mean that the Navajo were expecting a great chief who would arise in the East wearing twelve sacred feathers. Those feathers would represent his sacred principles. Under them, the peoples of the earth would unite.

But at the dance Annie explained that it was not that simple. The "he" was not so much a who as a what, in this case the path delineated by the Blessingway.

"We were told we weren't going to see God walking around on earth," Annie said. "Instead we've been given the Blessingway. The Peaceful Way. When we work with it, we'll find out that the prophecies are being fulfilled. This chief that will appear, we have only his blessings. His principles. We use these to keep on the path. The twelve principles are like the white light before dawn. The people waiting at the rim of the canyon and looking east will see it first. But by the time it is noon, it will be apparent to everyone.

"The time will come," Annie continued, "when people will become blind, deaf, and handicapped. He was talking about people being at war within themselves. Literally and figuratively blind. Lots of fighting among the people. They won't be able to see or hear. These things will happen to humanity because they no longer get up at dawn. They get up at noon. They'll forget that the baby and the old person are the same. That the mother is the center of the family and that two extremes make peace. 'I'll be standing there at dawn,' he said, 'holding gifts for them. And there'll be no one there. I'll try to talk with them, and they'll be asleep!' "

The number twelve is a holy one to the Navajos. It appears over and over again throughout their myths and legends. Were the ideas just mentioned some of those twelve principles? Were they the feathers in the great chief's headdress?

"Yes," she answered authoritatively. "We use them to keep on the path. Half are from nature, the other half are saintly teachers. Home God, Ripener Girl, White Corn Man, Yellow Corn Woman, and Pollen Boy—all of these teachers are represented by their own principles. From nature, we know East is male; a terrible person but a good teacher. South are the female teachings of perfume and softness. That there is male and female in all of us, this too is one of the twelve principles that derive from nature."

"But which principles are related to which saintly teachers?" a Paleface wanted to know.

She smiled enigmatically, refusing to pursue the matter. Pressed with more questions, she would not address them.

"If I tell you everything," she said with a gentle smile, "I'd just be giving you a bed and blanket to go back to sleep with. Allow the Great Spirit to complete it. Finding the principles shouldn't be hard work.''

"So the 'He' that is prophesized to come in the chant is the Blessingway," the Paleface summarized. "He is waiting for every new dawn.''

She nodded. "It walks," she explained. "It's walking already. It's renewed. The twelve principles are interdependent as a unit. It's like when I say, 'I see beauty before me, behind me, below me, above me, beauty all around me,' I actually see them in my mind, walking. That chief in the East, I use him as my guide. It's beautiful. It restores my strength. There is no word for the chief in English. Over the years, I've become comfortable with calling him Blessingway. At the moment we realize what is not a Blessingway, when we realize we're not in the peaceful way, then the prophecy has been fulfilled.''

•

There was a final prophecy related by the medicine woman. It involves a place in northwestern New Mexico called Chaco Canyon. Within this dry, isolated canyon lay the ruins of one of the most advanced civilizations of ancient America. From about A.D. 900 to 1115, in a remarkable display of sophisticated engineering and construction, the Anasazi people built over twenty-five hundred buildings, including thirteen "towns" with nine "Great Houses" of astonishing quality and elegant design, and some four hundred miles of graded roads, before abandoning the area—never to return.

Just how these people were able to construct their highly complex civilization without the benefit of the wheel, or why they would need roads that are in places as wide as a modern two-lane highway, are questions that vex scientists and scholars to this day.

The Navajos, however, in their legend of the Great Gambler, have an explanation for how the massive constructions that housed an estimated twenty thousand people came to be. As well, according to Annie, if we understand the phenomena of Chaco Canyon and how the Great Gambler ruled over it, we can also make sense of an ancient prophecy that contains a telling warning for those living today.

Prophecy of "Something Familiar"

Before White Shell Woman sent her people away, she told them that at the time of the end there will be something familiar about a stranger or a place. You will recognize it because it will be part of your liquid. That's how you'll know. Then search for it with your heart.

The Great Gambler

As told in a version of the legend recorded over a hundred years ago by Dr. Washington Matthews of the U.S. Army, there once was a man named Noqoilpi, or He-Who-Wins-Men, who a thousand years ago ruled over Chaco Canyon. Known most widely as the Great Gambler, he, like the Twins, was a child of the Sun. The Gambler developed his natural talent for black magic and used it to draw people toward him. Approached by anyone, he would challenge them to a game of chance. He engaged in several different kinds of games, though whichever one he played, he always won. For he had the favor of the Sun. From the men he first won their property, then their wives and children, and finally the men themselves. They became his slaves and he put them all to work building the houses and roads of Chaco Canyon.

In trying to judge how much truth, if any, this tale contains, there are several considerations. Although there is no conclusive evidence of Athapascan/Dineh wanderers who might have been present in the Four Corners region as early as A.D. 1150 to witness the Gambler's decline, it nonetheless seems likely that after the Anasazi abandoned Chaco, local survivors, hard-pressed though they must have been, passed along the oral histories of that terrible time to the Dineh when they did arrive. Stripped down to basic elements, there is likely more than a kernel of truth in the old legend.

Recent research seems to support the idea of a great ruler who revolutionized Chacoan society. Conducted primarily by the National Parks Service, analysis of the data indicates that at the beginning of the tenth century there was a sudden surge of development in the thirty-two square mile canyon. "In about A.D. 900," writes Douglas W. Schwartz in *New Light On Chaco Canyon,* a book that summarizes many of the conclusions of the Chaco Project, "some spark lit a fire of change in the Chacoan people, and the canyon became a focal point of interacting communities, all probably paying tribute or homage to the inhabitants of Chaco's greathouses. . . . A dramatic increase in population size and cultural complexity was achieved within a few generations, only to fail in less than two hundred years."

An intriguing point to contemplate is how the end of Classic Maya civilization occurred at the same time as the rise of Chaco culture and the Anasazi. The Mayan city of Seibal, for example, erected its final stelae in A.D. 889—within a generation of the "spark [that] lit a fire of change" in Chaco Canyon. Was the Great Gambler a Mayan refugee? Although the elaborate roadways and advanced construction and organizational techniques certainly seem to be similar to that practiced by the Classic Maya, there is no irrefutable evidence to support such speculation.

Why did the "interacting communities" of Chaco Canyon disintegrate and disappear? Most scholars will tell you the evidence points to a fifty-year drought. Yet many accede to the possibility that poor land-use management may have accelerated the process. According to Navajo legend, however, the fall of Chaco was caused by nothing less than the Gambler's pride.

Power, quite simply, went to his head. Noqoilpi began using his black magic more and more for evil ends like controlling the weather so that rain fell only on his land. To guard his property, he trained bears and terrible birds to devour all those who might challenge him.

One dark day, says the legend, the Gambler won the last, major prize from the people. It was a big, round turquoise as tall as a man with twelve sacred feathers. Previously, the Sun told his offspring, the Gambler, that when he won the great turquoise, he wanted it for himself. For the turquoise was the most precious item of all. But when the Sun came to claim the rock after the Gambler had taken possession of it, Noqoilpi refused and challenged him arrogantly, saying, "You will be the next I will gamble with. Come on!"

The Sun was angry. He said nothing in reply but returned to his home and plotted his revenge. In one version of the legend, the Sun chose a woman from the Mirage People to bear him another son. In a second version, his new champion was the son of the sacred being, Qastceqogan. Either way, the challenger was taught all of the Great Gambler's tricks. The young man, however, had the added advantage of having the Holy People as his allies, as well as many of the Gambler's pets and domesticated animals, for they were dissatisfied with their treatment and wanted greatly to be free.

When all was prepared, Niltci, the Wind God, blew a great gale so that the Gambler's animal guards would have an excuse not to sound the alarm when the Sun's new champion entered the area at dawn. The challenger, dressed like the Gambler from his headdress to his toes, waited by the spring for one of Noqoilpi's two beautiful wives to fetch some water. When one arrived carrying a water jar, the young man presented himself. Thinking he was her husband, the woman allowed him to approach. Soon, however, she realized he was an impostor. Worried about her own safety, she said nothing and allowed him to follow her into the Gambler's great house— said to be Pueblo Bonito—with two beautiful maidens who arrived with the challenger.

When the Gambler saw the young man enter behind his wife, dressed like him, he was immediately angry and jealous. Yet his only question as he rose to his feet was: "Have you come to gamble with me?" "No," the Sun's new champion quietly demured. As by this time the entire population of the region were slaves to the Gambler, he naturally thought that the newcomer was afraid to play a game of chance with him. So he began to recklessly challenge the young man, offering even to bet parts of his body. Finally, he offered to bet his wives and all his servants against the two maidens the young man had brought with him. To this, the young man agreed.

The first game played was called Thirteen Chips. It is played by throwing thirteen flat pieces of wood, painted red on one side, into the air. When the chips fall to the ground, the winner is determined by whoever has the fewest red sides showing. When it came time for the young man to throw his chips into the air, a bat grabbed them and threw down thirteen unpainted chips of wood so fast that the Gambler did not notice. Shaken at his first loss, Noqoilpi challenged the young man to another game. In this one, called the Rolling Ring, a snake was hidden inside the challenger's ring to make it fall where he pleased. When the Gambler saw that he was going to lose again, he angrily snatched the ring away and forfeited the game. The third game involved pushing over trees. The young man rejected the Gambler's first choices, and insisted instead on larger trees. When the contest began, the Gambler heaved and strained but could not push over his tree. But his challenger, how-ever, with the help of a gopher, shoved his tree over and won the third game. Noqoilpi was shaken but insisted on continuing. There followed a variety of contests on which the Great Gambler wagered everything he had—all his jewels, property, and most of his slaves—and lost every time.

Wet with sweat and very tired, the Gambler still would not give up. One last game, he demanded, believing his luck would return. As a wager, he bet the last of his slaves and added himself. The young man accepted and they began the final game; that of the ball. In this ultimate contest, all of those who were still the Gambler's slaves assembled on the far side of a line. On the near side stood an equal number who now belonged to the young challenger. With all his might, Noqoilpi hit the ball with his fist. But it did not cross the line. Then it was the young man's turn. Lightly, he tapped the ball and it flew through the air, secretly powered by a bird hidden within it. And as it crossed the line, the people jumped for joy! The Great Gambler was totally defeated.

The young man ordered all of his winnings, human and other-wise, to be assembled before him. Then, when the giant turquoise with the twelve feathers was brought out, the victor called down the Sun, and presented him with his prize. The Sun, of course, was very pleased.

Noqoilpi, meanwhile, sat brooding on the ground, cursing his former slaves, and threatening them with lightning and disease. Hearing his oaths, the new king called the once feared leader before him.

"Despite what you thought," the young man told him, "you are not a god. You are my slave and must do my bidding." He ordered the once mighty dictator to stand on the string of his magic bow and shot him into the sky as if he were an arrow. He disappeared from sight. But it was said that when he fell back to earth, he landed far to the south, where he came to rule over the people of ancient Mexico.

Then the young man turned to the Gambler's former slaves and told them to be cheerful, that he was a different kind of person.

"You are free to go," he said. "To your own country or wherever you wish."

One-by-one, the former slaves stepped forward to thank him. And that day, all the people moved away from Chaco Canyon and never returned.

•

Several years ago, Annie visited Chaco Canyon. In the museum, she saw the artifacts that archaeologists had collected from their excavations. On display are cups, bowls, spoons, hairbrushes, and combs. She contemplated five-story tall Pueblo Bonito, with its more than 650 rooms that covered three acres. And she thought to herself, there is something about this place that is very familiar.

"Chaco Canyon reminds me of Los Angeles or San Francisco," she says with a wry expression. "The same thing that happened in Chaco in happening right now in great cities around the world. Today, our so-called leaders are the Gambler's sons. They throw crumbs to humanity while making believe that everyone is happy."

The parallels between our civilization and the one that rose and fell in Chaco Canyon are intriguing, to say the least. Since the Industrial Revolution began, Western civilization has developed a god complex. We have separated ourselves from nature and thought of it as something to be conquered, or ruled, rather than as something to live with in sacred harmony. The Great Gambler was ruined because he forgot his place in the scheme of things. When he challenged the Sun to a game of chance, he set in motion a sequence of events that led to his own demise. Are we that much different today?

"Here, we live on so little," Annie says, referring to the reservation. "The cities, on the other hand, are just too extravagant. Each person in the city wastes so much. It's not equal. It doesn't balance out. I think it should be natural that people should see that. It was a paradise and now it's not a paradise. What happened? Where did it go?

"The land has a lot to say to the people. It speaks in a beautiful way all its own by having canyons and mountains, trees and flowers, the different colored dirt, and the eagles. Nature can heal the people. It can have a lot of influence.

"Abide by nature," warns the medicine woman. "It has the power to protect you."

CHAPTER SIX

THE HOPI:
WAITING FOR PAHANA

The world we now live in, say the Hopi of northern Arizona, is the Fourth World. Before this, we dwelled in a Third World inside the Earth.

"We lived [down there] in good ways for many years," the late Dan Katchongva, son of the great turn-of-the-century Hopi leader Yukioma, once explained. "But eventually evil proved to be stronger. Some people forgot or ignored the Great Spirit's laws and . . . began to do things that went against his instructions. They became materialistic, inventing many things for their own gain, and not sharing things as they did in the past. This resulted in a great division, for some wanted to follow the original instructions and live simply.

"The inventive ones, clever but lacking wisdom, made many destructive things by which their lives were disrupted, and which threatened to destroy all the people. Many of the things we see today were known to have existed at that time." Children were uncared for. Sorcerers directed their energies into harming those they were jealous of or disliked. The people became so enamored by their successes and self-importance that many decided they had created themselves.

"Finally, immorality flourished. The life of the people became corrupted with a social and sexual license which swiftly involved the leader's wife and daughters who rarely came home to take care of their household duties. Not only the leader, but also the high priests were having the same problems." People had no respect for anything. Life had become *koyanisqatsi*—a world out of balance.

The leader and the high priests gathered together to smoke and pray. They asked for guidance, and then the idea came to them to move. To find a new land and start fresh. As they had been hearing footsteps in the sky, a red racer snake, then various birds were challenged to investigate. Finally, a *tootsa,* or small sparrow hawk, found the *sipapuni,* or hole in the sky, and emerged into this, the Fourth World.

The bird found the Fourth World totally dark except for a dim fire in the distance. Flying toward the flames, it noticed a well-dressed, handsome, dark-skinned young man sitting next to the fire. Around his neck were four strands of turquoise and from his ears hung large pendants of the same stone. Streaks of black hematite ran from the bridge of his nose downward to each cheek. The young man identified himself as Maasaw, Caretaker of the Earth. The situation below was well-known to him. He had been expecting an emissary from down there to eventually show up. But since the people had brought trouble upon themselves due to their great plans of greed and ambition, Maasaw refused to grant them permission to enter the Fourth World.

The sparrow hawk winged back to the underworld with the disheartening news. Desperate, the leader and priests tried again. This time they sent along *paho,* or prayer feathers and instructed the bird to present the offerings to the strange young man. The leader, or *kikmongwi,* pledged that only good people would accompany them into the upper world. He loved his people as if they were all his own children and feared that they would not be able to endure such a crazy life much longer. So the next morning, the bird flew through the hole in the sky to try again.

Impressed by the prayer feathers and the people's persistence, Maasaw granted them permission. He said the people could come if they practiced his way of life. But the evil ones must stay behind.

The sparrow hawk relayed the message and those waiting were overjoyed. But being unable to fly, how would they get to the upper world? Again they smoked and prayed for guidance, then called upon the spirits of nature for help. Inspired, the *kikmongwi* and the priests planted a spruce tree. A squirrel brought them pine seeds and they also were planted. Then the leaders prayed and sang the creation songs. The trees shot into the air. But the branches were too soft to support the people all the way into the upper world. So a bamboo reed was planted.

All this was kept secret from the corrupt majority of the population. Only good-hearted people were informed of the plans to leave. As soon as they knew the project was successful, they began to climb up on the inside of the reed, resting between the joints as they worked their way up. The bamboo did not have sections in it at the beginning. The sections were created as the people rested during their long climb skyward. Finally, the pointed end of the bamboo pierced the sky and the people climbed through the emergence hole, or *sipapuni,* into this, the Fourth World.

In different versions of the emergence myth, the reed is either torn from its foundation and thrown over from above or chopped down by martyrs and destroyed from below. Then in the people's first real encounter with the supernatural Maasaw, who can change his appearance at will, he was seen not as a handsome young man but instead as the ghostly Spirit of Death. In this horrifying incarnation, Maasaw was almost bald with only a few strands of hair on top. His face was covered with layers of coagulated rabbit blood that he had poured over his head, making it appear quite monstrous. His eyes were hot coals and about him was an overpowering stench.

"It's up to you," Maasaw intoned to his frightened supplicants. "I have nothing here. I live simply. All I have is my planting stick and my corn. If you are still willing to live as I do, and follow the road plan which I shall give you, you may live here and take care of the land. And you will have a long, happy, and fruitful life."

The people were willing. So, in short order Maasaw opened up the sky to allow in the light of the sun that had been created earlier by Old Spiderwoman. He then introduced the immigrants to corn, watermelon, and squash, and showed them how to use a farming stick. "You can use the earth," Maasaw told them, "but you cannot keep it. For it is my responsibility to care for it."

Maasaw divided the people into groups, each with its own leaders, and laid before them ears of corn. Some say this was the origin of the races. Each group was told to pick one type of corn to take with them on their journeys. The corn represented all elements of life including food, culture, and religion. One by one, each group greedily picked out the longest and most perfect-looking ears until only the short blue corn was left. Little did anyone realize that this was a test of wisdom. The short blue corn was picked by the humblest leader. Then the Maasaw gave each group their names. The mockingbird, or *hopi-yaaba,* provided the languages by which they would be recognized. He who chose the short blue corn was named Hopi.

Maasaw then declared his famous *potskwani,* or rules for living a proper way of life. And in conjunction with those rules he gave them the *navoti,* or prophetic statements.

Gratefully, the people begged Maasaw to be their leader. With his guidance they surely could not fall into corruption again. But Maasaw declined. As a disciple of the Creator, Maasaw's assignment is to be caretaker of the earth. To fulfill this role, he was given the power to create the appropriate paths of life for humans to live in balance with nature, and to grant them the use of the earth's gifts. "For I was the first," he told them. "And I will be the last."

Maasaw instructed the Hopi to migrate to the four corners of the earth, and said that after their wanderings they would eventually link up at a common site. That site would be determined when one day, during migration, they would see a giant star. There they should found a village, name it Oraibi, and settle permanently. The features and locations of Oraibi were described in great detail by Maasaw, who also told the Hopi that after they built the village, they would become prosperous people who would gather eternal benefits from the land for the area is the "backbone of the earth."

Maasaw then gave a stone tablet to Old Spiderwoman, who had accompanied the people up from the Third World. Clever Old Spiderwoman magically inscribed the tablet with Maasaw's "road plan of life." Then, breaking it in two, Maasaw gave one half of the tablet to the Hopi and the other half to the Pahana, the Elder White Brother, who had emerged with them through the *sipapuni.*

The Pahana took off. Not running, mind you, but at a good clip. Everyone knew that the White Brother was heading off to settle where the sun rises in the East. And then, before Maasaw himself disappeared, he told them that the Pahana would return one day to unite with his Hopi brethren and all other righteous people not influenced by *koyanisqatsi.* On that day will come Purification.

•

Native Americans traditionally believed that their myths and legends are accurate records the past. Modern-day thinkers give this viewpoint little credence. Each clan within a tribe, after all, usually has its own versions of important clan legends. Oral traditions are thought instead to be relatively recent ways of explaining how the Hopi, for example, came to settle in nine villages—Oraibi, Hotevila, Bacobi, Mishongnovi, Polacca, Shipolovi, Shongopovi, Sichimovi, and Walpi—upon the fingerlike protrusions of First, Second, and Third mesas in what is now northern Arizona.

Accepting that modern point of view, it should be recognized nonetheless that understanding the essentials of the emergence myth, even in such a condensed and abbreviated version as above, is a key to understanding the still vital role of prophecy in Hopi culture. Isolated on their arid and rocky mesas, the Hopi have the longest authenticated history and the most complex and vibrant religion of any North American Indian culture. And more than any other Native American society, with the exception of the ancient Maya and Aztecs to whom they are connected, the Hopi are guided by prophecy.

Throughout their history, these "peaceful people," as they are often called, have been haunted by the meaning of their emergence myth and its related prophecies, the stone tablets—at least one of which still exists—and Maasaw's *navoti,* or prophetic statements, which have been passed down from one generation to the next. The legend of the Pahana and his anticipated return has also never been far from their minds. To fully understand their corpus of prognostication, however, one must first be mindful of the outlines of the harmonious culture from which these prophecies have sprung.

•

Southwest of Kayenta, Arizona, now located on the Navajo Reservation, archeologists have discovered cliff dwellings that contain the earliest known evidence of the Hopi's ancient ancestors. Carbon dated to A.D. 217, the rock shelter features a sandstone-lined storage pit where yucca-fiber sandals, jewelry, weapons, food, and finely woven baskets were stored. Similar havens have been found throughout the Four Corners region of Colorado, Utah, Arizona, and New Mexico. In the surrounding fields, these proto-Hopi people grew corn and squash in abundance. Sunflower seeds, piñon nuts, acorns, and cactus fruit, gathered in the wild, augmented their diet along with game such as deer, rabbits, and mountain sheep. The surplus in food permitted some leisure. And as they were intelligent people, they evolved.

Some time after A.D. 500, they began building pithouses, which were, as the name implies, dug into the earth. These pithouses had stone slabs for walls and roofs made of wooden poles and mud-covered brush. They also learned how to make ceramic pottery and began, for the first time, to use the bow and arrow.

By A.D. 800, the houses had moved above ground and were constructed of crude masonry. Connected to each other in the manner of apartment houses, they are referred to as "pueblos," from the Spanish word for villages. The pithouses evolved into the kiva, a type of underground ceremonial chamber still used by the Hopi today.

These early ancestors of the Hopi are called the Anasazi. Meaning "ancient ones," the word is Navajo in origin and the source of a long-standing joke among the Hopi. As they tell it, when white ethnologists first appeared in the Southwest, they saw the hundreds of ruins dotting the countryside and wondered who could have built them? The first Native Americans they encountered in the area were Navajos. The Navajos, when asked, were unwilling to admit anything positive about their enemies and said that the ruins were made by the Anasazi—the "ancient ones." But if the ethnologists would have asked the Hopi, they would have been told that the ruins had been left by the Hopi's ancestors. Their legends declare that their forebearers deliberately marked the paths of their migrations by leaving behind pottery shards and undisturbed dwellings. These dwellings are shrines and should be paid spiritual respect by the clans who once occupied these sites.

Hopi legends also tell us that sites including Hovenweep and Mesa Verde in Colorado, Chaco Canyon in western New Mexico, and Wupatki in northern Arizona, were all occupied by Hopi clans during the time of the great migrations. Such claims are backed up by pictographs of clan emblems found on the walls of many of these ruins. One cliff wall at Chaco Canyon, for example, is covered with symbols of the Snake, Sun, Bear, Eagle, Sand, Coyote, Lizard, Water, and Parrot clans among others. All of these clans are still active among the Hopi today.

Throughout their migration period, when it is believed that the complex rites of Hopi religion developed, the ancestors of the Hopi carried on trade with the more advanced civilizations to the south in Mexico. This commerce was not limited to goods such as tropical parrots and macaws, the remains of which have been found ritualistically interned beneath the floors of several pueblos. It included ideas, as well. Indeed the entirety of Hopi religion has its roots in the spectacularly successful agricultural religion based on corn that was originated by the Maya. The Hopi language itself is classified by linguists as a branch of Uto-Aztecan and is related, as are several other western Native American languages, to the old Aztec tongue of Nahuatl. There are also clear similarities between the legends of the Hopi's Pahana, Kukulcán of the Mayans, and the Aztec's Quetzalcoatl. All three of these cultural heroes were said to have gone to the East and who, it was prophesied, would one day return to reunite with their peoples.

Around A.D. 1100, the village of Oraibi was founded on Third Mesa by the Bear Clan. Old Oraibi still exists, though in an advanced state of decay, and vies with New Mexico's Acoma Pueblo for the title of the oldest, continuously occupied town in North America.

The highly evolved Anasazi culture suffered a mortal blow in the final quarter of the twelfth century when a severe drought squeezed the Southwest. Lasting more than a generation, the lack of moisture finally drove the Anasazi out of their honeycomb towns. The refugees wandered east, west, and south to find more dependable sources of life-giving water. Many gathered on the mesa-tops of northern and central New Mexico along the Rio Grande River. More to the south settled the founders of the pueblos of Laguna and Zuni.

According, once again, to Hopi legend, when their elders received instructions through premonitions from the Great Spirit, they continued their migrations until they reached Oraibi on the southern edge of Arizona's Black Mesa. Ever since then, their sacred lands have been roughly bounded by the Colorado and San

Juan rivers to the north, the San Francisco Peaks to the west, Chevelon Butte to the south, and the present Arizona–New Mexico border in the east. Hopi priests to this day visit shrines within this territory to perform rites, resupply themselves with herbs and minerals, and gather eaglets for their all-important religious ceremonies.

HOPI RELIGION

To truly understand the Hopi one must recognize how their lives center around their religion. More than a means of discerning good from evil, the Hopi believe their faith is nothing less than the force that keeps nature working and in balance. This is yet another similarity to the Mayans and Aztecs. The practice of Hopi religion is considered to be absolutely essential for the survival of everything on earth. And not just human beings. The Hopi also pray and dance for animals, minerals, vegetation. "We have to learn to live with all of them," says a Hopi priest from the One-Horn Society.

That is why Anglos and other visitors have traditionally been permitted to view many of their ceremonials which are held throughout the year. Because the Hopi dance and pray for everyone.

"The earth is referred to as our Mother," explains a member of the Reed and Snake clans. "Long time ago, and even now, no one was helping Hopi. So everything that the Hopi survived with came from the earth. Planting, crops, water, everything for sustaining life came from the earth. Now, when you still go out and plant a field, you talk to your cornfield just like you talk to your mother. Because these things come from her. Just like a child gets nourishment from its mother, the Hopi—and humans—get nourishment from the earth."

Each village has a priest assigned to observe the progress of the sun as it passes through the seasons. By this method of accurate scientific observation first developed by the Maya, the precise timing of planting and harvesting, as well as the Hopi festivals are determined.

Over the centuries, as migrating clans arrived on the mesa-tops and asked to join the Hopi, each was queried about what contribution it could make to the general welfare of the people. The price of admission, so to speak, was a ceremony that then became a perpetual civic duty. Each ceremony has since belonged to a certain clan, which maintains the ritual paraphernalia needed to carry it out in its clan house under the authority of a clan mother. The actual performance of a ceremony is done by one or more of the religious societies that cut across clan lines. None of the villages have ever possessed all of the clans. Today there are some twenty-seven or twenty-eight clans in existence and each has its own contribution to make to the benefit of society and humankind in its entirety.

The Eagle Clan is one of them. Symbolically, it perches up on top of the pueblo and watches out for any threats to the community. One of its primary responsibilities is the Clown Ceremony that is conducted in conjunction with the *kachina* dances. The *kachinas* can be considered to be Hopi saints. For half of the year, these supernatural beings live in the San Francisco Peaks north of modern-day Flagstaff. During the other half of the year, they come as clouds to the villages, take human form, and dance in order to bring rain and ensure abundant crops. Those participating in a *kachina* ceremony are thought to be the physical incarnation of *kachina* spirits. Their dances are formal and very serious. The clowns, on the other hand, act spontaneously in all sorts of amusing ways. Yet the ultimate philosophical foundation for the Clown Ceremony is a symbolic disciplinary process for all the people in the world.

"In effect," explains a member of the Eagle Clan, "the people have to be disciplined because there's a right way of living and a wrong way of living. So this ceremony provides for the fact that you people here are getting away from your primary responsibility as spiritual people. As you go into the other direction, you are practicing corrupting things. The ritualism of this public ceremony portrays this kind of drama. In the beginning when the clowns perform they're doing silly and bad things. And then Warrior Kachinas will periodically appear, and they will threaten the clowns who represent the people of the world. They threaten them symbolically and say, 'You people better straighten up. You're going the wrong way. And if you don't, we'll just have to come in eventually and straighten you out.' The Clown Ceremony culminates with the Warrior Kachinas attacking the clowns who sacrifice themselves on behalf of mankind."

Another responsibility of the Eagle Clan is the gathering of

Golden Eaglets. The Hopi are the only people permitted by the federal government to trap eaglets since their feathers are used in all ceremonies. Hopi clans from each of the villages are assigned various mountaintop nesting areas and collect the birds between the end of April and the summer solstice in June. In order to preserve their supply, they are careful to never take all of the birds.

"The eaglets are brought into a matriarch's home," explains the clan member. "And the bird is accepted just like a newborn. They baptize it in the Hopi Way, and they name it, and everything else. Then it's perched up on top of the roof until it's brought in for harvesting." The naked carcasses are then ritually buried to promote reincarnation.

In the village of Shongopovi on Second Mesa, where a complete cycle of ceremonials is still maintained, about two hundred days a year are devoted to religion. The calendar of major rituals begins in December with the Soyal, or winter solstice ceremony, participated in by all of the religious societies. The purpose of this pivotal ceremonial is to start the sun on another year's journey as well as renew the year. On December 21, prayer feathers are prepared and consecrated for everything on earth. The cycle ends the following November with the Wuwuchim ritual, one part of which entails the closing of all paths in and out of the village and the extinguishing of all fires. The head priest then rekindles a new fire which is carried to the people to reenergize the new year. This practice echoes the New Fire ceremony among the Aztecs. In its extended, sixteen-day format, young men are initiated into manhood during the Wuwuchim ceremony.

The annual cycle of major ceremonials occurs like this:

December	Soyal or "Winter Solstice"
February	Powamu or "Bean Dance"
July	Niman or "Home Dance"
August	Snake or Flute Dance
September	Marau or "Knee-High Dance"
October	Lolakont or "Basket Dance"
November	Wuwuchim

Each of these rituals is announced by a crier at sunrise. *Kachina* dances, on the other hand, are never announced ahead of time in order to maintain the masquerade that the spirits themselves decide when to visit the people. *Kachina* dances often last from sunrise to sunset. There is no fixed calendar nor any prescribed order in which the different kinds of *kachina* dances are performed, although they are now usually performed on weekends. At the end of the winter solstice ceremonial, any Hopi can present sacred corn meal to a society leader and ask to sponsor a certain dance. Such a request entails major responsibilities, however. A sponsor's family must feed the *kachinas* and provide them with fruit, nowadays often bananas and oranges, and other presents to give to the children.

Until initiated into a *kachina* society at the age of eight or nine, children are led to believe that the hundreds of different types of *kachinas* are real.

"The *kachina* is a tool," explains a man from Bacobi. "A learning tool. When a child cries, we tell him or her, 'Don't cry. Tsaveyo, the ogre *kachina* is going to hear you.' When I was a child, I remember going by the San Francisco Peaks on the way to Flagstaff. It looked like the clouds were coming out of the mountains and my mother told me that those were the *kachinas* coming out."

Adds the One-Horn Society priest from Hotevila: "When you get initiated into a *kachina* society at the age of maybe eight or nine, you transform this fantasy way of life into reality of life. You learn about the concept of *kachina,* and you dance, and you perform, and you develop your ability for a number of things. Like physical fitness and getting introduced into our tribal philosophy. Then you are no longer in this fantasy state. You become a man or a woman. But when parents neglect to make their children aware of these kinds of things, they're going to grow up not respecting anything."

Prophecy of the Kachina's Role in the Final Days

The practice of the Kachinas will be one of the last things that Hopi will be able to do. Today, not every village has the Soyal ceremony, the Wuwuchim ceremony, or the Snake Dance. At Walpi, for example, there's nobody trained to carry out the Snake Dance, which is a very sacred ritual. It is still done at Mishongnovi and Shongopovi. But in 1987 it died out at Hotevilla. They just refused to train the young people because of political confrontations. At other villages, they have members who are initiated into it. But they're not practicing it. Because they don't have the right people, they don't have the right paraphenalia, they don't have the right song, or they don't remember the right song. Or how it should be done. So, every village right now has the Kachina, but not every village has all of the other things that were there from the beginning of life. Again, it's another sign.

Return of the Pahana

The Old World first intruded into the harmonious Hopi universe in July 1540. In that month, Maasaw's ancient prophecy regarding the return of the Elder White Brother was finally put to the test in the Hopi's first encounter with the white man. It had been nearly twenty years since Hernando Cortez and an army of Spanish soldiers-of-fortune had conquered the Aztec Empire. After they had looted the vast golden treasure of central Mexico, the conquistadores, infected with "gold fever," spread out to look for more.

To investigate rumors of the golden "Seven Cities of Cibola" located far to the north, an expeditionary force was assembled at Compostela in the Mexican province of New Galicia. Led by a thirty-year-old nobleman, Francisco Vasquez de Coronado, the army of 336 Spaniards and several hundred Indians trekked northward across the great Sonoran Desert, eventually penetrating as far as modern-day New Mexico. But rather than the fabled seven cities of gold, they found only the mud-and-stone pueblos of Zuni.

Exhausted and bitterly disappointed, Coronado's interest was piqued nonetheless when the Zunis told him of "seven villages of the same sort as theirs" twenty-five leagues distant. The province was called Tusayan. Could these be the seven golden cities, Coronado wondered? Leery of dragging his entire army on another wild-goose chase, he instead dispatched Don Pedro de Tovar in command of a column of seventeen horsemen, three or four foot soldiers, and a Franciscan friar to learn the truth.

For centuries, the Hopi had been anticipating the return of their Elder White Brother. According to oral history translated by Oswald White Bear Fredricks and used by Frank Waters in his *Book of the Hopi,* the prophesied date of the Pahana's arrival was, strangely enough, the same as that of Quetzalcoatl's return to the

Aztecs: A.D. 1519 or Ce Acatl, the equivalent date by the Aztec calendar. "Every year in Oraibi, on the last day of Soyal, a line was drawn across the six-foot-long stick kept in the custody of the Bear Clan to mark the time for his arrival. The Hopis knew where to meet him: at the bottom of Third Mesa if he was on time, or along the trail at Sikya'wa [Yellow Rock], Chokuwa [Pointed Rock], Nahoyungvasa [Cross Fields], or Tawtoma just below Oraibi, if he was five, ten, fifteen, or twenty years late. Now the stick was filled with markings; Pahana was twenty years late."

Don Pedro de Tovar, however, appeared at none of these places. Instead, with great stealth, he arrived after dark and climbed up the rocky face of a cliff to await the dawn below the extinct village of Awatovi on westernmost Antelope Mesa. Castaneda de Nagera, chronicler of the Coronado expedition, tells us that the Hopis, who had never seen a horse, had heard that the Zuni had been "captured by very fierce people, who traveled on animals which ate people."

"Our men arrived after nightfall and were able to conceal themselves under the edge of the village, where they heard the natives talking in their houses," relates Castaneda. "But in the morning they were discovered and drew up in regular order, while the natives came out to meet them, with bows, and shields, and wooden clubs, drawn up in lines without any confusion. The interpreter was given a chance to speak to them and give them due warning, for they were very intelligent people, but nevertheless they drew lines and insisted that our men should not go across these lines toward their village. While they were talking, some men acted as if they would cross the lines, and one of the natives lost control of himself and struck a horse a blow on the cheek of the bridle with his club. Friar Juan, fretted by the time that was being wasted in talking with them, said to the captain: 'To tell the truth I do not know why we came here.' When the men heard this they gave the Santiago [war cry] so suddenly that they ran down many Indians and the others fled to the town in confusion. Some indeed did not have a chance to do this, so quickly did the people in the village come out with presents, asking for peace. The captain ordered his force to collect, and, as the natives did not do any more harm, he and those who were with him found a place to establish their headquarters near the village. They had dismounted here when the natives came peacefully, saying that they had come to give in the submission of the whole province."

Waters tells us that Tovar and his entourage were then escorted toward Oraibi. As directed by their ancient prophecy, the chiefs of the Hopi clans met the white men at Tawtoma, located below the mesa. Four lines of sacred corn meal were laid in the dirt between them. The leader of the Bear Clan stepped forward and held out his hand, palm up, to Tovar. The Hopis knew that if the Spaniard was their true Elder White Brother, he would hold out his own hand, palm up, and clasp the elder's hand "to form the nakwach, the ancient symbol of brotherhood." Unfortunately, the Bear Clan leader's gesture was misinterpreted as a demand for a gift and Tovar ordered that he be given a present. Perplexed, the Hopis wondered if the Pahana might not have forgotten their ancient agreement.

Uncertainly, they escorted Tovar and his men to Oraibi where they were given food and shelter. The pact made between the Hopi and their Elder White Brother after their emergence through the *sipapuni* was explained to their visitors. "It was understood that when the two were finally reconciled, each would correct the other's laws and faults; they would live side by side and share in common all the riches of the land and join their faiths in one religion that would establish the truth of life in a spirit of universal brotherhood," writes Waters. But Tovar, of course, even after double-checking the translation, could make no sense of what the Indians had told him. Disappointed with gifts of a few, meager pieces of turquoise, he soon saddled up and left.

Other than a brief visit later that month by more of Coronado's men, who would go on to "discover" the Colorado River and the Grand Canyon, the Spanish would not return for forty-three years. In the meantime, the Hopis continued to practice their religion high atop their dry and rocky mesas. Priests and priestesses exercised their powers to make it rain, to make the sun shine, to make the wind blow, to make life grow. Everything was done right. Life was in balance.

Then, early in 1583, enterprising Antonio de Espejo arrived in Hopi land with a friar and fourteen soldiers. Once again the Hopi were confronted with the question of whether Espejo was the true

Pahana. To honor him, they gave him corn and corn meal, venison and dried rabbit meat, and six hundred white and multi-colored cotton blankets. But Espejo was not the Pahana. In fact, he was wanted by the authorities and had been lured to Tusayan by the rumor of a lake of solid gold. When he left to continue his search, the Hopi were surprised and disappointed. Yet their faith was unshaken that one day their Elder White Brother would return with great benefits for the people.

Fifteen years would pass before the next white would appear in the person of Don Juan de Onate, the great colonizer of New Mexico and founder of Sante Fe. When Onate arrived at the mesas with a party of some sixty soldiers, the Hopi greeted him with sprays of sacred corn meal. Onate demanded their formal submission to King Phillip of Spain. And without resistance, the Hopis did what was asked of them. But Onate's response was another disappointment. He and his men moved on after six days with no sign of knowing anything about the Pahana.

Over the next thirty years, the Spanish visited only sporadically, preferring instead to concentrate on their colonization of New Mexico. The Catholic church directed its missionary effort at the Pueblos along the Rio Grande.

Finally, in 1628, the Franciscans embarked on a major program to convert the remote and isolated Hopi. Some of the villagers, wondering if the true Pahana had finally arrived in the person of Padre Francisco Porras, prime mover of the missionary effort, even agreed to help construct three mission churches at Awatovi, Shongopovi, and Oraibi, with branches at Walpi and Mishongnovi.

In *Truth of a Hopi,* Edmund Nequatewa, referring to the Elder White Brother as the *B*ahana, explains how deeply the legend had permeated society. "Most everybody was anxious to see the Bahana come, for they were so afraid that he might not come during their lifetime and they would not be able to enjoy all the benefits that he was to bring back with him—for the Bahana was supposed to bring great knowledge with him. These people were telling their children that the Bahana was wise and with his inventions had reached the rising sun and was coming back to them again, for they had seen the big eastern star and that was a sign and they were waiting for him. Every grandfather and grandmother was telling

their children that they were growing so old that they would not
see the Bahana. They would tell their grandchildren to go out in
the mornings before sunrise with sacred cornmeal to ask the sun to
hurry the Bahana along so that he would come soon."

Indeed, there was even a sort of test, according to Nequatewa,
for weeding out imposters.

A Test for the Bahana

If he ever did come they must be sure to ask him about his books,
which they thought would contain his secrets, and it was said that the
book of truth would not be on top, but at the very bottom, after
all the other books. If he asked the Hopi for the privilege of teaching
them his language and taught them how to write they must be sure
to ask that they would like to be taught in the book of truth, because
if he was a true Bahana he would quickly consent to teach them of
this book. For their belief is that if he is not the one they are looking
for he will refuse to teach them his religion. Now if they learned his
religion they would compare it with their religion and ceremonies,
and if these were alike they would know that the Bahana had been
with them in the beginning.

It did not take the Hopi long to realize their mistake in cooperat-
ing with the Franciscans. Catholic rites, though equally ornate, are
nothing like those of the Hopi. The elders were angry that the
headquarters church of San Bernardo was purposely being built
over one of their most sacred kivas at Awatovi. Five years after
work on the missions had begun, Padre Porras was poisoned. His
murderer was never identified but is thought to have been one of
the Hopi religious leaders. Rather than withdraw, the Franciscans
redoubled their efforts and backed them up with the lash. Acting
in concert with the Spanish military, over the next fifty years they
attempted nothing less than the elimination of the Hopi religion.
Friar Salvador de Guerra, for example, was so zealous in his faith
that in 1655, after catching a Hopi in what Guerra considered to
be a highly idolatrous act, savagely beat him bloody, then dragged
him inside his church where he doused him with turpentine and set
him on fire.

By 1680, the Hopi had had enough. Acting in league with other

Pueblo people in New Mexico, they rose up in a rebellion known as the Pueblo Revolt. The well-organized uprising had been planned for years and caught most of the Spanish by surprise. Four priests living among the Hopi were executed and all the missions were destroyed. The Spanish were driven completely out of the Southwest, back to what is now the Mexican border. Although they would attempt to reassert their authority, their dominance of the Hopi was effectively put to an end. Also ended for all time was the idea that one of the hated Castilians, or the Mexicans who would follow, might be the true Pahana.

Nearly 150 years would pass before the Hopi would encounter the next candidate for Elder White Brother and their first citizen of the then fifty-one-year-old United States of America. His name was William Sherly Williams. "Old Bill," as he came to be called, was a renegade Baptist preacher and mountain man who lived among the Hopi briefly in 1827. By all reports, he was as greedy and dangerous as the worst of the Spanish. Kit Carson, in fact, would later comment, "In starving times no man who knew him ever walked in front of Bill Williams." Although we cannot know for certain, it is probable that Williams was invited to stay long enough for his Baptist religion to be compared to the Hopi's own.

The two creeds, of course, were not alike. So Williams was escorted out. Seven years later, however, he returned like the plague as a guide for some two hundred mountain men, many of whom, among them Kit Carson, were employed by the Rocky Mountain Fur Company. To slake a hunger borne of their arduous backcountry trek, "Old Bill" led the ragtag army right to the Hopi corn and melon fields. When the farmers climbed down from the mesas, voicing their objections, the mountain men killed twenty of them before continuing on to Taos.

The American era officially dawned in June 1846 when some four hundred wagons and eighteen hundred soldiers of the new Army of the West left Fort Leavenworth, Kansas, under the command of General Stephen W. Kearny. President Polk had declared war on Mexico only the month before. Kearny's orders were to secure the broad expanse of land from New Mexico west to the Pacific. American businessmen and agents in Santa Fe worked hard in advance in order to convince important Mexicans that opposing the expansive young empire was dangerous and not to their benefit. As the American forces approached, Governor Armijo fled in panic to Mexico City. Just before sunset on August 18, the Army of the West encamped in the hills overlooking the town. General Kearny proceeded to the Palacio, where acting Governor Juan Vigil greeted him warmly. The next morning, the Stars and Stripes was flying over Sante Fe.

The rule of law, though, was still a long way off for most of the territory. Navajo, Comanche, and Ute raiding parties, arrogant and free on their swift ponies, would spill the blood of not just the Hopi, but Spanish settlers, Mexicans, and Americans as well, for years to come.

It would be three long years before the first Indian agent would be appointed to undertake the grueling overland journey to Sante Fe. That man was James Calhoun, a fair-minded and inquisitive individual who would be promoted to be the first governor of the territory of New Mexico by President Fillmore in January of 1851. Calhoun was intrigued by the Hopi from his earliest days as an agent. In his eighth report to the commissioner of Indian affairs in Washington, he wrote that the Hopi "are supposed to be decidedly pacific in their character, opposed to all wars, quite honest, and very industrious."

It did not take long for news of the powerful new white man to reach the Hopi. Fifteen months after his arrival, a seven-member delegation including two *kikmongwis* turned up in Sante Fe. They had risked the dangerous journey through Navajo country in order that they might peer into the white man's eyes themselves. Could he be the true Pahana who would be bringing them great benefits?

Seeking further understanding, a second delegation of thirteen Hopi men returned ten months later in August 1851. "Their object was to ascertain whether their Great Father, and they supposed me to be him, would do anything for them," wrote Calhoun to his superior. "They complained that the Navajos had continued to rob them, until they had left them exceedingly poor, and wretched, which indeed, they did look." Calhoun argued that "These Indians seem to be innocent, and very poor, and should be taken care of."

Many times Calhoun expressed his desire to visit Old Tusayan and investigate the situation there himself. But his request for a military escort was repeatedly denied. The U.S. was unable to project the forces necessary to protect him, let alone the Hopi, from marauding Navajo. The cavalry deemed the mission suicidal. So the Hopi were forced to rely on their own meager resources. Because of that, they paid dearly. From 1853 to 1861, smallpox and constant warfare combined to decimate their already diminished population by an estimated 60 percent.

When a party of Americans did finally show up in the fall of 1858, it was led not by an official of the U.S. government but rather by the soft-spoken "Apostle to the Lamanites," Jacob Hamblin. Hamblin was a tall, bearded Mormon with several wives who had previously been successful in ministering to the Paiutes and Utes. Chosen by Brigham Young, president of the Church of Jesus Christ of Latter-Day Saints, to lead a missionary effort to the Hopi pueblos, Hamblin and eleven others arrived with their Paiute guide in Oraibe after a bone-jarring, fourteen-day journey from their base camp at Santa Clara, Utah. Among them was a Spanish interpreter and a Welshman who had been sent along from Salt Lake City to see if the Hopi could be the descendants of the legendary Prince Madoc of Wales, said to have disappeared after sailing to the New World in the twelfth century.

The Hopi leaders counseled together while Hamblin and his Mormon brothers stood in Oraibi's main plaza. Waiting as they were for their Elder White Brother, they recovered quickly from their initial, understandable surprise and greeted Hamblin and his group graciously. The Spanish and Welsh interpreters were quickly found to be useless, but Hamblin was able to communicate in Ute, which he had learned previously. Shortly after his arrival, according to Hamblin's official Mormon biography, an elderly man informed him that when he was young, his father had told him that one day white men would appear among them and "bring them great blessings, such as their fathers had enjoyed, and that these men would come from the West." The enraptured old Hopi proclaimed that he believed he had lived to see the ancient prophecy fulfilled.

Despite the difference in the direction of arrival—west rather than the usual east—the old man's story was a clear reference to the prophecy of the Pahana. Two years later in a sermon in Salt Lake City's St. George Bowery, Hamblin would declare that he was escorted the day after his arrival to a strange, empty room that had been prepared "for the reception of whites . . . whom they had been expecting for years." He described the room as being whitewashed and located in a stone building measuring forty by thirty feet. Ushered inside, he was received in a solemn ceremony of song and prayer. Whether his story of the white room was a bit of hyperbole uncharacteristic of the reserved missionary, or, in fact, the room actually existed, we will probably never know for sure. No other reference to it has ever been found.

In the days after his arrival, Hamblin was led on a tour of the other villages by a chief named Tuba and regaled as the Elder White Brother who had finally returned. Hamblin, in turn, was impressed. He saw Hopi farmers putting in a day's labor, something that he had labored in vain to teach the Utes. The Hopi's mesa-top dwellings were as sturdy as his own. They were kind, intelligent, and civilized—the elite of the Lammanites, who, according to Mormon doctrine, were the descendants of the Israelites who had emigrated to America six hundred years before the birth of Christ. The idea that he and his brethren could be the fulfillment of the Hopi's prophecy stirred Hamblin deeply. Surely it was all supported by the *Book of Mormon* itself.

Hamblin did his level best during his stay to convince the Hopi to leave their harsh life upon the rocks and join the Mormon agricultural colonies north of the Colorado and San Juan rivers. But the Hopi politely refused, maintaining, Hamblin would later claim, that they could not abandon their towns until "the three prophets" who originally led them to the mesas returned and gave them instructions. Perhaps the number three was a mistake in translation, as once again there is no other reference to the Hopi waiting for three prophets. Three is, however, equal to the number of Nephite angels prophesied to appear prior to the Second Coming of Christ in the *Book of Mormon.* If this is also a case of Hamblin elaborating on the facts, his motives appear to be lost in an archaic maze of internecine politics.

Four Mormon brothers remained behind as missionaries when Hamblin returned to Santa Clara to complete a total journey of fifty-two days. But not long after submitting his report to Brigham Young, the downcast missionaries returned home unexpectedly.

After Hamblin had left, the Hopi had asked about the Mormons' "Book of Truth," then compared its doctrine to their own. Finding the religions dissimilar, the *kikmongwi*s and other leaders concluded that the missionaries could not be the white brothers foretold by their prophecy after all. The sacred white chamber was declared off-limits. The missionaries were stymied. Soon, their dispute escalated to such a level of intensity that they finally took the advice of Chief Tuba and left.

Hamblin returned undaunted, however, the next year with a Mormon brother who had been mystically "called" to teach the Hopi the new Deseret alphabet. Developed by the Latter Day Saints' University of Deseret, the alphabet was intended to be a means of universal communication. Hamblin's willingness to teach it was also one of the criteria for recognizing the true Pahana. Was he aware of this? It seems probable, since throughout his first visit to the mesas he was hailed as the true Pahana who had finally returned. All of the prophecies would have been related to him. The linguistic effort was soon abandoned, though, due to the targeted students' total lack of interest. The Hopi had already made up their minds about the Mormons and would not change.

Altogether, Hamblin would attempt six expeditions to the mesas before his death in 1870. But he was frustrated in all of his attempts to convert the Hopi to his faith. The Hopi remained quietly interested in trading, in politely learning new skills, and willingly incorporated unfamiliar Mormon farm products, like the pumpkin squash, into their diet. Yet when it came to matters of religion, the Hopi remained aloof.

Thinking that the Navajo threat had finally been eliminated by Kit Carson's campaign of 1863–64, other missionaries moved to set up shop on the mesas. In 1870, the Moravians established a mission at Oraibi. The Baptists returned in 1875, though their first unofficial evangelist, "Old Bill" Williams, had long been forgotten. The Mennonites arrived in 1893, and seven years later would open an imposing church in Oraibe. H. R. Voth, for many years its pastor, was the first to document in writing many of the most sacred Hopi ceremonies through his work for Chicago's Field Museum of Natural History. Yet paradoxically, as a missionary he was dedicated to their eradication. Despite the best efforts of scores of pious men and women, be they Catholic, Mormon, Moravian, Baptist, Mennonite, Presbyterian, or any of the myriad of other faiths that made an appearance and are now lost to memory, the Hopi applied the same test. Each of the religions and its "very bottom" Book of Truth was studied and examined and compared and found wanting.

On December 16, 1882, President Chester A. Arthur signed a one-sentence proclamation ordering a 3,863 square mile parcel of land be "withdrawn from settlement and sale, and set apart for the use and occupancy of the [Hopi] and such other Indians as the Secretary of the Interior may see fit to settle thereon." Considering the rabid condescension of Bureau of Indian Affairs officials at the time, it is not a surprise that no one ever consulted with the Hopi about the creation of their new reserve. If they had, perhaps the deleterious effects of the phrase "and such other Indians as the Secretary of Interior may see fit" could have been avoided. For by not setting aside a reservation solely for the Hopi, President Arthur permitted the land dispute with the Navajo to continue without end.

By the late 1880s, Navajo incursions into Hopi territory had again become so intolerable that Thomas Keam, a trader with a post some ten miles east of First Mesa, arranged for five Hopi leaders to travel to Washington, D.C., to ask for help. Although the results of their meetings were not what had been hoped for—government officials suggested the Hopi move off their mesas to escape the Navajo—the effects of the trip were far-reaching in an unexpected way.

The undisputed leader of the Hopi delegation was the *kikmongwi* of Oraibi, Lololomai. Lololomai was a quiet and devout man who had always been defiantly anti-American. But during his visit to Washington, Lololomai, who had previously never been east of Albuquerque, saw so many wondrous things that he underwent a conversion. Upon returning to his people, he declared that he had been wrong about the Americans. They were, after all, the true Pahana the Hopi had been awaiting for so long. To underline his faith, he sent his son and nephew to the government's hated, new boarding school at Keam's Canyon.

Although Lololomai buttressed his conclusion with details from Hopi emergence and migration myths, active opposition rose up against him immediately. And from that split come the factions known as "traditionalists" and "progressives." The angry traditionalists insisted that Lololomai had been duped. If the white man was the true Elder White Brother, what happened to his half of the sacred Stone Tablet? No, they insist to this day. The true Pahana is still to come.

"Up 'til this point, there have been a lot of white people," says the Reed and Snake clans member. "Is this the right white person? Is that the right white person? Most of them nowadays come as lawyers. We know that this person is going to come from the East. So far," he adds with a gentle laugh, "we've had lawyers from Utah and Colorado. But no one from the East! All the attorneys are acting like, 'I am the White Brother who is going to speak up for the Hopi!' " His voice trails off in a chuckle.

"Whoever he is, maybe he's not born yet. Maybe he's around someplace. Never been to Hopi. Apparently, he's never been to Hopi. So, it's still believed that this white person is going to come and speak up for the Hopi, speak on our behalf."

MAASAW'S DOWNFALL

Attempts by sanctimonious and sometimes vicious officials of the Interior Department's Bureau of Indian Affairs to "civilize" the Hopi by finding a way to put an end to their practice of religion was a reoccurring theme for decades. To assist in this "noble" struggle, the General Allotment Act, thought by reform-minded easterners to be an important new tool in raising the Indians out of their primitiveness, was signed into law in 1887. Sponsored by Senator Henry L. Dawes of Massachusetts, the act mandated that communally owned lands be broken up into individually owned parcels. "Surplus lands" would then be free to be bought and sold.

The allotment program reached the mesas three years later in 1890. Seeing surveyors peering through their theodolites and planting stakes made the Hopi angry. Their sacred land, upon which they had been allowed by Maasaw to stay, was in danger. Once the surveying parties departed, the chiefs had the stakes pulled up and burned.

By June of 1891, the government had reached the limit of its tolerance. A detachment of five men led by Lieutenant L. M. Brett was dispatched to Oraibi from a cavalry company encamped at Keam's Canyon with orders to arrest the chiefs. Relations between the feds and the twelve hundred people of Oraibi were already at a low point due to the government's insistence that Hopi children be sent to the boarding school at Keam's Canyon. Most of the Hopi had responded by hiding their children.

As the cavalry approached Oraibi, they were stopped below the mesa by Lololomai, who asked them to go no farther. Lt. Brett ignored him and led his men forward. When the detachment entered Oraibi's main plaza, accompanied by the schoolteacher, the agent, and an interpreter, they found the entire pueblo prepared for war. Warriors were stationed on rooftops and behind barricades, armed with bows and arrows, and a few, rusty, old firearms. Lt. Brett ordered his men to dismount, then informed the people of his intentions. But before the orders to arrest the chiefs could be carried out, a figure stepped out from the shadows to confront the troops. It was Old Spiderwoman, or a man dressed up to incarnate her. Spiderwoman warned the soldiers that they must leave immediately, or trouble would result. But the cavalrymen would not withdraw. A moment later a more awesome personification appeared: Maasaw, Spirit of Death and Caretaker of the Land. Wearing a heavy black mask painted with spots, the Maasaw carried a number of sacred objects, including a liquid-filled medicine bowl. Stepping closer to the line of soldiers, he dipped a feather into his bowl, and sprayed each with drops of the elixir. Then, in his most terrible voice, he ordered the whites to leave at once or hostilities would commence.

The appearance of the deity did not have quite the affect the Hopi had been expecting. Brett and his men found the grizzled old figure mildly ridiculous. More than a few chuckled and grinned. Yet the lieutenant was keenly aware of the influence the comical, masked figure seemed to have over the armed warriors that surrounded his men. In light of Maasaw's vociferous declarations, and the fact that they were badly outnumbered, Brett wisely chose to withdraw. Though he warned them that they would surely be punished for defying the authority of the U.S. government.

As threatened, two companies of cavalry under the command of a Major Corbin arrived eleven days later at the spring below Oraibi. Four Hotchkiss guns, of the kind made famous at Wounded Knee only six months before, had been trundled along. At least one of them was fired in an intimidating display of firepower. Above, the Hopi were watching. They had never seen so many soldiers before. Their guns were like lightning; an attack could be disastrous. A courier was sent up with the demand that six leaders present themselves to be placed under arrest.

Nothing after that, quite literally, was ever the same again. Five leaders were jailed that day. One got away, for a time. The Hopi could not overcome the firepower of the U.S. military. Instead they tried passive resistance. Yet despite their tenacity, the allotment program would go forward, their children would be hunted down and taken away to school. A few "longhairs" would be tied up with barbed wire and have their hair forcibly cut. The split between the progressives friendly to the government and the traditionalists trying to preserve the ancient path would grow to the point that, in 1906, Yukioma and the old believers would move out of Oraibi to found the religious stronghold of Hotevila. A year later, a splinter group from Hotevila that wanted to return to Oraibi would be rejected. These gentle people would go on to found the village of Bacobi.

The biggest change of all was in the Hopi's perception of Maasaw. After the epic clash with the U.S. Cavalry in which the age-old deity was mocked and ultimately defied, it was no longer possible for Maasaw to appear in human form without the risk of being laughed at. In order to prevent the structure of Hopi religion from crumbling, its foundation—Maasaw—had to change. But rather than be cast aside, Maasaw was promoted to a higher status. Over the last century, he has been transformed in the Hopi mind into the Great Spirit, or Creator known as "the one who is supposed to be our father," "the one who is invisible," or "this being that lives unseen."

"He still shows himself in one way or the other," says the One-Horn Society priest from Hotevilla. "A lot of times people will observe a ball of fire going through some other place at different times, showing itself to different people; not everybody. That's Maasaw."

Stone Tablet

When the six leaders from Oraibi climbed down from the mesa as demanded by Major Corbin, one of them handed the major a stone tablet. Corbin passed the flat stone to famed anthropologist J. Walter Fewkes, who was living at the time at Walpi and had accompanied the troops to Oraibi. When Fewkes asked the Hopi elder what the tablet meant, he was told that "it was the testament given to his ancestors by the gods securing to the clans of Oraibi control of all the country about their town. This stone," Fewkes writes, "was later passed to other officers and then returned to the Indians. A search was made for it subsequently, but it was impossible to find it or to gain any further information regarding its whereabouts."

This documented encounter was the first time non-Native Americans had ever been allowed to gaze upon the Hopi's sacred Stone Tablet. Other than Dr. Fewkes and the handful of officers who saw it briefly on that fateful day, and perhaps some unknown government officials who may have seen it when Lololomai carried it with him to Washington, only two other non-Hopis have ever seen the Stone Tablet. They are the late Mischa Titiev of Harvard, who was allowed to examine the tablet in the mid- to late-1930s; and Frank Waters, to whom it was presented in December 1960. Both men had the opportunity to study it in detail. Waters is the only scholar to claim to have seen four tablets, although Dan Katchongva also refers to there being more than one. Most Hopis, it should be noted, have never seen any of them, as they are jealously protected by their delegated guardians from profane observation and are considered to be among the Hopi's most sacred objects.

Reported by Ekkehart Molotki as made of compressed corn meal, and by the others as hewn from some sort of rock, the tablet in question is one and a half inches thick, eight inches wide, and ten to sixteen inches long. Both sides are flecked with what Waters calls "intrusive blotches of rose," and Titiev says are "irregular red dots which the chief interprets as points of land."

"One surface is covered with miscellaneous symbols," Titiev continues, "including a row of eight little scratches, said to stand for the eight-day period during which the Soyal is observed; cloud and lightning emblems in a random arrangement; an unidentified *katchina* figure; two or three sets of bear claws; an old-age crock; a poorly executed serpent, said to represent the Little Colorado River; and eight circles, arranged in two parallel rows, which the chief explains as thunder because the sound of a thunderclap is like that of a number of objects being struck in succession. Along the edge of one of the long sides of the relic there runs a series of little lines which are not interpreted; and along the other edge there is a succession of conventional cloud and rain symbols to indicate that . . . there was [once] always plenty of rain. The pictures on the other surface of the stone tell a connected story. A double rectangle in the center is supposed to represent the Oraibi domain. Around this are grouped six figures which depict the Soyal officers. Reading from the bottom in a counterclockwise circuit, they refer to the Village, Pikyas, Parrot, Tobacco, Crier, and War chiefs. Each figure stands with the left hand across the chest and the right extended downward to cover the genitalia. This posture is said to indicate that the chiefs are claiming the land enclosed within the central rectangles. Along the edge representing the east, there is a line of small scratches, interspersed with occasional circles or crosses, which depicts the proper Hopi path that the chiefs are supposed to travel. The War chief brings up the rear to make sure that no one turns aside from the correct road."

The tablet is reportedly brought out from its repository annually during the closing day of the Soyal ceremonies. Bear Clan elders, according to Titiev, "examine it closely and then reaffirm their rights to hold office and their claims to the land."

After Yukioma died in 1929, the tablet passed into the possession of his nephew, James Pongyayaoma, who was also a member of the Fire Clan and the last known *kikmongwi* of Hotevila. His departure from his post came about due to the widening split between the progressives and traditionalists, which reached a decisive stage on December 14, 1936, when Bureau of Indian Affairs Commissioner Alexander G. Hutton gave his official approval to the "Constitution and By-Laws of the Hopi Tribe." The Constitution had been approved in an election in which the traditionalists refused to take part. The Tribal Council that was formed in its wake is a matter of controversy among the Hopi today. Many traditionalists still refuse to recognize its authority.

Pongyayaoma, meanwhile, "the one they should be doing the

dances around," hated the turn of events. So one day, the arch-traditionalist deviated from his sacred duty, which is considered to be a never-ending responsibility for a *kikmongwi*. "Once a *kikmongwi* deviates from that, he is done. He can never get that authority back," explains an elderly man from Bacobi. Pongyayaoma "gathered his bag of seeds, and he gathered his bag of earth, and he left."

The fallen leader went to live quietly in small town of Parker, Arizona, where he resided in obscurity for many years. But his intentions were not quiet. What he had attempted to achieve by abandoning his post and hiding the seeds and bags of earth was nothing less than the starvation of his people and the ending of all life on earth. "Because it was also prophesied long ago that the *kikmongwi* himself would deviate from the path because of the Pahana's bad influence," explains the old man from Bacobi.

Life, as we all know, did not end. So the tablet was placed in the custody of another Fire Clan elder, Pongyayaoma's nephew, whose first name is Martin. Around 1957, Martin and another Fire Clan member are reported to have taken the tablet to Washington, D.C. "People donated money and things, and then put them on the train," says the priest from Hotevila. "They were going to try to either present it to the federal government and inquire about its meaning, or ask if anyone knew of the existence of the other half." The results of the trip are unfortunately unknown. Nothing more was ever said about it again.

In 1970, Fire Clan leaders decided to show the tablet to the Tribal Council in the Hopi Tribal Chambers. At the time, the land dispute with the Navajos was at a climactic phase. It was thought by many that the tablet could prove the Hopi's claim to their land. Many, though not all, believed then and now that the tablet conveys upon the Hopi a sort of sacred deed.

Prophecy of the Tablet

The instructions on the tablet say that this land belongs to Hopi. "When you are being closed in, when you are being challenged by other people about your land, all you need to do is show this tablet. When the other people recognize this, when they see this, they'll know that this land is Hopi."

Other Hopi vehemently disagree. "People will claim that the tablet describes what the spiritual boundaries of the Hopi land is," says the One-Horn Society priest. "But the ultimate philosophical foundation for the cultural values that exist in Hopi culture is that nobody owns the land. You have the right to use it. If you have the energy, the motivation, and the ability to provide the necessary food or whatever from working this earth, and take care of it, you have the right to use it. That's all. You can't claim this acre is mine; or that two acres. No! You can't do that."

The priest's seriousness is reflected in his eyes. "The Stone Tablet only really means that this is a path of life and instruction for people to exist with the elements on the earth. If you interpret it this way, that tablet only means that whenever people get together and figure out a way to establish a situation where they can live in harmony, then the path will have been followed."

Unveiling the Stone Tablet in the Tribal Chambers, unfortunately, only made matters worse. The tablet, to most everyone's surprise, could not be completely interpreted by anyone present. The markings on one side seemed to be an aboriginal map of the Hopi landbase, with the *sipapuni,* or place of emergence, and area of migration. But beyond that, the meaning of other lines and figures were a mystery. One source relates that from what he has heard, "it is probably written in Spanish."

Now it is feared by some that no one other than the true Pahana might be able to interpret the tablet. Many in the Fire Clan and others believe that it may have been the wrong time to have exposed it. So the rock writing may not be shown again.

Prophecy of the Lights

One of our oldest prophecies that came true is that we were told one day we would be surrounded by lights. One day, people would be closing in on Hopi, because they know Hopi is going to be the last tribe to go. We can sustain life. We can prolong our life. And it was prophesied that, "You will be surrounded by lights." As a result, we have Flagstaff, Winslow, and the Navajo closing in today.

Letter to Nixon

The "Hopi Traditional Village Leaders," as they called themselves, comprised of Dan Katchongva from Hotevila, Mrs. Mina Lansa of Oraibi, Claude Kawangyawma of Shongopovi, Starlie Lomayaktewa of Mishongnovi, with an interpreter, wrote a seven-paragraph letter to President Richard Nixon on August 4, 1970. Perhaps better than any other document, the letter embodies the essence of what many Native Americans have been trying to tell us. Reprinted here in part, it can be considered a manifesto of humankind's struggle to save our planet.

DEAR MR. PRESIDENT:

Those of us of the Hopi Nation who have followed the path of the Great Spirit without compromise have a message which we are committed, through our prophecy to convey to you.

The white man, through his insensitivity to the way of Nature, has desecrated the face of Mother Earth. The white man's advanced technological capacity has occurred as a result of his lack of regard for the spiritual path and for the way of all living things. The white man's desire for material possessions and power has blinded him to the pain he has caused Mother Earth by his quest for what he calls natural resources. All over the country, the waters have been tainted, the soil broken and defiled, and the air polluted. Living creatures die from poisons left because of industry. And the path of the Great Spirit has become difficult to see by almost all men, even by many Indians, who have chosen instead to follow the path of the white man.

We have accepted the responsibility designated by our prophecy to tell you that almost all life will stop unless men come to know that every one must live in Peace and in Harmony with Nature. Only those people who know the secrets of Nature, the Mother of us all, can overcome the possible destruction of all land and life. . . . This must not be allowed to continue, for if it does, Mother Nature will react in such a way that almost all men will suffer the end of life as they now know it.

Today, almost all of the prophecies have come to pass. Great roads like rivers pass along the landscape; man talks to man through the cobwebs of his telephone lines; man travels along the roads in the sky in his airplanes; two great wars have been waged by those bearing the swastika or the rising sun, man is tampering with the Moon and the stars. Most men have strayed from the path shown us by the Great Spirit. For [Maasaw] alone is great enough to portray the correct way back to him.

It is said by the Great Spirit that if a gourd of ashes is dropped upon the Earth, that many men will die and that the end of this way of life is near at hand. We interpret this as the dropping of the atomic bombs on Hiroshima and Nagasaki. We do not want to see this happen to any place or any nation again, but instead should turn all this energy for peaceful uses, not for war.

Before his death of natural causes in February 1972, Dan Katchongva wrote down other traditional Hopi prophecies that he hoped would be "spread to the four winds" in the book, *Hopi: A Message for All People.* Considered by his opponents to be obstinate and unyielding, and by others a brave warrior in the struggle to stay true to the Hopi Way, his love for humanity was genuine. His faith, too, was unswayed that the unfulfilled prophecies attributed to Maasaw, known as the *navoti,* would come to pass. One of these *navoti* details more of the signs that will appear when we are near the end of this world.

End of the Fourth World

The people will corrupt the good ways of life, bringing about the same life as that from which we fled in the underworld. The sacred body of the female will no longer be hidden, for the shield of protection will be lifted up, an act of temptation toward sexual license will also be enjoyed. Most of us will be lost in the confusion. An awareness that something extraordinary is happening will develop in most of the people, for even their leaders will be confused into polluting themselves. It will be difficult to decide whom to follow. . . . Those gifted with the knowledge of the sacred instructions will then live very cautiously, for they will remember and have faith in these instructions, and it will be on their shoulders that the fate of the world shall rest.

Finally, Katchongva related what is perhaps the most complex and obscure prophecy of all. Incorporating elements from a number of other forecasts, this one predicts natural disasters and three great wars and substitutes the name Bahanna for Pahana. The final war will bring forth either purification or destruction of all life on earth.

Prophecy of Moha, the Sun Symbol, and the Red Symbol

Time passed on, people passed on, and prophecies of things to come were passed from mouth to mouth. The stone tablets and the rock writing of the road plan were often reviewed by the elders. Fearfully, they waited as they retold the prophecy that one day another race of people would appear in our midst, and would claim our land as his own. We now call those people Bahanna. He would try to change our patterns of life. He would have a sweet tongue, fork tongue, like snake, and many good things by which we would be tempted. He would use force in an attempt to trap us into using weapons, but we must not fall for this trick. For then we would be conquered and brought to our knees, from which we might not be able to rise. Nor must we ever raise our hand against any nation.

We have teachings and prophecies informing us that we must be alert for the signs and omens which will come about to give us courage and strength to stand on our beliefs. Blood will flow. Our hair and our clothing will be scattered over the earth. Nature will speak to us with its mighty breath of wind. There will be earthquakes and floods causing great disasters, changes in the seasons, and in the weather, disappearance of wildlife and famine in different forms. There will be gradual corruption and confusion among the leaders and the people all over the world, and wars will come about like powerful winds. All of this has been planned from the beginning of creation.

We will have three people standing behind us, ready to fulfill our prophecies when we get into hopeless difficulties: the Moha (swastika-shaped symbol, like the leaf of a certain plant which has a long root, milky sap, and grows up again after being cut down), the Sun symbol, and the Red symbol. The Bahanna's intrusion into the Hopi way of life will set the Moha symbol into motion so that a certain people will work for the four great forces of nature (the four directions, controlling forces, original forces) which will rock the world into war. When this happens, we will know that all our prophecies are coming true. We will gather strength and stand firm. It will fall, but because its subsistence is milk, and because it is controlled by the four forces of nature, it will rise again to put the world in motion, creating another war in which the Moha and the Sun Symbol will be at work. It will again be defeated or come to rest, and this time, it will rest in order to rise a third time. Our prophecy foretells that the third event will be the decisive one. Our road plan foretells the outcome.

This sacred writing speaks the word of the Great Spirit. It could mean the mysterious life seed with two principles of tomorrow, indicating one, inside of which are two. The third and last, which will it bring forth, purification or destruction?

This third event will consist of the Sun, the Moha, and the Red symbol. It will depend on the Red symbol; he will take command, putting the four great forces of nature in motion for the Sun. When he sets those forces in motion, the whole world will shake and turn red and turn against the people who are hindering the Hopi cultural life. To all these people, Purification Day will come. Humble people will run to him in search of a new world, and the equality that has been denied them. He will come unmercifully. His people will cover the earth like red ants. We must not go out to watch. We must stay in our houses. He will come and gather the wicked people who are hindering the red people who were here first. He will be looking for someone whom he will recognize by his way of life, or by his head (haircut?) or by the shape of his village (dwellings). He is the only one who will purify us.

When this happens, the symbol of the Rising Sun will be seen. Since he is the brother of the Hopi, he will join the others. Commanded by the Red symbol, with the help of the Sun and the Moha, the purifier will weed out the wicked, who will have disturbed the way of life of those who are following the Hopi way of life, the true way of life on earth. The wicked will be beheaded and will speak no more. This will be the Purification for all righteous people, the earth, and all living things on the earth. The ills of the earth will be cured. Mother Earth will bloom again and all people will unite into peace and harmony for a long time to come.

But if this does not materialize, the Hopi traditional identity will vanish by pressure from Bahanna. Through the white man's influence, his religions, and the disappearance of our sacred land, the Hopi will be doomed. This is the Universal Plan, speaking through the Great Spirit, since the dawn of time. . . .

The Hopi have been placed on this side of the earth to take care of the land through their ceremonial duties, just as other races of people have been placed around the earth to take care of her in their own ways. Together, we hold the world in balance, revolving properly. When the Hopi Nation vanishes, the earth motion will be interrupted or disturbed. The water will swallow the land, and the people will perish. Only a brother and a sister will be left to enter a new life. . . .

I am forever looking and praying eastward to the rising sun for my true white brother to come and purify the Hopi.

Like all cultures that consider themselves to be the center of the world, the Hopi run the risk of being dismissed by stronger powers. Yet their beautiful view of the earth and humankind's place upon it is one that needs to be taken to heart. Their vision is far-reaching and stretches well beyond the borders of their parched and isolated reservation. Keeping the world in balance, after all, is their sacred duty. For when the Hopi dance, they dance for all of us.

CHAPTER SEVEN

SUN BEAR: SAVE THE PLANET

The earth is our mother,
  we must take care of her
The earth is our mother,
  we must take care of her
Hey younga, ho younga, hey young young
Hey younga, ho younga, hey young young
Her sacred ground we walk upon with
  every step we take
Her sacred ground we walk upon with
  every step we take
Hey younga, ho younga, hey young young
Hey younga, ho younga, hey young young

—from "The Dawning: Chants of the Medicine Wheel"
                    by Bear Tribe Medicine Society

As the second millennium of our era winds to a close, the scope of our global environmental crisis has assumed staggering proportions. Traditional rivalries between nation-states are receding and, in place of the struggle between East and West, a common front is emerging to save the planet. Native Americans, with their reverence for the Earth Mother, have a lot to teach the rest of us about avoiding environmental apocalypse. Yet some, nursing hatred borne out of centuries of white genocide, bitterly resent their brothers and sisters who share what is considered sacred medicine.

One man who has chosen to ignore the critics and work tirelessly to warn of the error of our ways and the coming earth changes is Sun Bear, medicine chief of the Bear Tribe Medicine Society.

"I don't go around shaking my fist at the white people saying, 'You nasty people. You did all these horrible things to the land,'" says Sun Bear during a summer visit to his rustic home on Spirit Mountain, fifty miles northwest of Spokane, Washington. "I try to reach out and share with them spirituality to get them back into balance so they're no longer doing these nasty things. I feel this is my spiritual responsibility to the earth and to human beings."

Spirituality is a word that makes many people nervous. But it is precisely that which Sun Bear believes is missing from the contemporary environmental movement. "I believe that environmental issues have to become a spiritual thing," he says in a characteristically quiet voice. "People have to think of the earth in a spiritual way. Taking responsibility for the earth must be ingrained from the time they're still children."

The morning light illuminates the crags in his broad face as he stands, sipping tea, on the porch of the Longhouse and surveys part of the eighty acres of mountainside owned by the tribe. Two months shy of his sixtieth birthday, Sun Bear's long, dark hair is beginning to gray. He is dressed in sneakers, jeans, and a sweater, and takes a moment to listen to the gentle rushing of the wind through the surrounding ponderosa pine trees. He has returned home to plot strategy with the nineteen other members of the tribe and to rest after his latest speaking tour. These days, 95 percent of Sun Bear's time is spent on the road. In the preceding six months, he has lectured and held workshops in Florida, Philadelphia, and New York, as well as across the Atlantic in Germany, Austria, Belgium, and the Netherlands.

Sun Bear's message revolves around his belief in the inevitability of coming "Earth Changes." His warnings about what he sees as happening in our near future spring less from science than from Native American spirituality and earth wisdom. The Indian people of America are the sources of his prophecies. They may be Chippewa, Manitoba, Hopi, Puyallup, or from some other nation. They can also be a synthesis of divinations, as is his central message. There are even a few predictions, as we shall see, that have stemmed from his dreams.

Prophecy of Earth Changes

Native people have had prophecies that go back hundreds of years. They tell how if humans don't take a responsible position in regards to relating to the earth, then the time would come when major changes would happen. I feel that we are into that now. Most people think of the earth as just here. That they can do anything they want to it. It's just dumb nature. But to native people, the earth is an intelligent, living being. It has power. I believe that the earth will make the necessary changes if the humans won't. That's what is happening right now. And it's going to happen with greater intensity all the time.

Sun Bear meanders down the trail from the Longhouse to observe a flight of flickers playing in the cool, clean air. On the way, he pauses to scratch a favorite dog behind his ear.

"The human being is just another species on the planet," he says. "No different from the animals or anything else. But their arrogance has kept them from acknowledging this fact. We feel that for the planet to survive, nature has to start taking its position.

"My work is to teach native and nonnative people to come back to balance and harmony with the earth, and work with the healing of the planet. From now until the year 2000, and beyond that a bit, we're going to be seeing major changes. But the greatest change has to happen within humans. They have to make a change of consciousness and perspective of how they treat the earth and show respect for it. Otherwise," he adds, "they aren't going to survive and the planet may not either."

•

Born on the last day of August 1929 to a Norwegian-American woman and a Chippewa Indian man, the prophet-to-be spent most of his first twenty years on the White Earth Reservation in northern Minnesota. Given the name Vincent LaDuke, his formal education ended after the eighth grade. Yet throughout his early years, the lively lad was schooled in a different kind of knowledge by two wise uncles, both of whom were practitioners of the *Midewiwin,* the Grand Medicine Society of the Chippewa.

"My uncle Bill Burnett was the more powerful medicine man," says Sun Bear to a visitor in the living room of the Longhouse. "He did all kinds of medicine things. He had the power to see things before they happened. He was a successful gambler, and worked on the railroad so he could go places and gamble. He was very respected all around the area. People would come from miles around to see him because he was a very powerful medicine man with tremendous ability.''

Little Vincent's other medicine man uncle, Bo Doge—meaning, Like the Wind—began instructing his nephew while he was still a boy. "Bo Doge was a quiet person, more of a woodsman," Sun Bear explains. "He had a real strong love of nature and creation and things around him. I remember him taking me down by the lake and other places in the summertime. My learning from him was on a more quiet basis. He could be hard. He would take me for a walk in the woods and show me a herb, and point to the herb, and I would go over and look at it real carefully. If I asked him a question at that time, he'd give me a dirty look. But that night when we'd sit down, and have some of my mother's big oatmeal cookies, he'd tell me about it. What it was, how he used it, and so forth. That's where I gained my knowledge. He also taught me songs and chants.

"When I was seven years old, Bo Doge gave me my Indian name. It's Gheezis Mokwa in my language, or Sun Bear.'' The name once belonged to a friend of his uncle, and his uncle wanted it passed along. He adds: "I wasn't given permission by him to use it, though, until I was actually doing the work that I'm doing.''

Although Sun Bear's uncles were the two most important spiritual influences in his early life, his mother, Judith, also taught him important lessons. Born in a sod hut in South Dakota, she was surrounded by Native Americans throughout her life and had great feeling for their wisdom. "My mother always encouraged me to be open to everything," states Sun Bear. "Like even when we'd have something to eat, she'd be serving up something different. We'd be eating salads and stuff. Up in the country where I was, with all the German-Norwegians, they were all meat and potatoes people. And they'd say, 'That's rabbit food!' But she didn't care. My mother would always say when she'd have some new dish, 'Well, try a little bit of it and see if you like it.' She'd put a bit of it on my plate. This way, I learned how to enjoy just about every type of food. Except, maybe, fried parsnips.''

As the Great Depression tightened its grip, Sun Bear's father, Louis, was unable to find work as a lumberjack. So, the family took to the road while he looked for a job. Hopscotching through the Dakotas and into Idaho, they landed briefly in Clarkston, Washington, before returning to Minnesota in 1937. But the economic hardship took its toll, and the following year Louis and Judith's marriage ended. The boy stayed with his mother and his sister, La Vonne.

The Minnesota forest was rife with game. When his family needed food, young Vincent would often grab his .22 rifle or slingshot, and bring home a gray squirrel, ruffed grouse, or rabbit. He also ran a twenty-five-mile-long trap line and caught weasels, muskrats, and raccoon; although later in life he would disavow trapping.

In his biography, *Sun Bear: The Path of Power,* the medicine man writes about his overriding memory of those early years. "The thing I loved most at White Earth was the land. The gently rolling hillsides were very green in summer, and snow-covered in winter. I loved to sit under the trees, to watch the snow come swirling out of the clouds. The fall was beautiful with all the red oak trees, and when we walked through the woods, kicking up the leaves, we'd see the gray squirrels scurry up into the branches. . . . To me, that is true wealth . . . sitting on the Earth Mother . . . seeing, smelling, tasting the freshness of it all. It was at that early age when I first realized what nature is all about."

In the summer of 1944, when Vincent turned fifteen, he left the reservation with several neighbor boys in search of adventure. From spring through fall, he toiled as a farmhand in the grain fields of North Dakota, hauling and stacking wheat and oats for the trip to market. When the snows of winter forced it, he returned home to Minnesota. But having tasted freedom, the young man was off again at the first thaw. Over the next few years, Vincent kept moving, usually stopping only long enough to earn some money picking potatoes, cooking for a railroad, working in a bakery, even landscaping a cemetery. At the age of eighteen, he made his first visit to Los Angeles but found the city disconcerting. There was too much noise and clatter for someone reared on the land. His stay in the burgeoning postwar metropolis was short, but he would be back. In 1948, he hitchhiked north, stopping in Fargo, North Dakota, where at the age of nineteen he took a job as a real estate salesman and fell in love. When the love affair turned sour, the young man headed east to Kentucky, where he landed a job in a cigarette factory.

By the time Vincent returned home to Minnesota in 1950, the Korean War was in full swing. Advised by friends and relatives to enlist to avoid the draft, he decided first to appeal to the draft board to grant him conscientious objector status. The refusal was prompt. Despite serious doubts about his ability to be an obedient soldier, he nevertheless joined the army and was shipped off to Fort Chaffee, Arkansas, for basic training.

Boot camp forced the young Chippewa to reexamine his life. The great visions that would steer his life in unforeseen directions were still years in the future. But some things became very clear during those weeks of arduous army training. Paramount was the realization that there was simply no way he could go and kill Koreans in Korea. He was sick with the thought, miserable and feeling trapped. So, on the ninetieth day of his military career, heart pounding, he left his post on the base. For the next four years he lived life on the run.

Having rejected the white man's war, he found himself drawn ever more deeply into the waiting arms of Indian spirituality and culture. And as he followed that path, he abandoned his "white" name in favor of his Indian name—Sun Bear. He got a ride first to North Dakota, back to the land that he knew, where he earned enough money by doing odd jobs to buy a rusty, old car. Motoring eastward, he soon ran out of money in Omaha, Nebraska, and ended up on skid row. There he met a large number of other Indians, many of whom were lost in the bottle. Young, healthy, and willing to work, it was not long before the Chippewa from White Earth found a job at a wholesale market. There, he met two Winnebago Indian brothers who were members of the Native American church.

As part of their sacrament, members of the Native American church ingest peyote. The practice is an ancient one, dating back at least to the Mayan Chilam, or "prophet," priests. Use of the hallucinogenic north of the Rio Grande River began with the Indians of Texas. By the 1870s, it had spread to the Mescalero Apaches of Arizona; and to the Kiowa and Comanche, who popularized it throughout the plains. On October 10, 1918, the state of Oklahoma issued a certificate of incorporation for the Native American church to founder Quanah Parker. Since then, the church has become the fastest growing spiritual movement among Native Americans in the U.S. and Canada.

Church members have frequently been forced to battle for their freedom of religion in court. Until recently, the right to use peyote had always been upheld. But in April 1990, the United States Supreme Court delivered the church a crushing blow when it ruled that states may ban the use of peyote without violating the constitutional right of freedom of religion. To Native Americans, the court's ruling is only the latest in a long series of attacks meant to amputate their spirituality.

Sun Bear, however, did not need to have anyone explain the church to him. When the brothers invited him to participate, he readily agreed. The peyote meeting was at the home of an Omaha Indian by the name of Ballantine Parker and got underway around 9 P.M. More than a dozen other Omahas and Winnebagos were present and they welcomed their Chippewa brother to share in the sacrament. After eating some of the dried, green buttons, Sun Bear embarked upon a journey that included an intense feeling of oneness with all creation. Spurred on by the rhythmic beating of a drum, each of those present chanted and prayed in turn, asking for the Great Spirit's intervention in problems large and small. Sun Bear fell into a visionary trance in which he saw through the eyes of an eagle soaring high above a lake. The ceremonial singing and praying lasted through the night and ended at dawn.

In later years, Sun Bear would share the energy of the dried buttons a few more times with other members of the Native American Church. "The peyote is a healer both spiritually and physically," he says in *Sun Bear: The Path of Power*. "But it is a sacrament and, I feel, should be used only ceremonially under the direction of people who have been properly trained in its use. Otherwise you don't get the full power of it. Taking it by yourself isn't the same, and I don't recommend it as a thing to play around with."

Although his experience with the church proved powerful, what left a more indelible mark on him were the Omaha and Winnebago people themselves. "The whole way that they treat each other," he reminisces. "As brother and sister, always with great respect and always gentle and giving each other gifts. I learned from them how a person's religion or philosophy reflects how they treat other people."

Sun Bear eventually left Nebraska and traveled with a Winnebago Indian named Willard LaMere to Wichita, Kansas, where they staged Indian dances twice a month with a powwow club known as the Wichita Warriors. Native Americans from many different tribes residing in the former Indian Territory of Oklahoma poured north along the highway into Wichita for the dances, providing the Chippewa an opportunity to meet a colorful cross section of his people.

A few months later, Sun Bear and LaMere bought an old Chevy sedan and drove to Phoenix, Arizona, where they visited LaMere's relatives and spent some time at the Phoenix Indian Center. Then they headed south to the Papago Reservation. When trouble broke out there, Sun Bear assisted some of the local forces of good citizens in kicking a gang of drug runners and criminals off the reservation. Later, the bad guys got him back when they caught him walking alone in the desert, dragged him to a mesquite tree, and tied him by his thumbs to an upper branch. He dangled there with his toes barely touching the ground for several hours before his friends rescued him. His thumbs still bear scars from the torture.

From the Papago Reservation, it was on to Las Vegas to unload boxcars, landscape another cemetery, and wash cars. They traveled north to Reno, and after a short time, the friends went their separate ways.

Sun Bear followed the setting sun into California, where he found work picking strawberries. When his funds were replenished, he drifted a bit before landing near the town of Sebastapol, northwest of San Francisco. There, he got a job in an apple cannery. Living in a nearby trailer park, Sun Bear sought out the local Pomo Indians whose families had inhabited the coastal area for centuries. One he met was an artist named James who taught him about the Pomo's Bear Medicine Society. Another was an attractive Pomo girl with whom the young traveler revived his then-sporadic love life. Rejuvenated, he soon moved on to the Feather River country, where he studied with the medicine chief of the Wichipek tribe.

"I was traveling around and learning," says Sun Bear. "If some-body gave me a job painting a house, I painted the house. If I was stacking hay bales out in the fields, that was what I was doing at the time. I was just living. And to me, that's the way a person has to learn. I don't believe you've got a right to teach people about life unless you know about it. Any medicine person that I know really has to have balance by actually experiencing life first."

Luckily, alcohol has never held much of an attraction. "I was usually looking after my friends, making sure they got home okay after they drank too much," he explains in a somber tone. "I never liked the feeling of losing control of myself, so I didn't get drunk. Maybe if I had a couple of drinks, that was it. I used to like to drink blackberry brandy or something like that. I always liked something that tasted good. But I never could handle tequila or whiskey. Who'd want to drink that stuff? It tastes nasty!"

In 1954, Sun Bear headed east to Nevada where he stayed for a while with a cousin and dabbled in acting at an arts program conducted by the Reno Sparks Indian Colony. Comprised of Washo, Paiute, and Shoshone people, the colony, like most reserva-tions, was a poverty-stricken place. Institutionalized racism per-vaded Nevada at the time. Signs that read, "No Indians Allowed" were posted near the doors of a lot of restaurants and other estab-lishments. Sun Bear certainly experienced a great deal of racist treatment. But he also encountered decent, unbiased white people like those of the Nevada Historical Society and the folks at the Salvation Army, who helped him through the winter when he could not find work.

The spring of 1955 saw Sun Bear on the move again. In desper-ate need of a job, and being sought by the FBI as a deserter from the army, he headed back to the Golden State, where he happened into a job as a bit-player in Hollywood westerns. Introduced to the assistant producer of CBS's "Brave Eagle" television series, Sun Bear waited out a strike by the Screen Actor's Guild, then went to work. Aside from his small roles in "Brave Eagle" portraying war-riors on horseback or the occasional medicine man, he was also given the title of technical director. In that capacity, he was respon-sible for making sure the scripts and staging were as authentic as possible.

After "Brave Eagle" was canceled, Sun Bear returned to the

Reno Sparks Indian Colony to organize a series of self-help projects. One was to paint all eighty-seven houses in the settlement. With publicity from a columnist at the *Los Angeles Mirror-News,* paint donated by the Paramount Paint Company, free trucking to haul the supplies from Los Angeles to Reno, and the participation of dozens of volunteers, that is just what happened. The local alcoholics, and even the painter's union joined the bandwagon. Once the painting was completed and the trash hauled away, everyone was feeling better.

Then, while reroofing a building in Sparks, Nevada, Sun Bear was finally arrested by two FBI agents. At his court-martial, his army-appointed defense counsel, Major David S. Padnitz, displayed remarkable sensitivity toward the Chippewa deserter's situation. The attorney argued that during his period of desertion Sun Bear had not sought to enrich himself or lose himself in debauchery, but instead "went out to study the Indian problem . . . and he did help the Indians." Fearing a possible prison term of up to twenty years, Sun Bear was rather relieved when, after the tribunal found him guilty, he was sentenced to one year in prison at hard labor and given a bad conduct discharge.

Six months later, due in large part to the intercession of Nevada's Democratic Congressman Walter Baring, he was released on parole. Flown back to Reno, he was warmly received by his Native American friends and thanked them for their support. Yet, above all others, there was one friend he wanted to thank the most. As night fell, he drove into the desert, stripped off all his clothes, made an offering, and rubbed himself all over with wild sage and brown earth. He gave thanks to the Earth Mother for her eternal goodness and wonder. He prayed to the Great Spirit to purge him of bitterness and make him worthy of the support so many had extended to him. With the dawn, the Native man felt a strong sense of renewal.

Broke and with few prospects for a decent job in Reno, Sun Bear headed back to Hollywood in 1957. The connections he had made during his work in "Brave Eagle" served him well. Over the next eleven years, he worked fairly regularly in television and the movies, doing bit parts with no dialog, often riding a horse. His first job after his return was with Twentieth Century Fox's "Broken Arrow" television series. Aside from Indian roles, which were his staple, he was cast in a variety of character roles. In one episode of "Wagon Train," he played a Mexican bandito attacking a stage carrying Debbie Reynolds. In the series "Desert Rats," he portrayed an Arab camel herder. In "Hawaiian Eye," he was an oxen driver. With a change of wardrobe, he became a Cossack in the movie *Taras Bulba.* And in *Spartacus,* he played several different parts, including a bearded Jew. He built up an impressive résumé over the years. Among his other television credits as either actor, extra, or technical director are "Rawhide," "Bonanza," "Daniel Boone," "Cheyenne," "The Rifleman," "Maverick," and "Adventures in Paradise." As for the movies, he can still be seen in old reruns of *The Greatest Story Ever Told, The Story of Ruth, Comanche Station,* and Blake Edward's *What Did You Do During the War, Daddy?*

Throughout this period, Sun Bear remained actively involved in Native American affairs. Through the Los Angeles Indian Center, he helped to solicit donations of food and clothing for the hundreds of destitute Indians from throughout the nation who had ended up in the city. Many tribes were represented in Los Angeles then, with especially large concentrations of Navajos, Blackfoot, and Lakotas. With little if any economic opportunity on the reservations, and in some cases, with no reservation at all, many of them had migrated into an even more desperate situation. There was no food stamp program then; no government medical aid. Strangers in their own land, too many ended up losing all sense of self and wasted their days in alcohol-induced stupors.

Although he was never a household name, Sun Bear's face was recognizable to many due to his on-screen performances. Because of this semicelebrity status, the Los Angeles Indian Center would send him out to speak about Native American concerns. He spoke to Quakers, Jaycees, and Kiwanas clubs, and managed to raise funds, especially around the holidays. Still, there was much bigotry and ignorance to confront.

"One time I was talking at a Kiwanas Club," says Sun Bear. "And this guy got up and said, 'I don't know what you Indians are complaining about. We give you free land.' I said, 'Whose land did you give us? They took all the land. If I come up and stick a gun at the back of your head and say, I want all of your money, and I take thousands of dollars from your pocket, then you say, here, I want to be good to you. I want to give you five bucks to go home on. Would you be happy? That's what has happened to the Indian.' And that guy had no response.''

Sun Bear's activism naturally led him into politics. In 1957 the Eastside Democratic Club elected him vice president, and the following year he hitchhiked to Washington, D.C., wearing a warbonnet and carrying a poster that read, "Have Blanket, Will Travel." His publicity stunt gained a fair amount of media coverage in newspapers along the way and Sun Bear used every opportunity to lobby for Native issues including more reservation housing. Unfortunately, he could do little more than chip away at President Eisenhower's anti–Native American policies. In 1960, he served on the endorsement committee of John F. Kennedy's campaign for president. But by and large, Sun Bear has been disappointed with politicians time and again and especially reviles former President Reagan for his total ignorance of Indian issues.

"President Johnson, with his War on Poverty, was one of the best shots to do some real good things for Native people," Sun Bear says in a rapid-fire voice. "Most of the time the approach is of big city people trying to tell people who are trying to be on the earth how to live and not understanding the fact that Native people want to be Indians.''

Upon leaving Washington, D.C., Sun Bear took a side trip to New York City. There in the megalopolis, he met a dark-haired, blue-eyed artist by the name of Betty Bernstein and fell in love. After a month, they took summer jobs as counselors at a camp for kids in the Catskills called Bass Lake Farm.

At the end of the summer of 1959, Sun Bear and Betty set off on a cross-country trip in an old panel truck and, after stopping in Minnesota, ended up once again in Los Angeles. Unable to find work at the time in film or television, Sun Bear got a job managing a Christmas tree lot near the old MGM studios. And it was there, in the back of the panel truck, that their daughter Winona LaDuke was conceived.

It was not long before Sun Bear was once again employed as an actor. In his spare time, while Betty went back to college to obtain her teaching certificate, he became involved again with the Indian

Center and a group called the Federated Indian Tribes. The federation was made up of Indians from all over the country who abstained from alcohol and were trying to restore the traditional way of life. The leader of the group was a medicine man named Doc Spotted Wolf, who was also a practicing medical doctor. Doc had built a sweat lodge in his backyard and there, concealed from the prying eyes of nosey neighbors, the group held ceremonies and shared knowledge.

By this time, Sun Bear's own philosophy had coalesced into the belief that "power can be a quiet thing."

"It's the strong, gentle people who really are giving something to humanity rather than the loud noisemakers," he points out in an interview with the author. "The loud noisemakers, we allow them to bully us into doing things often in life. These are the politicians and others who are always pushing. But they are not really the people who help others most. It isn't the loudest or the noisiest, but rather the person who sits quietly and in a sacred manner."

Once Winona was born, Sun Bear spent more time around the house helping with the housework and taking care of the baby. The macho concept of "women's work" had no meaning for him. Besides, while Betty was studying, he had time to teach his daughter about the earth. The intelligent little girl learned quickly. "Once," the medicine man relates, "when she was about three years old, we were up at the Grand Canyon. Whenever I would come to a place to camp, I would pick up all of the paper and trash. People would leave newspapers, toilet paper, and paper plates, and I would use them to start my campfire. Winona was used to seeing me clean up everything around the campsites. She'd help, too, by going and picking up cans and everything. So one day, these people came along and started kicking garbage out of their car onto the ground. Winona walked right up to them, this little three-year-old girl, and she said, 'My daddy don't like it when people put garbage on the earth.' And they picked up the garbage, put it back in their car, and left. I was proud of her," he adds. "Children have to grow up with this sense of consciousness for the earth."

Betty was offered a teaching position at Southern Oregon State College at Ashland soon after graduation and decided to accept. Sun Bear, however, had other plans. So the couple separated, with

Winona going with her mother. Betty became a professor of art. Little Winona went on to graduate from Harvard, become an activist in the Native rights and antinuclear movements, a principal of an alternative high school on the White Earth Reservation, and director of the Land Recovery Project.

Now that he had something to say, Sun Bear began to seek the proper forum. In 1961, he made his first foray into publishing with *Many Smokes,* a newsletter published in Los Angeles. Targeted at Native Americans, the paper featured notices of weddings, births, and upcoming powwows and sold for only fifteen cents. As time went on, the focus would change to earth awareness, self-reliance, and other issues of national and international importance. *Many Smokes* would also provide an important outlet for the concerns of other Native American writers. Except for two and a half years in the mid-sixties, and a brief respite in the early seventies, publication has been continuous ever since.

After Betty left with Winona, Sun Bear sought to establish an inner-city Indian center. He was given the use of a house in Altadena, a suburb of Los Angeles. But the dream soon spun out of control and evolved into a half-way house where alcoholism and strife among the residents overwhelmed all hopes for what might have been. Around this same time, Sun Bear also took over an automobile service station. But he had spread himself too thin. By 1964, he had lost his investment in the service station. And his ardor for acting had cooled. So he left Los Angeles and moved back to Reno.

While there, Sun Bear gambled a bit. Gambling has been a Native American sport dating back at least to the Classic Maya. To Sun Bear, it was natural to work on his "gambling medicine" whenever he was in Nevada. In fact, in 1983 he claimed to have won sixteen thousand dollars up to that point in his life. "I didn't have gambling fever, like so many people get," he writes in his biography. "I could take the dice or leave them. It just felt really good, bringing in big chunks of green energy, one after another. Medicine power is good for all things, you see; if the Great Spirit wants me to win at craps or keno, I figure who am I to turn down the opportunity?"

Dream of the Numbers

One night in May of 1965, Sun Bear was asleep in his bed when he had a prophetic dream about the game of keno. In the dream, he saw specific numbers. The next day, after awakening, he went to the Cal Neva casino and played the numbers. All but one of the eight hit—winning him a jackpot of $1,100. It was not the first time and it would not be the last that Sun Bear would listen to his dreams.

Flush with "green energy," Sun Bear headed to Berkeley to check out the Free Speech movement in the summer of 1965. Berkeley was a heady place in those days. The Vietnam War was taking the lives of thousands of American boys and polarized politics, free love, and drugs were pillars of the day. Although Sun Bear indulged in the political debate, and the make-love-not-war atmosphere, he avoided drugs. The ceremonial use of peyote, as part of a religious experience, he understood. But he had observed that the use of LSD and marijuana, on the other hand, were too often crutches used to irresponsibly escape the hard battles of life. And Sun Bear wanted to change society, not hide from it.

Bit by bit, Sun Bear was clarifying his vision. Increasingly, he felt he wanted to bring together a group of people made up of all races to live and work together in a single place. Upon that base, a community would be built that would work for the healing of human beings and the earth. But how could he turn such a vision into reality?

One important piece of the machine fell into place when Sun Bear met Annie Ross at a party in Berkeley. A gentle and attractive journalism student who would become Sun Bear's principal partner in the years to come, Annie entered with a man on each arm. Sun Bear was taken by her and she was encouraging of his vision. The two linked up and traveled for a while, to Reno, then to L.A., then back to Reno where they rented an apartment and revived *Many Smokes.* Before long, she took on the name Nimimosha; Chippewa for "woman with a heart of love." To supplement their income, she went to work as a receptionist while Sun Bear drove a cab and worked on his gambling medicine.

Then one day Sun Bear was offered a job by the Intertribal

Council of Nevada as a community development specialist for the Reno Sparks Indian Colony. It was a dream come true to finally be able to help better the lot of his Native brothers and sisters with government matching funds from the Office of Economic Opportunity (O.E.O.). Sun Bear's first project was to organize the disposal of the colony's household trash. Then he built a park, put in a water and sewer system, and transformed two old church buildings into an Indian center. The O.E.O. bureaucrats who oversaw his work were impressed by his commitment and energy.

Sun Bear was then approached by the owner of a trailer park in nearby Sun Valley and offered the entire operation at a very low price. Sun Bear was tired of apartment living, and after he'd consulted with Nimimosha, he and the seller agreed to terms. It was not long before he realized why the old landlord had sold out so easily: There were problems galore with tenants who would skip out without paying rent and steal anything that was not nailed down. Two women once rented a trailer and returned with four roommates who were members of the Misfits motorcycle gang. The din their "hogs" produced was disturbing enough. But when a contingent of Hells Angels swooped in to settle a grudge, only the Misfit's absence and Sun Bear's quick thinking averted violence.

Hippies began arriving at the trailer court wanting to study with Sun Bear, and he was loath to turn them away. Over the years, he had come to the belief that if anyone came to him and sincerely wanted to learn the medicine ways, he would teach them no matter what color their skin. He even arranged to reduce trailer rent for some. But few of the flower-power people were willing to take responsibility for their lives, let alone the earth. The length of their hair, getting stoned, and haunting the hippy hangouts of Reno was of far more interest. Sadly, Sun Bear saw that the road to realizing his vision of a dedicated community would be a long and rocky one. Kindly but firmly, he kicked the hippies out.

The work for the Intertribal Council, meanwhile, was going exceedingly well. Before long, Sun Bear was promoted to supervisor of community developers, responsible for programs on twenty-three reservations throughout Nevada. His job required him to travel throughout the state and he enjoyed that. Not everyone he met liked him, though. Once, in Elko, Nevada, Sun Bear walked into a tavern and ordered a Coke. Moments later, he was insulted and punched in the mouth by a big fellow who ran the local stock-yard. Refusing to be drawn into a brawl, Sun Bear mopped up his bloody lip in the rest room. When he returned to the bar, his attacker had gone. The man made it his business to punch Indians around, Sun Bear was told. He had been encouraged by the fact that no one had ever dared to press charges. But he had never before encountered Sun Bear. Eventually, the bigot was arrested, tried, and found guilty. He received a five hundred dollar fine and a six-month suspended sentence.

Sun Bear was promoted to the position of economic develop-ment specialist in 1968 and charged with bringing industry and employment to the reservations of Nevada. The position, however, was a desk job that involved a lot of writing of grant applications and intercession with the Bureau of Indian Affairs (B.I.A.). Neither was much to Sun Bear's liking. One project that did turn out well involved the Paiutes on the Moapa Reservation. The tribe had been leasing 570 acres of prime agricultural land to a dairy. The lease, worked out by the B.I.A., generated only twenty-one hundred dollars a year for the tribe. Sun Bear encouraged the Paiutes not to renew it, and they followed his advice. With an eighty-thousand dollar loan arranged in cooperation with officials of the Mormon church, they created employment for their people and built a prof-itable, working farm.

In the summer of 1969, Sun Bear resigned from the Intertribal Council and accepted a position offered by Jack Forbes of the University of California at Davis to help develop a Native Ameri-can Studies Program. Sun Bear thought it would be a good way to educate not only his Indian brothers and sisters but also white students about Native culture. At the same time, he was assisting a group of Native American and Chicano students with an experi-mental college named Deganawidah Quetzalcoatl University in an abandoned air force base in Winters, California. After about three months of teaching journalism and Native American philosophy at Davis, the faculty pushed him out. Despite the fact that he was the publisher of *Many Smokes* and had put out his first book, *At Home In The Wilderness,* the year before, they objected to an Indian with only an eighth-grade education teaching at their university.

The late sixties was a period of widespread social upheaval and soon it spread to the Native American community. In late November 1969, seventy-eight Indian activists occupied Alcatraz Island off San Francisco in an angry attempt to draw the world's attention toward the plight of Native Americans. Outrage over how Indians in the United States were being treated fueled the occupation to the point that after a month more than fifty tribes were represented at the abandoned prison. In his capacity as publisher of *Many Smokes,* Sun Bear, accompanied by Nimimosha, drove to San Francisco and interviewed the radicals. It did not take long to see that the occupiers had not thought through the practical considerations. The island had no fertile soil, no potable water, not even any food.

Though *Many Smokes* printed a number of articles supportive of the activists' demands, Sun Bear came to feel quite strongly that the way to improve things was not through anger and hostility but through love and harmony. "To walk in balance," as he would come to say, "in a sacred manner on Mother Earth."

A core of students from the experimental college who were interested in alternative life-styles and Sun Bear's ideas of an "international community" began meeting with him regularly after he returned from Alcatraz. Their desire to know of Native American ways was sincere, and Sun Bear had long been committed to sharing with anyone who was serious in wanting to know medicine ways. His vision was emerging ever more clearly

Sun Bear's Vision

I saw earthquakes and cities where they were no longer functional. Nothing was happening there. Cars were rusted. Very powerful things had happened. Spirit told me that I should go out and start teaching people about coming back to harmony, understanding the powers and forces around us. I started teaching these things. How to survive in a sacred manner.

I was told to do this, so first I went out teaching these things to people who were interested in coming and living with me, permanently, and being part of the Bear Tribe. Spirit said, no that's not enough. You got to go out and lecture all over the world, wherever people will have you. Wherever you are invited. Because the only place you can go is where you're invited. Because if you go some-places before you're invited, you're sticking your nose in other people's business.

Spirit told me that I should reach out to share with people, but they shouldn't be drawn to me out of fear. People who come to this should be reaching for a higher level of consciousness. Because that's what it's about. It's processing time upon the planet. The people who are going to be getting through into the Fifth World are the people who have reached a higher level of consciousness and wanting to live in and be part of a better world. To have a better world, you have to have a better people.

Through the heartfelt discussions that followed Sun Bear's elucidation of his vision, a surprising degree of unanimity emerged. Word of mouth brought others from the Davis area and beyond who wanted to join the experimental community. As the movement's spokesman, Sun Bear had by definition become a prophet. His ideas of a better way of living energized the group.

A milestone was reached on winter's solstice, 1970, when upon a piece of loaned land in Placerville, California, Sun Bear extinguished the camp fires, relit them ritualistically, thanked the sun for earth's renewal and the gift of life, then inducted twenty people including himself as members of a new, intentional community of like-minded people called the Bear Tribe. The name Bear Tribe had been chosen not only because it referred to Sun Bear's cognomen, but also because the bear is a sacred medicine animal with strength and endurance to the Chippewa and other Native American peoples. Assisted by his medicine helper, Tommy Gun, a Flathead Indian from Montana, Sun Bear led the tribe in prayer and chants. After they cleansed themselves in the sweat lodge there was a feast and singing:

> Kee ay wahtay lenyo lenyo mohoytay
> Hiano hiano hiano
> Kee ay wahtay lenyo lenyo mohotay
> Hiano hiano hiano
> We are one with the infinite sun
> Forever and ever and ever
> We are one with the infinite sun
> Forever and ever and ever

The motivation behind creating such an organization was simple. "The reason the Bear Tribe came into existence," Sun Bear says, "is that when a medicine man or woman has more work than he or she can do by themselves, they have to create a medicine society of people who can help them do the work: people who are committed to the same direction and purpose."

Word spread quickly through the counterculture of the founding of the Bear Tribe. Sun Bear began to receive invitations to speak at schools and churches and other gatherings. Jerry Garcia and the New Riders of the Purple Sage, Country Joe, and other bands staged a benefit in San Francisco for the Bear Tribe and called it Mother Earth Rock. The *Berkeley Barb* and other underground newspapers ran stories on the Bear Tribe. Quicker than you can say, "psycadelicized," some two hundred had joined and were reestablishing their personal ties to nature in seventeen camps in California.

"I believed in the tribe so much that I took all of the money I had saved and used it to support the tribe," says Sun Bear in *The Path of Power.* "I even sold some of the trailers in Reno to supply more money when it was needed. I purchased food, and sleeping bags, sometimes for people who were missing them simply because they had forgotten where they left them. I fixed cars, bought gas, paid for postage and phone calls. Some of the other people with me also put in their money to support the tribe. Nimimosha was even willing to stay in Reno most of the time, running the trailer court, so that we could have the income from that."

In the summer of 1971, Sun Bear, Nimimosha, and Caron Klare, who had taken on the name Morning Star, set out on a cross-country speaking tour. Problems at the trailer court soon forced Nimimosha to return to Reno, however, and the reports Sun Bear was receiving from the tribe's camps were worrisome. By the time he returned in late summer, Sun Bear found the communities in chaos. Interpersonal squabbles and turf battles combined with rampant drug abuse had spawned oceans of irresponsible behavior.

The medicine man looks back ruefully: "I didn't have anyone with me who was organizationally minded. And I was all heart and no head. I thought everybody was going to come and live together, and share equally living upon the land. I thought they were going to live together sharing work as well as everything else. But the basic thing of it is that some people are willing to work hard, and some people want to sit and live off other people's work. That was a problem. A lot of people would show up at the breakfast table, but they weren't out there when it was time to pick fruit."

By November, Sun Bear had concluded that his social experiment was not going to work. The problem was in the irresponsible behavior of so many who were unable to raise their consciousness beyond drugs and petty jealousies. Throughout his life Sun Bear had had problems with people who could not manage to stay sober. But this topped them all. He told the two hundred that they were on their own and disbanded the first attempt at creating the Bear Tribe.

Broke and disillusioned, Sun Bear drove to a hill outside of Vacaville, California, climbed to the top, stripped off his clothes, and prayed and asked the Great Spirit for guidance. It was his practiced method in times of crisis. Marlise James, a New York writer who would join Sun Bear the following year, explains in the forward of Sun Bear's biography, *Sun Bear: The Path of Power,* what happened next:

Slowly, from the south, a golden eagle circled. It flew above the hilltop, circled lower and lower, closer to him. He raised his hands and watched the circling bird; it seemed the eagle's eyes were so close he could see into them, into the soul of this holy messenger. . . . The Indian prayed for guidance. He gave thanks for this holy sign; then, the eagle began to fly away. It circled higher and higher, and the man's face grew pained once again. The eagle disappeared. The man was thankful for the messenger; yet, the message still eluded him. He knew the eagle looked into his soul, even as he had looked into the bird's. He prayed again for direction, for another sign. From the southwest a great cloud materialized and moved toward him. The rest of the sky was clear. The Indian watched as the cloud grew in mass, in height, and hovered in white and dark texture above the hillside. The cloud sailed toward the northeast, and a small puff of it separated off from the rest and started to spin. It whirled faster and faster, and, as the Native watched it, his mind began to spin, back, back, back to the beginning, back to the beginning of the vision that brought him to this time and place. . . . The small cloud continued to spin, seemingly caught in a whirlwind of the heavens. It spun like his mind had a few minutes before; then, it separated in two. One piece evaporated into the sky; the other returned to the large cloud. The man knew this was his answer, this was how his vision would go on to fulfillment. His first attempt to form a tribe of medicine teachers who would help to bring balance and harmony back to the Earth Mother seemed to have failed. He knew know, however, that in time it would succeed.

Sun Bear retreated back to the trailer park in Sun Valley, Nevada, to ruminate. Nimimosha welcomed him, despite having developed a relationship with another man. Morning Star arrived shortly afterward and, along with a few others from California, concentrated on the production of *Many Smokes.* In January 1972, Marlise James arrived from New York to interview Sun Bear for a magazine article. The connection between her, Sun Bear, and the rest of the group was immediate. Sun Bear's vision of a world in balance sparked James's imagination like it had the others. Except everyone knew that if there was to be a next time, the key to success was in personal responsibility.

Holy Pyramid Lake, a sacred site to the Paiutes long before Wovoka's dances, was the chosen spot at which Marlise James was adopted as a full member of the tribe. She took on the name Wabun, which in Chippewa means Spirit Keeper of the East. For much of the next three years, she and Sun Bear traveled the pow-wow circuit of Native American dances and fairs, seeking out Indian brothers and sisters, reconnecting with old friends, while selling Native jewelry and craft items.

The winter of 1973 saw the Native American occupation of Wounded Knee. It was the eighty-third anniversary of the massacre of the half-starved and frozen Sioux ghost dancers and the spirit of the people had yet to recover. Sun Bear traveled to the Pine Ridge Reservation as publisher of *Many Smokes* and was allowed through the barricades by the FBI. They knew all about him; a worrisome prospect in itself. He interviewed those involved, ran stories in support of charges by the independent Oglala nation and the American Indian Movement (AIM) of murder, intimidation, and inhuman treatment. Though short-term gains were slight, the greatest accomplishment of the occupation that ended on May 8 was that it united young and old Sioux people as nothing else had in generations. That unity would reverberate positively for years to come.

All in all, though, Sun Bear was not an absolute supporter of the violent confrontation. When you are angry, he maintains, you give away your power. He argues instead for peace and harmony with Mother Earth.

It had become clear by this time that in order for the Bear Tribe to gain any stability and long-term influence, a piece of land would have to be found that could be called their own. So, after a thorough discussion with his people, Sun Bear traded the Sun Valley trailer park for eleven acres of land near Los Gatos, California. When it was learned, too late, that the land was sitting on a major earthquake fault, he sold it.

Dream of Spirit Mountain

> I had a dream at night in which I saw a mountain with great rocks on it and big trees and ponds and water. And the Spirit told me that this is the place we had to move to because this would be the place that we would have water and be able to produce food when other people would be starving in other parts of the world.

Sun Bear had a prophetic dream about a mountain on which the tribe would build its base camp. That dream set the band into motion. It was a hopeful time full of bright optimism when six adults, one child, and a dog loaded into a car and an old yellow truck and headed north into Oregon searching for their Shangri-La. During the next year and a half, living on ten loaned acres near Klamath Falls that belonged to a remaining member of the Klamath tribe, the Bear Tribe publicized Edison Chiloquin's land fight with the U.S. Forest Service. Meanwhile, Sun Bear incorporated the Bear Tribe as a 501(c)3 nonprofit organization, making it the first Native American medicine society ever granted that designation.

Unable to get the Forest Service to budge, and having more dreams about the mountain, Sun Bear once again pushed the tribe onto the road. They drove to Seattle, back to Oregon, then on to northern Idaho hunting for their mountain. No spot felt just right.

But when the caravan arrived in the Spokane, Washington region, a warm, abiding feeling came over Sun Bear. He knew they were close. Then one day, checking out an ad in a local newspaper, he found the mountain with the rocks and water he had seen in his dream. The tribe's first purchase in 1978 was eighteen and a half acres. Later, he learned that the peak had been sacred to the Spokane Indians for hundreds of years. And that its name, loosely translated, is Vision Mountain.

•

"Up here, it's teeming with wildlife," Sun Bear points out to a visitor as they walk along a worn path to a house trailer that serves as the educational center. "You see many things up on our mountain. Because we love them, you see more birds and butterflies and all sorts of living things. These creatures are here because we respect them. There's deer all around. It's like the Garden of Eden."

Nearly fifteen years have passed since the Bear Tribe Medicine Society arrived. During that time, Sun Bear and his merry band of teachers have made remarkable progress toward realizing his vision. More land has been purchased and now totals eighty acres. But Sun Bear is not the owner.

"I don't think I have a right to own the land," he states flatly. "Nobody has a right to own the land. I believe what I have belongs to the Great Spirit and Mother Earth. I have a right to use it. And so I felt very strongly that it should belong to a nonprofit group, namely the Bear Tribe, rather than myself."

The mountain sits on the edge of the Columbia Basin high desert, east of the Cascades, where rainfall averages eighteen inches a year. Farthest up a winding mountain road is the Longhouse. Nestled amongst the ponderosas and overgrown natural vegetation, the metal-roofed homestead has been expanded twice over the years and today is home for many of the society's twenty current members. At the end of the porch running the length of the structure is the "earth changes storage shed," with its stockpile of beans, grains, and a special purple barley from Egypt. In the other direction, a path leads from the Longhouse to the education center, a hundred yards away. The loudest sound here is the wind rustling the trees. Chickens, four dogs, two cats, and two sows litter the area in between along with a number of small wooden buildings. About a mile down the mountain is the lower farm, where a two-acre organic garden abuts a small clapboard house and a large tipi.

If the Longhouse is the heart of the tribe, then the Circle Center is the brain. Located fifty miles away in a transitional neighborhood near downtown Spokane, the center is where most of the programs, activities, and workshops sponsored by the Bear Tribe Medicine Society are organized. Installed here is the wholly-owned Turtle Island Bookstore, as well as the offices of *Wildfire* magazine, the glossy-cover quarterly that in 1984 grew out of *Many Smokes.*

"Now I have a good, strong organization," the medicine man says proudly. "I have a very centered, hard-working group of people and we get a lot done because they want to do it. My feeling is that people should do things out of love and wanting to do it. That's what we've got now. People who have a sense of commitment, a permanent basis with us, and have a particular skill that fits in with what we're trying to do. In the Bear Tribe, we want people who are capable of carrying their own weight. That means if they're a part of us, when they're working with us, be willing to have a sense of commitment beyond themselves. To me, that's what the old tribal structure was all about. People who had a sense of giving of their energy toward helping something beyond themselves. To me, that's true spirituality. That's what I'm reaching for in the tribe."

An increasingly large number of compatriots live either on adjacent tracts of land on Spirit Mountain or nearby. Most are Sun Bear's apprentices. They participate in events with the regular members and work with the tribe on different ideas and projects. Others visit just for the pipe ceremonies and sweat lodges.

Monthly, the Bear Tribe Medicine Society's board of directors meets at the Circle Center in Spokane. As chairman of the board, Sun Bear conducts the meetings when present. When he is not, Executive Director Beth Davis is in charge. Aside from the income Sun Bear receives from his books, and occasional residuals from past TV shows and movies, he receives a stipend of one hundred dollars a month. Many other members of the tribe work on the same basis. "I get my room and board if I'm here," says the medicine man. "Or if I'm out on the road, my expenses are covered. Then all the rest of the money goes to the Bear Tribe. We use it to make the payments on the land, or build the buildings that we need, or for covering whatever else is needed. We have animals and people to feed. Books to publish. We have a structure. We have a person who counts the money—a bookkeeper—and so forth. Makes sure it goes in the right place. Some years back we were audited by the I.R.S. to see if we were doing everything we claimed to be doing. And we came out clean. They told us that we could become a church or continue as we are, either one."

Medicine society members who live in some place other than the longhouse or another facility owned by the corporation get a larger stipend because they rent houses and have other kinds of expenses. "We have to pay for our cars to run back and forth and all the rest of that stuff," says Sun Bear, adding with a laugh: "But I haven't seen any of them driving any Rolls Royces! I don't think they're taking any money away!

"I feel that a person can eat only one meal at a time, sleep only in one bed at a time, and that's about all you're going to get out of it anyhow. So why get into big amounts of money stashed around?"

Sun Bear's books have been translated into German, Dutch, Greek, and Turkish. The German following is undoubtedly the largest outside of the United States and may, in fact, eclipse it in size.

"I had a feeling that with the kind of message he has, that he was going to be successful," says Erica Malitzky, RN, aka Thunderbird Woman, a German member of the tribe who accompanied Sun Bear on his first trip to Germany. "Because in Europe, and especially in Germany, a lot of people are interested in Native Americans. Why that is, I don't know," she adds with a laugh.

The Green environmental movement, born as a political movement in Germany, shares Sun Bear's attitude toward the earth. Both appeal to the traditional German love of nature. "Native American philosophy has the tendency to tell people that we have to go back to nature," Thunderbird Woman continues. "Work with nature, rather than against it. The movement has always been strongest in West Germany. It is now strong in other countries, too. There are a lot of people working for Sun Bear in the Netherlands, in England, and Switzerland."

When Sun Bear first went to Germany, he presented two sold-out lectures in Vlotho. After a couple of days, he felt so closed in in the superurbanized environment that he asked someone drive him to the Black Forest. There, to the amazement and admiration of many Germans, he hugged a fir tree until he felt himself recharged with natural energy.

"The Europeans have been industrialized up to their eyebrows and they're looking for a breath of fresh air," says Sun Bear. "They're looking for reality and spirituality. They haven't found that in old religions, by that I mean Catholicism and Lutheranism. They've also looked and seen all of the bigotry and arrogance in them. Those religions have been used as a whip over the people rather than a way of teaching them. To me, I believe people should come to spirituality out of love rather than out of fear."

Living communally and following a charismatic leader has not, however, made the members into mindless automatons. When asked if they are, Sun Bear finds the question humorous.

"People who have been with the tribe for long periods of time are now in other parts of the country. They still work with us and most are still members of the tribe. One of them is becoming a doctor. I encourage them. We encourage them to use the knowledge we give them to grow. It's not a cult that locks people into little boxes with all the 'Thou Shalt Nots.' We don't hold them prisoner. They're here to learn and take the knowledge with them and use it in the world.

"Native spirituality is one of empowerment," he declares with conviction, "empowering the individual, teaching them how to come into their fullest sense of power. In Native religion, you're taught to go out and fast, and pray, and find out what your purpose in life is supposed to be. To have a vision. In the other religions, they don't want you to go out and find out what you personally should do. They want you to listen to what they put in a little book, and obey that. Native spirituality helps you to become a whole, balanced human being. And it's a participatory religion. It isn't something where the preacher sits up there and points to the audience down there someplace. In it, each person is praying for themselves and taking responsibility for themselves. This is why I feel it is a very powerful thing.

"Religion is often used as a weapon over people," he continues. "And people murder other people because they don't believe the same way. To me, this is the difference between religion and spirituality. I see what's happened in Iran and some of these other places where the people are totally dogmatic. They put people in prison and exterminate them because they're following a different belief system. The only thing I'm afraid of is human conditioning. Human conditioning that has been built into people to where they march to anybody's tune. You had a man, Ayatollah Khomeini, who said Allah is on the other side of the mine fields. He marched off thousands of young people to slaughter."

Prophecy on Iran

Now I had this dream some time back. A very powerful dream. In the dream I saw a map of Iran, and the word vanished completely off of the map. Spirit told me that what would happen would be that Iran would be destroyed by its neighbors or by major earthquakes.

Sun Bear has also experienced dreams regarding future earthquakes in California. At a seminar in Malibu, California, on October 31, 1987, he addressed a room full of people and began by telling them, "The earth is an intelligent, living being! Before any major changes ever happen upon the Earth Mother, it's warned people. In 1973, there was a tidal wave off the coast of a country called Bangladesh. Before the wave the gurus and the holy men were telling the people, 'Move away from here, go far away! There's going to be a disaster! A big flood is coming through here!' And the people would say, 'No. You're just trying to get us to leave our land so your relatives can move in.' Two weeks later, the tidal wave hit and five hundred thousand people perished."

Then, he told the Californians what he foresaw for their state.

Prophecy of California Earthquakes

You're going to be seeing more major changes here. I have asked the Spirit about what is happening. I pray about areas, then do a dream ceremony. When I asked the Spirit about the earthquakes, and whether these things could be changed, and what would happen? Spirit said it's already sealed. It's already happening. You speak of sevens and eights on your Richter scale. We speak of tens and twelves.

"I've had dreams many times that have told me things. I've seen things ahead of time through dreams," he relates in the living room of the Longhouse.

Dream of the Burning Airplanes

On December 1, 1988, I had a dream in which I saw two airplanes catch fire in the sky and burn. I told my friend about it. Within three weeks, both of them had happened. One was Pam Am flight 103, [blown up by terrorists over Lockerbie, Scotland] and the other was that British Airlines airplane over London.

Though there is an obvious difference between dreams and visions, both can convey prophetic information. "A dream is something you have at night while you're sleeping," says Sun Bear. "A vision is something that you can have when you're just sitting, looking out. It can come at any time." These visions are directed by the Great Spirit. "Sometimes you have spirit helpers who help you bring your vision in. Visions aren't necessarily limited to Native Americans. All people can go out on vision quests. I think it's kind of powerful," he says.

In the late seventies, Sun Bear had another vision. This one was about the return of the ancient American medicine wheel.

Vision of the Medicine Wheel

I saw a circle of rocks on the top of a hill, and an inner circle. And I saw what I thought at first were animals coming to the circle. But as I watched, I saw they were human beings and they had on animal costumes. Wolf masks and stuff like that. As they came to the circle, a voice in the middle of them said, "Now comes the time for the return of the medicine wheels. Now comes the time for the healing of the Earth Mother."

Sun Bear shared this vision with his people. Out of it was born the Medicine Wheel Circle, a small wheel that explains earth astrology. Two years later, in 1980, Prentice-Hall published *The Medicine Wheel* as a book. That year the tribe held the first Medicine Wheel Gathering in a U.S. Forest Service campground at the base of Mount Rainier and Sun Bear lectured for the first time in Europe.

By the end of the 1980s, four or five gatherings were being held each year. The first one in Europe was held in 1990. Sun Bear explains: "We have maybe five hundred to one thousand people come, to learn and share with different Native and other spiritual teachers. This goes back to the ancient way. Because in the old way, there were some twenty thousand of these medicine wheel circles in North America. The same thing is over in Europe, at Stonehenge and so forth. These were places were people would gather for spiritual gatherings and they would do ceremonies there and share knowledge. The medicine people would open up their medicine bundles and different things and they would share how they used this herb or that plant for healing. Or what ceremony they did, or what prayers they felt were powerful. To heal or bring in the rain or whatever it was.

"Medicine Wheels are a way of bringing Native and non-Native people together to teach. Because we feel that this knowledge is what's going to heal the earth and bring us all back into balance," says the prophet.

Some of the prophecies that Sun Bear has related have already been fulfilled and proven frighteningly accurate. One of them involved a prophecy that is said to have been handed by Smoholla. In January 1979, not long after the Bear Tribe had *The Medicine Wheel* published and had relocated to Spirit Mountain, Donald Matheson, a leader of western Washington State's Puyallup tribe told Sun Bear that he was moving his people to Idaho.

Prophecy of the Volcanoes

He told them that the time had come for the fulfillment of the Indian prophecy. The prophecy he spoke of was one that said, "The time will come when Little Sister will speak, and Grandfather will answer. And the land will be swept clean to the ocean." In March 1980, the mountain that we call Little Sister began to whisper. May 18th of 1980, the Little Sister spoke with a cubic mile of mountain. A cubic mile of mountain that was spread over the northwest area, and many other parts of the world. . . . That was the Little Sister that was speaking to us. The Little Sister is called Mount St. Helens. Soon, the Grandfather is going to answer so much bigger. That one is called Mt. Rainer.

Two hundred and ninety miles away from the volcanic eruption, Sun Bear and the Bear Tribe members were hard at work on their mountain acreage. "We had made our prayers and planted our gardens," explains the medicine man. "We planted a pasture up there. And we were praying for rain, to drive the seed down into the pasture. Instead the creator did us one better. He gave us a half an inch of topsoil from the heavens! Then the rains came. We had the best crop we've ever had.

"Recreation of the earth!" says Sun Bear full of wonder. "To Native people, it was the Earth Mother doing a process of recreation. Earth Mother was rearranging the real estate!"

In the winter of 1980, Sun Bear had another powerful dream that would influence him greatly.

Dream of the Apprentices

I had a dream that the earth was dark. And every time I would point my finger, a light would come on. The lights were many different sizes, and shapes, and colors. I asked the creator spirit what these lights were. The spirit told me these were people who would come and study with me as apprentices. That they would be like bright lights in the universe during the changes.

Out of Sun Bear's dream came the apprentice program. Begun in 1982, by the end of the decade some 550 people had gone through the ten-day intensive training program. They represent nearly every state in the nation and a good portion of the world, including Germany, Switzerland, Austria, France, England, the Netherlands, Canada, New Zealand, and Australia. Sun Bear explains to his visitors that the students "learn how to work with the pipe and the sweat lodge. They don't have the authority to do sweat lodges as a result of this training. But they learn how to do these things. Then they learn how I work with the Thunder Beings, call in the forces, the spirits and so forth. If they feel the spirits are open to them, they can work with these things. They learn, basically, preliminary self-reliance skills. How to find power spots on the earth and how to communicate with the earth and the forces around them. They also learn respect for the Native traditions, which is very important. The reason some non-Native people get into trouble with Native people is because they don't respect their traditions. They come into a Native ceremony and want to do their thing instead of sitting respectfully and learning what the Native thing is about.

"The apprentices are people who are full-time, long-term students with me who are growing in their power and knowledge in a sacred manner," he declares.

Early one Saturday in July 1989, Sun Bear led a caravan of three vehicles loaded with his latest batch of apprentices, a visiting writer, and Jaya, his lady of several years, on a field trip to harvest herbs. Off Route 2 near Davenport, under the sparkling pale blue, wide open skies of eastern Washington, Sun Bear halted the group. Everyone piled out. Across the fence was a field of sage, its pungent aroma evident fifty yards away.

"We use this in our ceremonies for smudging, and for getting good medicine out of that," said Sun Bear to his new apprentices. "Sage is also a good drink if you need it for colds and flu. Of course, it's also good for seasoning, as well. This is good, you can smell it. It's strong sage here. We'll do a ceremonial offering. I think we're going to offer that big fellow over there. It looks like the grandfather. We'll go across the fence, so walk carefully."

The group, almost two dozen strong counting tribe members Simon Corn Man and Michelle Buchanan, crossed a ditch and climbed over a wire fence.

"Be aware of where you're at," the medicine man warned the more severely urbanized. "Everything is beautiful. There are things that stick and bite occasionally, so keep aware of that. You'll find a lot worse things in the big city. Hawk brother is over there, so it's sacred medicine. Sometimes, some of my little brothers the owls live down over here. You get to see them every once in a while, so it's good medicine."

He led the group over to one particularly grand specimen and addressed the plant. "We come here in a sacred way. We come here to honor you, and tell you that we're going to use some of your people, use some of your leaves, for our sacred purpose. We ask that you grant this to us, give it to us to help our people, so that we can prepare it in a sacred manner and use it in a sacred way. Ho!" Only then did Sun Bear cut the bush.

Dalmation toadflax and Saint-John's-wort, both of which make powerful healing oils, were also harvested before the troop turned back toward Spirit Mountain. Along Route 2, Sun Bear sighted a dead racoon in the road and asked Corn Man, who was driving, to pull over. The chairman of the Bear Tribe jumped out of the van and approached the smashed, little critter. Quickly, he pulled it by its tail onto the roadside. A quick prayer was said before the caravan continued on its way.

Over the years, the old Chippewa has accumulated his share of critics. Professor Ward Churchill of the University of Colorado at Boulder, writing in *The Bloomsbury Review* (September/October 1988), is an example. Churchill, who is of Creek/Cherokee descent, accused Sun Bear of being a huckster guilty of the "selling of ersatz sweat lodge and medicine wheel ceremonies to anyone who wants to play Indian for a day and can afford the price of admission."

When asked about the charge as he was eating a bowl of oatmeal on a sofa in the Longhouse, Sun Bear swallowed and responded without rancor. "Many Native people charge for healing. They charge any sum they want from a horse to whatever. For all the history of my tribe, medicine people have charged for knowledge. A person came to study with one of the medicine men in Minnesota, he brought him a horse and some blankets and $150. This was back in the 1930s. And he worked for the medicine man all winter, carrying wood and water at the same time. So to me, I don't see anything wrong with charging for these things.

"Any time I go to a medicine man or woman, and I need something from them, I bring them money. I give them $50 or $100 if I'm asking to do a healing with them because that's my respect for them. I go to a doctor, it's the same way. When people come to me for consultations, I charge a fee and that goes to the Bear Tribe.

"That man [Churchill] in Colorado who works with Indian Studies there receives a regular salary from his university for teaching people Indian traditions and philosophy. How do we explain that?" he demands.

More to the point, perhaps, is the charge that Sun Bear has blurred his Chippewa Medewiwin medicine roots and turned it into a mishmash that represents nothing accurately. But Sun Bear brushes such criticisms aside. He has always said that he is a "universal medicine man."

"The Creator wants us to grow and learn from everything around us," he maintains. "I don't feel that you're supposed to be locked into things. There are religions that take on a dogmatic approach and say, 'I'm right and everybody else is wrong.' But that's not the way of it. True Native spirituality—and this isn't true of all Native people, many of them are as locked up as anyone else—but to me, true Native spirituality is acknowledgement of other people's belief systems.

"For example, when I sit down, I make a pipe. I do it my way and that's good. Somebody else does it another way, and that's okay, too. There's not a right or wrong about it. It's the same way with the sweat lodge. Many people do the sweat lodge. Some do it differently. That's okay. Don't get dogmatic, in other words. Don't get locked into something. I believe the Spirit put us here to learn and to grow to our fullest consciousness. That's what we're supposed to be doing."

Among Natives, Sun Bear usually encounters criticism only around the big cities. "The big city Indians," he sighs and shakes his head. "Some of them have grown up, they've got Indian blood, but have never seen the reservation. The other Indians call them 'the loafers about the fort.' These people who are bad-mouthing me sit on their butts, half the time getting drunk, and not doing anything for anybody. Nothing for their own people. They're the biggest noisemakers around.

"I've tried to create self-help projects for Indian people," he continues. "And I've tried to get money from grants and different people. Lately, all I get is bullshit. Because they don't understand. If I had the resources for it, I'd like to help get fish farms going on the Indian reservations. I've been looking for what I call a conscious capitalist. Somebody who has some money who is willing to make an investment in helping Native people to get enterprises going that are harmonious with their life-styles and to their relationship with the earth. You don't have to have smokestacks out there. You can create some kind of nonpolluting industry to provide employment for people. Native people are very skilled crafts people and there are a lot of possibilities along that line."

Prophecy of the People from Across the Great Water

My people were told of the coming of the Europeans to this continent. . . . And we were told that if they came in here in a sacred manner to learn the spiritual teachings from us, then we would come together and live in harmony. Each one of us would bring a gift . . . and it would be a beautiful thing between us. But if the people from across the Great Water didn't accept our spiritual teachings or acknowledge them, then a time would come when the Native people would lay as if they were dead in the dust . . . and our teachings would be forgotten by many of us and even our young people wouldn't listen to us. Then after a period of a hundred years or more, we would stand up again, we would be walking on our hind legs and we would be as if we were earth spirits that had sprung up from the earth again. We would have power again to work with the natural forces, with the beings and powers and at that time our children would turn to us and seek this knowledge. Not only would they do it, but the people who had come from across the Great Waters, their sons and daughters would be doing it and they would say to us, "Teach us, because we have almost destroyed the earth."

On earth, all is sacred. City people too must realize the truth of this and act accordingly, Sun Bear maintains. But how can a person who lives in a city act with the earth in mind? He suggests solutions. "People have to start being conscious of these things in a very real way. I don't want us using styrofoam cups when we're having programs. Up here on the mountain, everyone washes dishes. It doesn't matter if they're a banker or a housewife that's come to study with us. They wash their dishes so they take responsibility for expanding pollution. Other places, they may be talking about holy things. But if they're still using styrofoam cups, they still aren't getting the message.

"Add to nature," Sun Bear pleads, "rather than take away from it. Learn how to buy organic food that isn't costing a lot in packaging. One of the products I'm now marketing is a shopping bag with 'Save a Tree' on it. One of the reasons is that I believe people should have a shopping bag that lasts five years, rather than a bunch of paper and plastic bags that are chucked every day!"

Human beings are going to have to raise themselves up into a higher level of consciousness. "Man has a responsibility as a keeper or protector of the planet. We may have different belief systems, but the basic belief that the earth is the mother of all living creation is all over the world. Ancient Europeans, all of them, had this same idea. That's why they spoke of it as the 'Mother of Religion.' This is real! It doesn't change simply because it's 1990 and you have computers. It still goes back to 'what do you eat?' You don't eat computer ribbons. You eat things that come from the earth. You have to eat food that is raised out of that living soil that brings forth life. Humans have gotten so far away from the planet."

Prophecy of the Surviving Quarter

I see major changes coming. I see that they're necessary. The planet has a lot of people on it that really don't take responsibility for the planet. And that has to change. If it is necessary that a lot of people die off during the major changes, and that the people that survive are conscious people that are responsible for the earth and are living on it in harmony and love and respect, then that is what is supposed to happen. . . . Up to a fourth of the people will survive.

"By the year 2000," says Sun Bear, "you're going to see some very major changes. By the year 2012, it's going to get very interesting, very, very interesting to watch. Because the people who are going to survive are going to be the people who are really working on this higher state of consciousness and responsibility. That's the thing about it. Not just consciousness. If you're going to go and sit under a tree and meditate on your navel and say, 'Well, I'm great and holy and I'm becoming so pure!' That's not it! You've got to be able to exercise your spiritual muscle. You've got to be able to use that in an everyday basis with your fellow human beings. That's what real consciousness is, being able to answer this world. To me, that's what a spiritual warrior is. I'm not interested in wimps or almosters."

•

Americans are not well known for honoring intellectuals of color. History is replete with examples of how such national treasures are paid more respect abroad than at home. With his growing overseas following, Sun Bear may well fit into this pattern. Hopefully he will achieve the stature that he deserves before it is too late. Exactly what will happen to the Bear Tribe once Sun Bear passes from the scene is an open question. What will happen to the earth if his message is ignored is not. Nature will take its rightful place and human beings will be left to cope as best we can on a planet greatly diminished by our lack of respect for it.

BIBLIOGRAPHY

INTRODUCTION

"4 of 5 in Poll Believe Pollution Threatens Quality of U.S. Life," *Los Angeles Times,* June 12, 1990, Part I - page 4.

Hultkrantz, Ake. *Native Religions of North America.* New York: Harper & Row, 1987.

Maugh II, Thomas H. "Global Warming Storm Link Probed," *Los Angeles Times,* September 20, 1989, Part I - page 16.

Montalbano, William D. "Green Wave Surging Over West Europe," *Los Angeles Times,* May 11, 1989, Part I - pages 1, 22 & 23.

Stammer, Larry B. "Air Gains May Be Undone by Ozone Harm, Panel Is Told," *Los Angeles Times,* May 21, 1989, Part II - pages 1 & 8.

Stammer, Larry B. "Global Environmental Threat Largely Ignored, Experts Say," *Los Angeles Times,* September 17, 1989, Part I - page 4.

Summary of 1989 Air Quality Management Plan, "The Path to Clean Air: Attainment Strategies." A publication of the South Coast Air Quality Management District and the Southern California Association of Governments.

THE MAYAN ROOTS OF PROPHECY

Aveni, Anthony F. *Skywatchers of Ancient Mexico.* Austin: University of Texas Press, 1980.

Brinton, Daniel G. "Maya Chronicles," in *Library of Aboriginal American Literature, No. 1.* Philadelphia: D. G. Brinton, 1882.

Coe, Michael D. *The Maya.* London: Thames and Hudson, 1966.

Knorozov, Yurii. *Maya Hieroglyphic Codices.* Albany, New York: Institute for Mesoamerican Studies, 1982.

Landa, Diego de. *The Maya: Account of the Affairs of Yucatan.* Edited by A.R. Pagden. Chicago: J. Philip O'Hara, Inc., 1975.

Leon-Portilla, Miguel. *Time and Reality in the Thought of the Maya.* Boston: Beacon Press, 1973.

Makemson, Maud W. *The Book of the Jaguar Priest: A Translation of the Book of Chilam Balam of Tizimin.* New York: Henry Schuman, 1951.

Maugh II, Thomas H. "New-Found Site in Jungle May Be First Maya City," Los Angeles Times, Sec. A - p. 1, November 14, 1989.

Men, Hunbatz. *Secrets of Mayan Science/Religion.* Santa Fe, New Mexico: Bear & Company, 1990.

Morley, Sylvanus G. and George W. Brainerd. *The Ancient Maya.* Stanford, Ca.: Stanford University Press, 1983.

Nicholson, Irene. *Mexican and Central American Mythology.* London: Paul Hamlyn, 1967.

Pearce, Kenneth. *The View from the Top of the Temple.* Albuquerque: University of New Mexico Press, 1984.

Peterson, Natasha. *Sacred Sites.* Chicago: Contemporary Books, 1988.

Roys, Ralph L. *The Book of Chilam Balam of Chumayel.* Norman: University of Oklahoma Press, 1967.

Sten, Maria. *The Mexican Codices and their Extraordinary History.* Mexico, D.F.: Ediciones Lara, 1974.

Thompson, J. and Eric S. *The Rise and Fall of Maya Civilization.* Norman: University of Oklahoma Press, 1966.

THE AZTECS: CULT OF THE FIFTH SUN

Anaya, Rudolfo A. *Lord of the Dawn.* Albuquerque: University of New Mexico Press, 1987.

Brinton, Daniel G. *Ancient Nahuatl Poetry.* New York: AMS Press, 1969.

———. "On the Words 'Anahuac' and 'Nahuatl.' " *The American Antiquarian* 15, no. 6 (November 1893): 377–82.

Broda, Johanna, David Carrasco, and Eduardo Matos Moctezuma. *The Great Temple of Tenochtitlan.* Berkeley: University of California Press, 1987.

Carrasco, David. *Quetzalcoatl and the Irony of Empire.* Chicago: University of Chicago Press, 1982.

Caso, Alfonso. *Los Calendarios Prehispanicos.* Mexico, D.F.: Universidad Nacional Autonoma de Mexico, 1967.

Cortez, Hernan. *Letters from Mexico.* A.R. Pagden, ed. New York: Grossman Publishers, 1971.

Davies, Nigel. *The Aztecs.* London: Macmillan London Ltd., 1973.

———. *The Toltecs.* Norman: University of Oklahoma Press, 1987.

Diaz del Castillo, Bernal. *The Discovery and Conquest of Mexico.* New York: Harper & Brothers, 1928.

Duran, Fray Diego. *The Aztecs: The History of the Indies of New Spain.* New York: Orion Press, 1964.

———. *Historia De Las Indias De Nueva Espana E Islas De La Tierra Firme.* Mexico, D.F.: Editora Nacional, 1951.

Hultkrantz, Ake. *The Religions of the American Indians.* Berkeley: University of California Press, 1979.

Leon-Portilla, Miguel. *Aztec Thought and Culture.* Norman: University of Oklahoma Press, 1963.

Moctezuma, Eduardo Matos. *Informe de la revision de los trabajos arqueologicos realizados en Ichcateopan, Guerrero.* Instituto de Investigaciones Historicas, Dictamenes Ichcateopan: 6. Mexico, D.F.: Universidad Nacional Autonoma de Mexico, 1980.

Moctezuma, Eduardo Matos. *The Great Temple of the Aztecs.* London: Thames and Hudson, 1988.

Prescott, William H. *The World of Aztecs.* Geneva, Switzerland: Editions Minerva, 1970.

Sahagun, Fray Bernardino de. *The Florentine Codex: General History of the Things of New Spain.* Books 2, 3, and 12. Arthur J. O. Anderson and Charles Dibble, eds. Sante Fe, New Mexico: School of American Research and the University of Utah, 1969–1975.

Soustelle, Jacques. *The Daily Life of Aztecs on the Eve of the Spanish Conquest.* London: Weidenfeld and Nicolson, 1961.

Time Magazine, "Slow Count: A Winner and Some Angry Losers in a Historic Race," July 25, 1988, page 50.

Townsend, Richard F. *State and Cosmos in the Art of Tenochtitlan.* Studies in Pre-Columbian Art and Archaeology Number Twenty. Washington, D.C.: Dumbarton Oaks, Trustees for Harvard University, 1979.

3. DEGANAWIDAH: PEACEMAKER OF THE IROQUOIS

Bowen, Catherine Drinker. *The Most Dangerous Man in America.* Boston: Little, Brown & Company in association with the Atlantic Monthly Press, 1974.

Colden, Cadawallader. *The History of the Five Nations Depending on the Province of New York in America.* 1727 and 1747. Ithaca, N.Y.: Cornell University Press, 1958.

Fenton, William N., ed. *Parker on the Iroquois.* Syracuse, N.Y.: Syracuse University Press, 1968.

Grinde, Donald A., Jr. *The Iroquois and the Founding of the American Nation.* San Francisco: Indian Historian Press, 1977.

Henry, Thomas R. *Wilderness Messiah: The Story of Hiawatha and the Iroquois.* New York: William Sloane Associates, 1955.

Hewitt, J. N. B. "Legend of the Founding of the Iroquois League." *American Anthropologist* 5 (1892): 2.

Jennings, Francis. *The Ambiguous Iroquois Empire.* New York: W. W. Norton & Company, 1984.

———. *Empire of Fortune.* New York: W. W. Norton & Company, 1988.

Johansen, Bruce E. *Forgotten Founders: Benjamin Franklin, the Iroquois and the Rationale for the American Revolution.* Ipswich, Mass.: Gambit, 1982.

Labaree, Leonard W., ed. *The Papers of Benjamin Franklin.* New Haven, Conn.: Yale University Press, 1959.

Parker, Arthur C. *The Constitution of the Five Nations.* Albany: University of the State of New York, 1916.

Reynolds, Wynn Robert. *Persuasive Speaking of the Iroquois Indians at Treaty Councils 1678–1776: A Study of Techniques as Evidenced in the Official Transcripts of the Interpreters' Translations.* Ph.D. diss., Columbia University, 1957.

Tooker, Elizabeth. "The League of the Iroquois: Its History, Politics, and Ritual." In *Handbook of North American Indians,* vol. 15—Northeast. Washington, D.C.: Smithsonian Institution, 1978.

————, ed. *An Iroquois Source Book.* Vol. 1. New York: Garland Publishing, 1985.

Van Doren, Carl. *Benjamin Franklin.* New York: Garden City Publishing Co., 1941.

Van Doren, Carl, and Julian P. Boyd, eds. *Indian Treaties Printed by Benjamin Franklin.* Philadelphia: Pennsylvania Historical Society, 1938.

Wallace, Paul A. W. *The White Roots of Peace.* Philadelphia: University of Pennsylvania Press, 1946.

4. WOVOKA: PAIUTE GHOST DANCER

Bailey, Paul. *Wovoka, The Indian Messiah.* Los Angeles: Westernlore Press, 1957.

Barney, Garold D. *Mormons, Indians, and the Ghost Dance Religion of 1890.* Lanham, Md.: University Press of America, 1986.

Brown, Thomas D. *Journal of the Southern Indian Mission.* Salt Lake City, Utah: Deseret Book Company, 1972.

Cannon, George Q. *Life of Joseph Smith the Prophet.* Salt Lake City, Utah: Deseret Book Company, 1958.

Dockstader, Frederick J. *Great North American Indians: Profiles in Life and Leadership.* New York: Van Nostrand Reinhold Company, 1977.

Du Bois, Cora. *The 1870 Ghost Dance. Anthropological Records* 3. Berkeley: University of California Press, 1939.

Hittman, Michael, "The 1870 Ghost Dance at the Walker River Reservation: A Reconstruction." *Ethnohistory* 20 (1973): 247–78.

Miller, David H. *Ghost Dance.* New York: Duell, Sloan and Pearce, 1959.

Mooney, James. *The Ghost Dance Religion.* Extract from the Fourteenth Annual Report of the Bureau of Ethnology. Washington, D.C.: Government Printing Office, 1896.

Moses, L. G. " 'The Father Tells Me So!' Wovoka: The Ghost Dance Prophet." In *American Indian Prophets,* edited by C. E. Trafzer. Sacramento, Cal.: Sierra Oaks Publishing Co., 1986.

Parker, Z. A. "The Ghost Dance at Pine Ridge." *Journal of American Folklore* 4, no. 13 (April–June 1891): p. 160–62.

"Rosebuds Ready to Fight." *New York Times,* November 30, 1890, p. 2.

Secretary of the Interior. *Annual Reports.* Washington, D.C.: Government Printing Office, 1890–92.

Secretary of War. *Annual Reports.* Washington, D.C.: Government Printing Office, 1890–91.

Thornton, Russell. *We Shall Live Again.* Cambridge, Eng.: Cambridge University Press, 1986.

Utley, Robert M. *The Last Days of the Sioux Nation.* New Haven and London: Yale University Press, 1963.

Vander, Judith. *Ghost Dance Songs and Religion of a Wind River Shoshone Woman.* Los Angeles: University of California Press, 1986.

Watson, Elmo S. "The Last Indian War, 1890–91—A Study of Newspaper Jingoism," *Journalism Quarterly* 20, no. 3 (September 1943): 205–19.

5. WHITE SHELL WOMAN: BELOVED OF THE NAVAJO

Brugge, David M. *A History of the Chaco Navajos.* Reports of the Chaco Center, no. 4. Albuquerque, N.M.: Division of Chaco Research, National Park Service, 1979.

Dorris, Michael. *The Broken Cord.* New York: Harper & Row Publishers, 1989.

Evers, Larry, ed. *Between Sacred Mountains: Navajo Stories and Lessons from the Land.* Vol. 11, *Sun Tracks: An American Indian Literary Series.* Tucson, Ariz.: Sun Tracks and the University of Arizona Press, 1982.

Gill, Sam D. *Sacred Words: A Study of Navajo Religion and Prayer.* Westport, Conn.: Greenwood Press, 1981.

Haile, Berard. *The Navajo Fire Dance.* Saint Michaels, Ariz.: St. Michaels Press, 1946.

Kahn, Annie, Olin Karch, and Blu Mundy. "Interpretations of Ancient Navajo Chants." In *Four Remarkable Indian Prophecies.* Happy Camp, Calif.: Naturegraph Company, 1963.

Kluckhohn, Clyde, and Dorothea Leighton. *The Navajo.* Cambridge, Mass.: Harvard University Press, 1951.

Link, Margaret S. *The Pollen Path.* Stanford, Calif.: Stanford University Press, 1956.

Matthews, Washington. "Noqoilpi, The Gambler: A Navajo Myth." *Journal of American Folklore* 2, no. 5 (April-June 1889):89–94.

Noble, David G., ed. *New Light on Chaco Canyon.* Santa Fe, N.M.: School of American Research Press, 1984.

O'Bryan, Aileen. *The Dine': Origin Myths of the Navaho Indians.* Bureau of American Ethnology, Bulletin 163. Washington, D.C.: Government Printing Office, 1956.

Perrone, Bobette, H. Henrietta Stockel, and Victoria Krueger. *Medicine Women, Curanderas, and Women Doctors.* Norman: University of Oklahoma Press, 1989.

Roessel, Ruth. *Women In Navajo Society.* Rough Rock, Ariz.: Navajo Resource Center, 1981.

————, ed. *Navajo Stories of the Long Walk Period.* Tsaile, Ariz.: Navajo Community College Press, 1973.

Underhill, Ruth. *The Navajos.* Norman: University of Oklahoma Press, 1956.

Wyman, Leland C. *Blessingway.* Tucson: The University of Arizona Press, 1970.

6. THE HOPI: WAITING FOR PAHANA

Bailey, Paul. *Jacob Hamblin, Buckskin Apostle.* Los Angeles: Westernlore Press, 1948.

Calhoun, James S. *The Official Correspondence of James Calhoun.* Annie H. Abel, ed. Washington, D.C.: Government Printing Office, 1915.

Corbett, Pearson H. *Jacob Hamblin, The Peacemaker.* Salt Lake City, Utah: Deseret Book Company, 1952.

Courlander, Harold. *The Fourth World of the Hopis.* New York: Crown Publishers, 1971.

————. *Hopi Voices.* Albuquerque: University of New Mexico Press, 1982.

Eiseman, Fred B., Jr. "Notes on the Hopi Ceremonial Cycles." *Plateau* 34, no. 1, (July 1961). Flagstaff: Museum of Northern Arizona.

Ellis, Florence H., "The Hopi: Their History and Use of Lands." In *American Indian Ethnohistory: Indians of the Southwest,* edited by David A. Horr. New York: Garland Publishing, 1974.

Euler, Robert C., and Henry F. Dobyns. *The Hopi People.* Phoenix: Indian Tribal Series, 1971.

Fewkes, J. Walter. "Contributions to Hopi History, II: Oraibi in 1890," *American Anthropologist* 24, no. 3 (July-August 1922).

James, Harry C. *Pages from Hopi History.* Tucson: University of Arizona Press, 1974.

Katchongva, Dan. *Hopi: A Message for All People.* Rooseveltown, N.Y.: White Roots of Peace, Akwesasne Notes, 1972.

Kennard, Edward A. *Hopi Kachinas.* New York: Museum of the American Indian, 1971.

Malotki, Ekkehart, and Michael Lomatuway'ma. *Maasaw: Profile of a Hopi God.* Lincoln: University of Nebraska Press, 1987.

Nequatewa, Edmund. *Truth of a Hopi.* Flagstaff: Museum of Northern Arizona, 1936.

Titiev, Mischa. *Old Oraibi.* Papers of the Peabody Museum of American Archeology and Ethnology, Harvard University, vol. 22, no. 1. Cambridge, Mass.: Peabody Museum, 1944.

Waters, Frank. *Book of the Hopi.* New York: Penguin Books, 1963.

Winship, George P. *The Coronado Expedition: 1540–1542.* Washington, D.C.: Government Printing Office, 1896.

SUN BEAR: SAVE THE PLANET

Churchill, Ward. "A Little Matter of Genocide: Native American Spirituality & New Age Hucksterism," in The Bloomsbury Review, Vol. 8, Issue 5, September-October, 1988: p 23.

La Barre, Weston. *The Peyote Cult.* Hamden, Conn.: Shoe String Press, 1970.

Sun Bear. *At Home in the Wilderness.* Happy Camp, Ca., 1968.

Sun Bear. *Buffalo Hearts.* Spokane, Wash.: Bear Tribe Publishing, 1976.

Sun Bear, with Wabun. *The Medicine Earth Astrology Wheel.* New York, N.Y.: Prentice Hall, 1986.

Sun Bear, with Wabun and Nimimosha. *The Bear Tribe's Self-Reliance Book.* New York, N.Y.: Prentice Hall, 1988.

Sun Bear, with Wabun and Barry Weinstock. *Sun Bear: The Path of Power.* Spokane, Wash.: Bear Tribe Publishing, 1983.

Sun Bear. "Interview with Sun Bear on Earth Changes," in Wildfire Magazine, Vol. 2, Nos. 3 and 4, n.d.

Sun Bear, Crysalis Mulligan, Peter Nufer, and Wabun. *Walk in Balance.* New York, N.Y.: Prentice Hall, 1989.

INDEX

Nequatewa, Edmund, 173–174
Neutrals, 83
Nevada Historical Society, 201
New Fire ceremony, 11, 37–38
New Galicia, 170
New Indian Age (prophecy), 99
New Light on Chaco Canyon
(Schwartz), 153–154
New York State Museum Bulletin, 69
New York Times, 119
Newberry Library Center for the
History of the American Indian, 84
Newhouse, Seth, 69
Nezahaulpilli (astronomer-king), 23;
prediction of, 24
Niltci, the Wind God, 155
Nimimosha, 207, 210, 212, 214
"Nine-night scene," 148–152
Nixon, Pres. Richard M., 188–189
"No sleep" ceremony, 150
"Noble Savage," 87
Nohpat, 8
Noquoilpi (He-Who-Wins-Men),
153, 154–157

Ocelot (warrior society), 34, 46, 57
Ododarhol, 67, 70; and
Deganawidah, 71–72
Office of Economic Opportunity
(O.E.O.), 208
Ogalala Sioux, 105, 112
Oglala nation, 214
Old Spiderwoman, 161, 182
Old Tusayan, 176
Olid, Cristobal de, 60
Olmedo, Fray Bortolome de, 44
Omaha Indians, 199–200
Omaha World Herald, 119
Ometeotl (Aztec god), 37, 38–39, 42
Onate, Don Juan de, 130, 173
One-Horn Society, 166, 169, 183,
187
Oneida Indians: as American allies,
89; and Great Peace, 70, 71; in
Iroquois Confederacy, 64, 72
Onondaga Indians: as firekeepers, 74;
and Great Peace, 71; in Iroquois
Confederacy, 64, 72; vs. Mohawks,
67; reservation, 89

Oraibi, 162, 163, 165, 172, 173,
177, 179, 184, 188
Orenda (magical power), 68, 71
Otomi Indians, 30
"Outfits," 146
Overwhelming Vagina, 140
Owl, 140

Padnitz, Maj. David S., 202
Pahana, the Elder White Brother:
legend of, 162–163; return of,
170–181; similarity to, 165. *See
also* Bahana; Bahanna
Paho (prayer feather), 160
Paiute Indians, 91, 92, 96, 97, 201,
209; celestial intervention, 99–100;
Ghost Dance, 115
Palace of the Governor, 8
Palmer, Perain P., 118
Papago Reservation, 200
Paramount Paint Company, 202
Parker, Arthur C., 69
Parker, Ballantine, 199
Parker, Quanah, 199
Parker, Z. A., 114–115
Penis perforation, 17
People from Across the Great Water
(prophecy), 227
People of the Longhouse, 72
Peten, 2, 8
Peters, Hendrick, 63
Peters, Richard, 85
Peyote: outlawed, *xvi;* Sun Bear on,
199; use of, 198–199
Phillip, King of Spain, 173
Phoenix Indian Center, 200
Piegan Indians, 107
Pine Ridge agency, 112, 113
Pine Ridge Reservation, 214
Pit River Indians, 100
Pithouses, 164
Place of Melting into One, 135
Plan of Union, 86–87
Pleiades, 11; calendar of, 13; and
New Fire Ceremony, 37–38
Polacca, 163
Polk, Pres. James K., 175
Polygamy, Mormons renounce, 120
Pomo Indians, 200